ISLE OF WIGHT

A HISTORY AND CELEBRATION

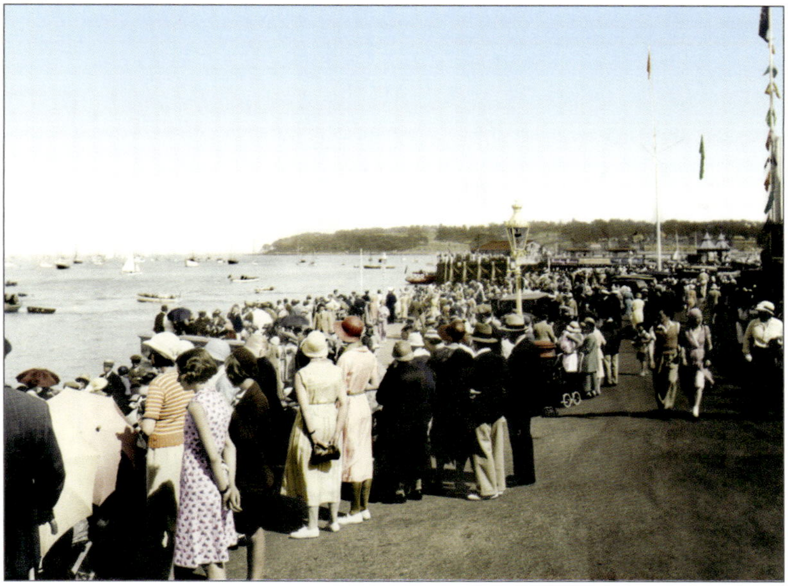

ADRIAN SEARLE

Produced by The Francis Frith Collection
exclusively for

OTTAKAR'S

www.ottakars.co.uk

First published in the United Kingdom in 2005
by The Francis Frith Collection®

Hardback Edition 2005
ISBN 1-84567-747-1

British Library Cataloguing in Publication Data

Isle of Wight - A History and Celebration
Adrian Searle

The Francis Frith Collection
Frith's Barn, Teffont,
Salisbury, Wiltshire SP3 5QP
Tel: +44 (0) 1722 716 376
Email: info@francisfrith.co.uk
www.francisfrith.co.uk

Printed and bound in England

Front Cover: **COWES, WATCHING THE RACING 1933** 85896t

Additional modern photographs by Matt Searle unless otherwise stated.

Domesday extract used in timeline by kind permission of
Alecto Historical Editions, www.domesdaybook.org
Aerial photographs reproduced under licence from
Simmons Aerofilms Limited.
Historical Ordnance Survey maps reproduced under licence from
Homecheck.co.uk

The colour-tinting in this book is for illustrative purposes only, and is not intended to be historically accurate

AS WITH ANY HISTORICAL DATABASE, THE FRANCIS FRITH ARCHIVE IS CONSTANTLY BEING CORRECTED AND IMPROVED, AND THE PUBLISHERS WOULD WELCOME INFORMATION ON OMISSIONS OR INACCURACIES

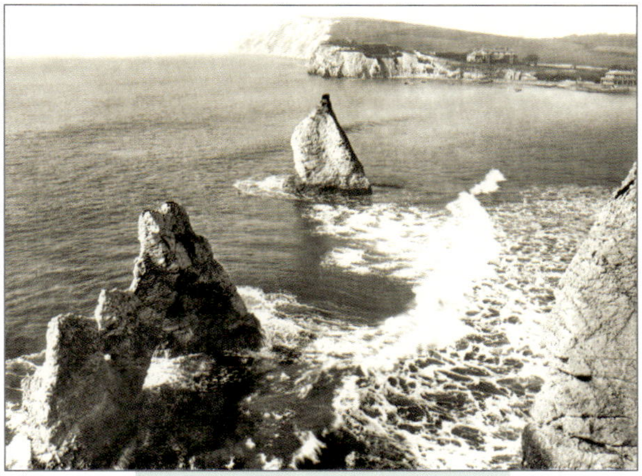

Contents

6 Timeline

8 Chapter One: Footprints to the Normans

30 Chapter Two: Norman Fiefdom - French Target

58 Chapter Three: Pestilence, Politics and Prosperity

76 Chapter Four: Victoria - The Icing on the Cake

98 Chapter Five: Adjustments - The Modern Wight

117 Acknowledgements & Bibliography

121 Free Mounted Print Offer

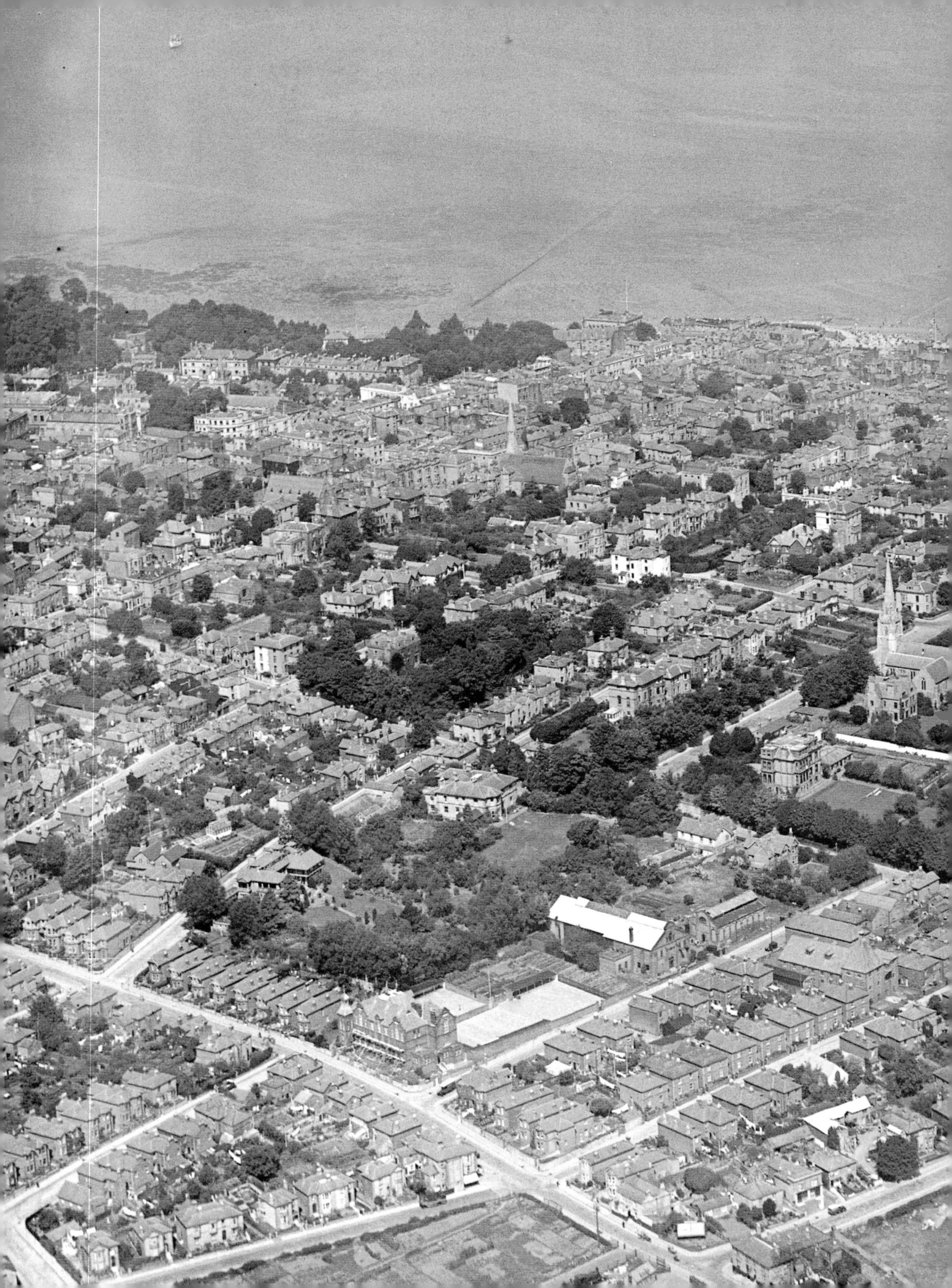

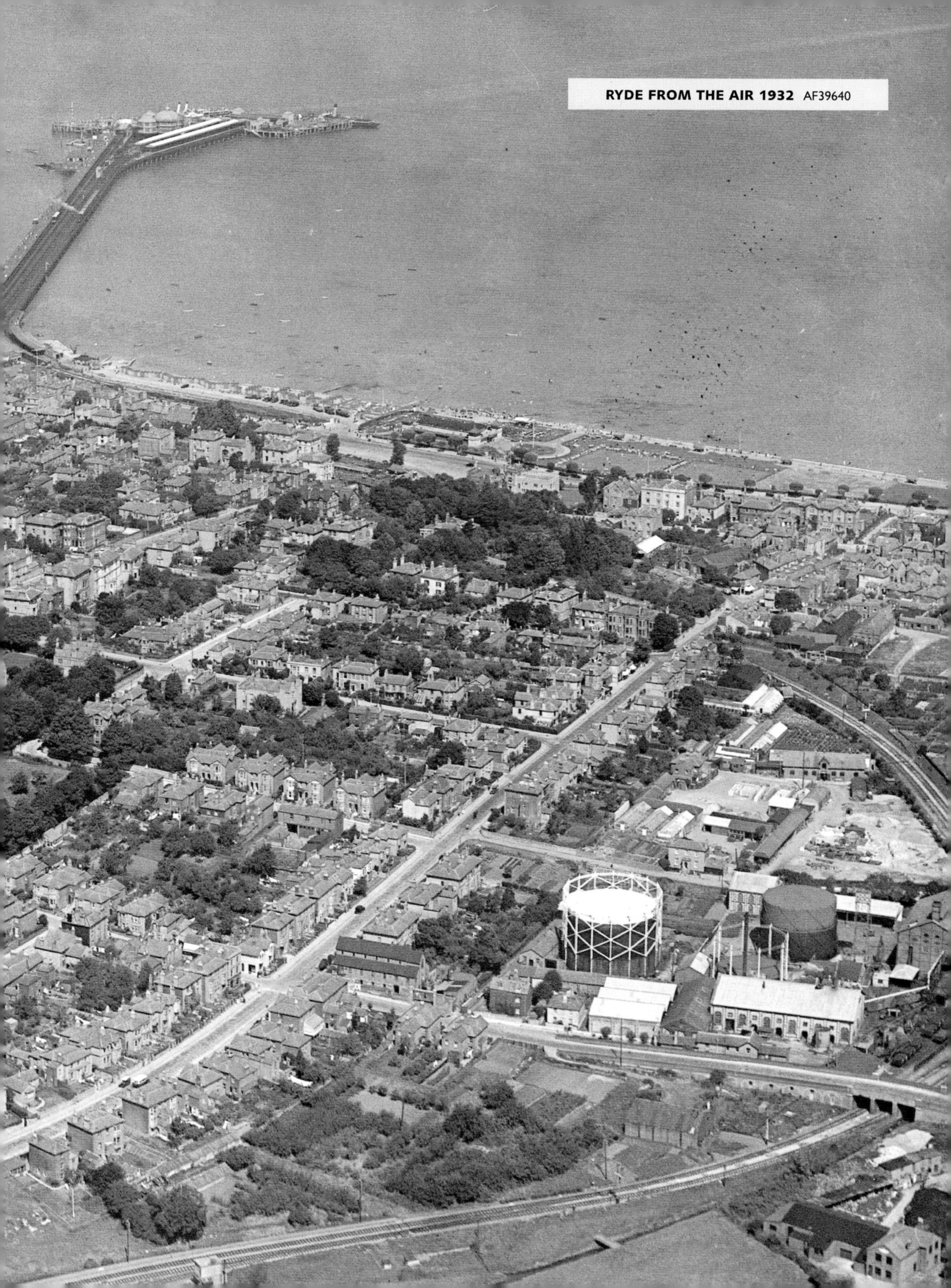

RYDE FROM THE AIR 1932 AF39640

Historical Timeline for Isle of Wight

Prehistory

c7,000-6,000BC End of Ice Ages - Wight becomes an island

c3,000BC Arrival of Neolithic farmers - first settlers

Roman Britain

49BC Julius Caesar crosses the Rubicon

AD43 2nd Legion captures Wight for Rome

AD79 Eruption of Vesuvius destroying Pompeii

AD122 Emperor Hadrian orders Hadrian's Wall to be built

AD280 Building of Roman villa at Newport

AD455 Vandals sack Rome

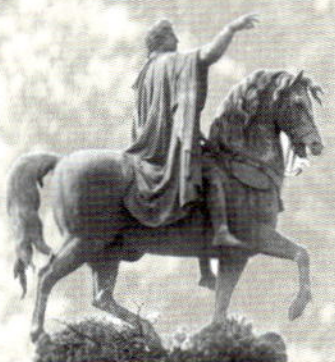

Dark Ages

AD520 Possible period of King Arthur legend

AD524 Wihtgar controls the Island

AD686 Island's late conversion to Christianity

AD871 King Alfred and Danelaw

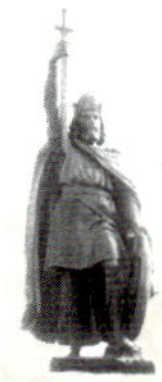

Tudor Period

1509 Henry VIII becomes king

1536 Dissolution of Quarr Abbey

1558 Accession of Elizabeth 1

1582-1584 Plague runs riot in Newport

1588 Spanish Armada defeated

1600 Founding of East India Company

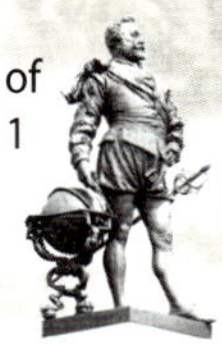

Stuart Britain

1605 Gunpowder Plot

1647-1648 Charles I held at Carisbrooke Castle

1649 Charles I executed

1650 Death of Princess Elizabeth at Carisbrooke

1666 Great Fire of London

Victorian Britain

1837 Victoria becomes queen

1838 Opening of first prison at Parkhurst

1845 Victoria and Albert buy Osborne House

1846 Repeal of Corn Laws

1851 Great Exhibition at Crystal Palace

1862 First railway links Cowes and Newport

1882 Reclamation of Brading Haven

1885 Karl Benz designs first automobile

1899-1902 Boer War

1901 Queen Victoria dies

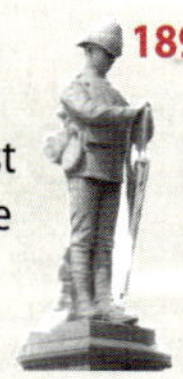

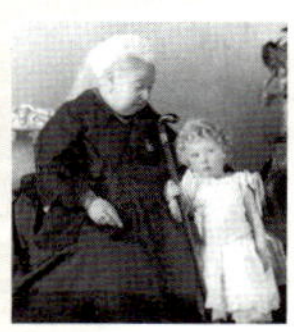

Edwardian Era

1903 Campaign for women's suffrage begins

1904 Nation's first public library opens in Newport

1910 Edward VII dies

Middle Ages

1066 William FitzOsbern becomes Lord of the Island

1078 FitzOsbern's rebellion - Crown assumes control

1132 Founding of Quarr Abbey

1293 Wight sold to England by Isabelle de Fortibus

1337 French destroy towns / Siege of Carisbrooke

1066 Battle of Hastings. Norman rule begins

1086 Domesday Book

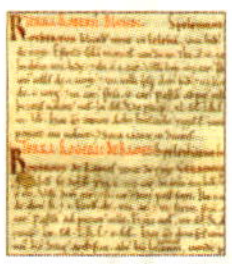

1170 Murder of Thomas à Becket at Canterbury Cathedral

1215 Magna Carta

1306 Robert the Bruce declares himself King of Scotland

Late Medieval

1445 Henry Beauchamp crowned King of the Wight

1348 Black Death kills 25 million in Europe

1415 Battle of Agincourt

1485 Battle of Bosworth Field marks end of Plantaganet dynasty

Georgian Era

1780 Union Street links Upper and Lower Ryde

1782 Worsley trial scandal/ end of paid Governors

1803 Thomas White begins shipbuilding at Cowes

1814 Opening of Ryde Pier

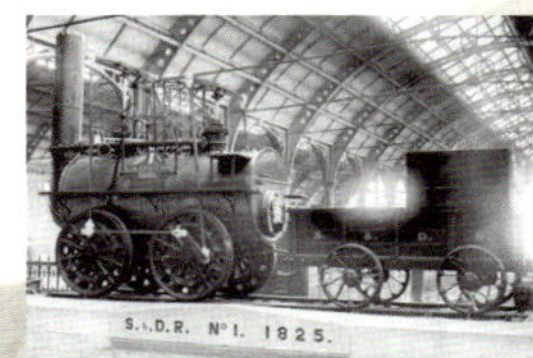

1739 John Wesley founds Methodist church

1762 Mozart performs at the age of 6

1789 French Revolution

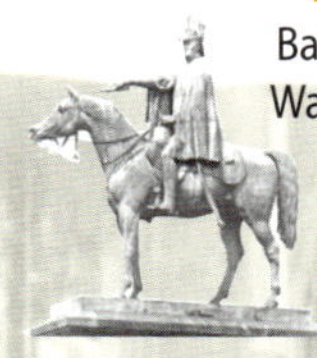

1815 Battle of Waterloo

1825 Stockton to Darlington Railway

20th Century Britain

1959 World's first hovercraft unveiled by Saunders-Roe

1927 First car ferry service launched at Fishbourne

1928 Saunders-Roe formed at East Cowes

1940 Invasion alert and attack on radar station

1942 Cowes Blitz claims many lives

1965 Closure of J Samuel White's at Cowes

1968-1970 Massive pop festivals rival Woodstock

1994 First unitary authority set up

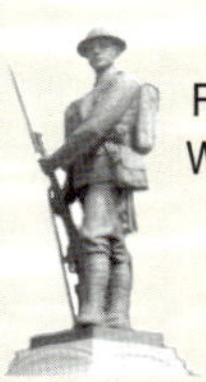

1914 First World War begins

1926 John Logie Baird obtains first television picture

1939 Outbreak of Second World War

1956 Suez Crisis

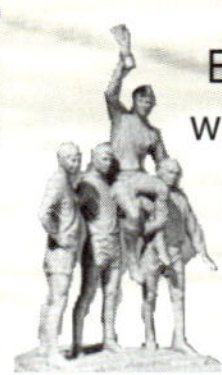

1966 England win World Cup

1969 First man on the Moon

1982 Falklands Conflict

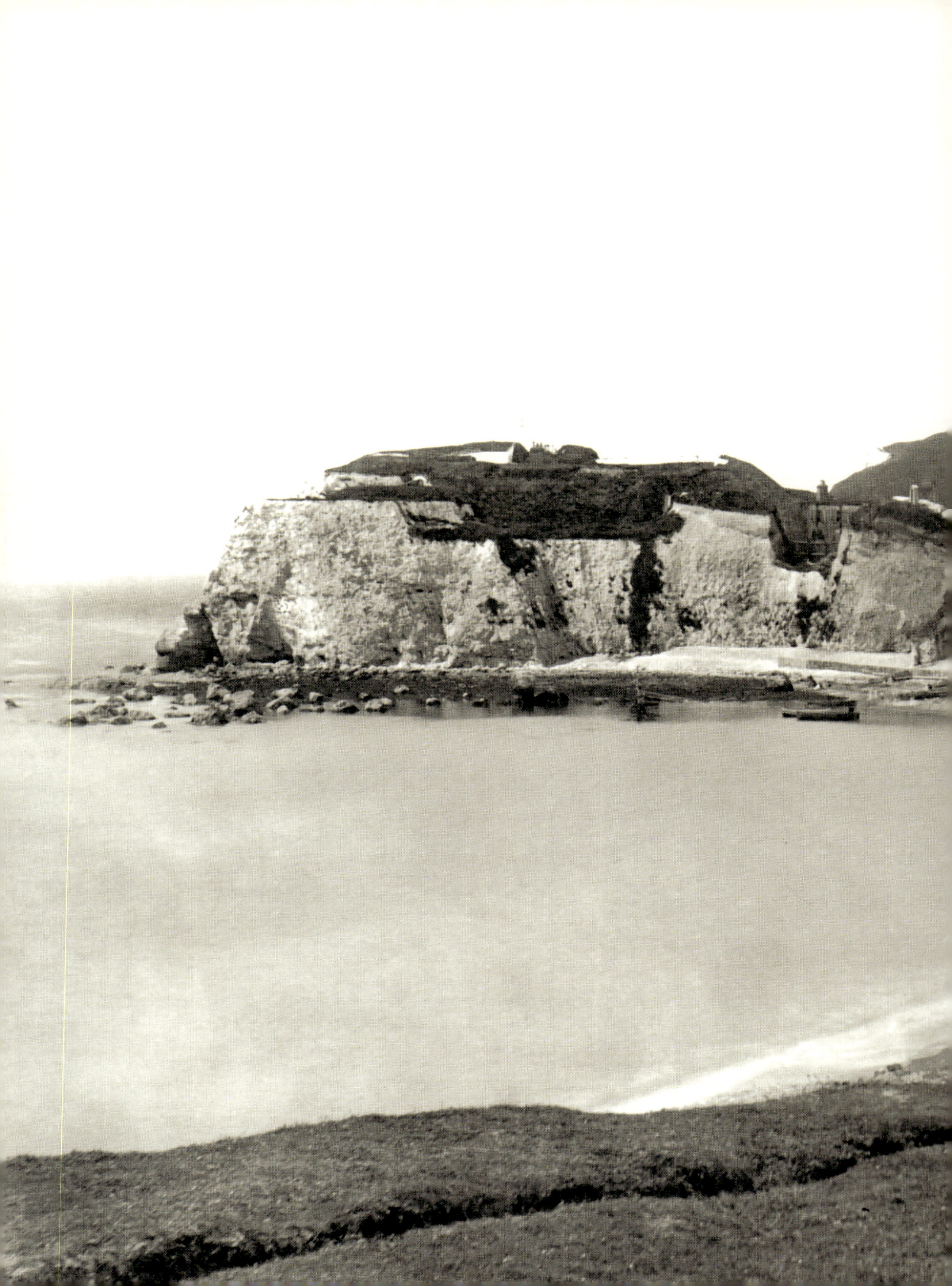

CHAPTER ONE

Footprints to the Normans

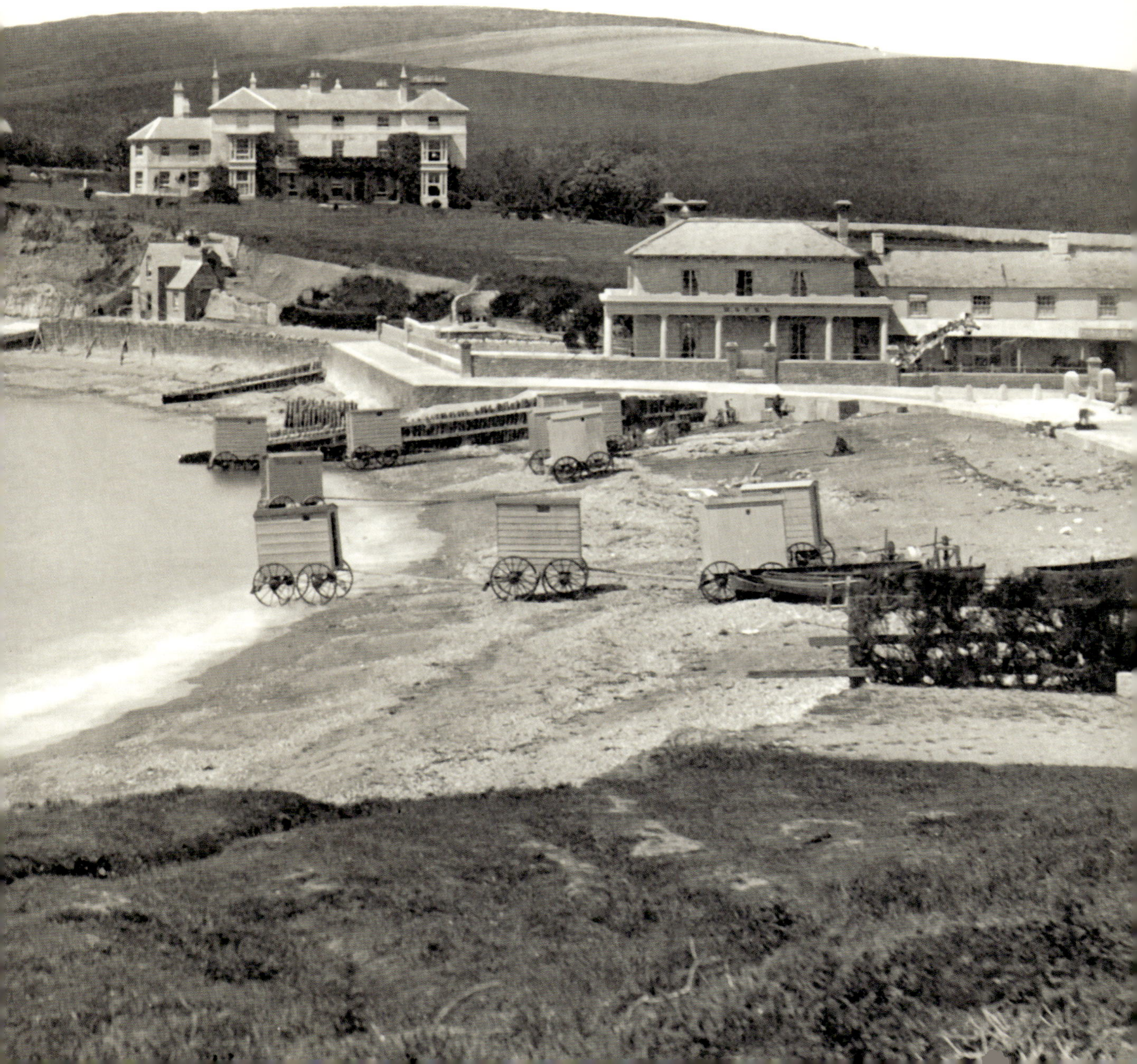

A FUNDAMENTAL QUESTION awaits anyone who attempts to tell the story of the Isle of Wight - where to start?

Extending 23 miles from Bembridge's Foreland in the east to the famous Needles rocks jutting out from the western tip, and just 13 miles north-south between the extremities at Egypt Point and St Catherine's, the shape of Wight resembles a rough-cut diamond - the clichéd jewel of England's south coast. Nestling a comfortable five or so miles offshore from mainland Hampshire, the Island - the use of the capital 'I' is seen as something of a God-given right by its

Did you know?

The Missing Needle

There is nothing very thin and sharply pointed about any of the three chalk stacks making up The Needles. The one stack that did resemble the sewing implement - the Needle Rock itself - disappeared after crumbling into a storm-lashed sea as long ago as 1764. The gap it left is obvious.

THE NEEDLES 1890 26173

The Needles are the Island's most famous landmark - follow their line and you'll arrive in Dorset.

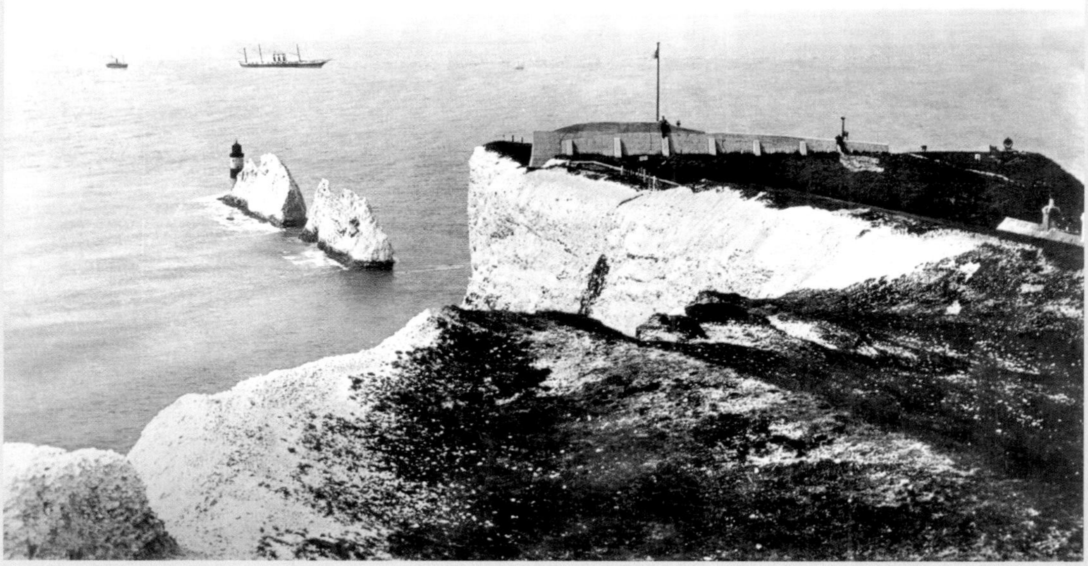

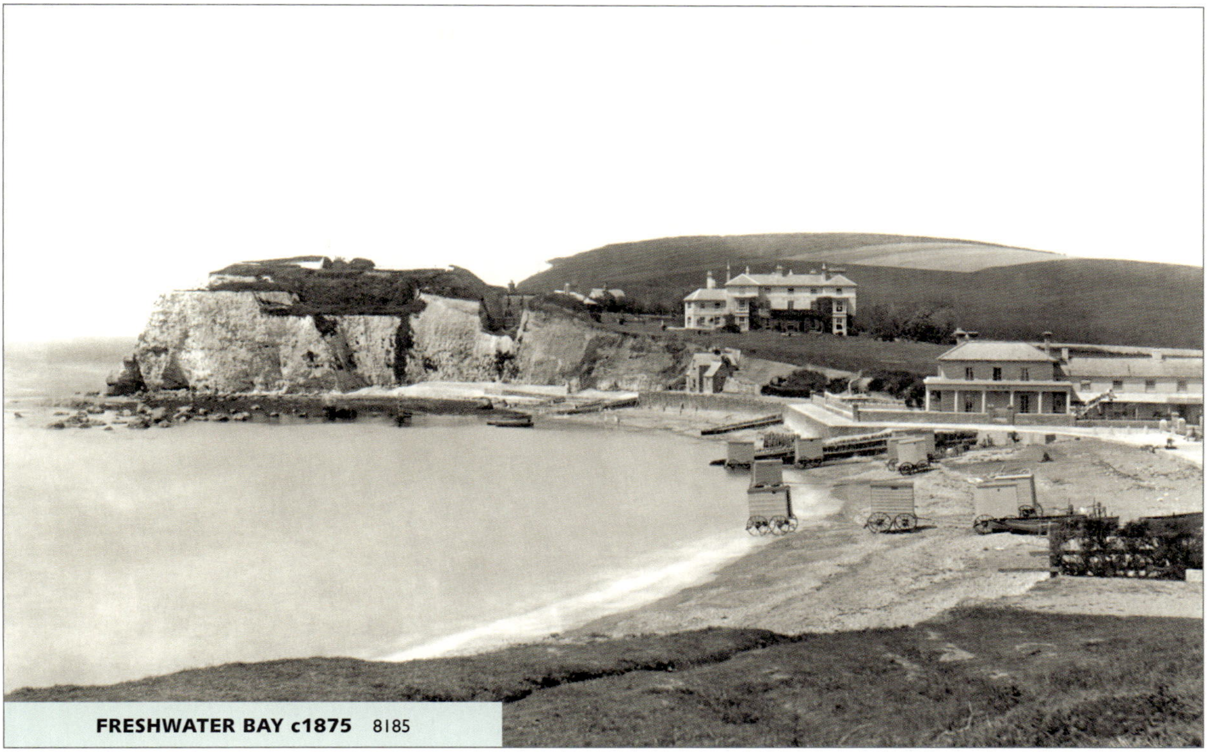
FRESHWATER BAY c1875 8185

Old maps refer to the 'Isle of Freshwater', virtually divided from the rest of Wight by the Western Yar. The only way to reach it used to be via the narrow strip of land between the river and the bay.

people - emerged gradually over thousands of years into the basic form we recognise today. This was after the final melting of the Ice Ages spelled the end for the massive chalk ridge linking Wight with a British mainland that was itself in the throes of divorce from continental Europe as global warming re-drew the map of the world.

The narrow, increasingly precarious, barrier between the old Solent river and the sea finally gave up the unequal struggle against the constant scouring of the rising tides. Dramatically breached, its disintegration allowed the sea to pour into the western Solent between Wight and what we know today as Dorset, joining the river flowing down present-day Southampton Water, which had already found an exit to the sea via the channel of the eastern Solent. At low tide, the depth of the water in the river-turned-sea would at that stage, and for some time to come, have been insufficient to prevent movement across the Solent on foot. But, essentially, Wight was now an island.

Precisely when this occurred is impossible to say with any certainty. The best guess is probably some time between 7,000 and 6,000 BC. At either end of the gap in the chalk, The Needles and Old Harry Rocks at Swanage remain as spectacular, if forlorn, evidence of this defining 'moment' in history.

However, to begin the story of Wight at this point is to ignore the millions of years, deep into prehistory, that preceded it. Wight may not actually have been an island before the chalk ridge was breached, but it certainly existed as part of a landmass, the 'Dinosaur Island' beloved by today's television documentary makers. Much of the extensive prehistoric evidence - usually the odd bone or two, but occasionally spectacularly complete skeletons - is unearthed at fairly regular intervals along or near the south-western coastline, the Back of the Wight. Here, the oldest rocks of the Cretaceous period, classified today as the Wealden Beds, were formed amid freshwater lagoons and estuaries before the dinosaurs' earthly dominance ended so abruptly around 65 million years ago.

Before there was Wight, before there were any British islands, before there was even a self-contained European continent, iguanodon and the huge brachiosaurus were among the dinosaurs who plodded and chomped their way in lush, humid conditions through a landscape about as far removed from today's as it is possible to imagine. Massive conifers towered above giant cacti, palms, cycads and other plant life akin to the modern Caribbean. Astonishingly, the primeval forest can still be seen off the Back of the Wight today, though barely recognisable to the untrained eye, in the form of the Island's Pine Raft. Twisted trees lie at the foot of Hanover Point, long since turned to stone.

Consensus among the archaeologists of prehistory has it that the forest died as the climate markedly cooled, causing the decline of the trees. Trunks, boughs and branches were then carried some distance along the course of a river until ending up, literally log-jammed, submerged in sand at the mouth of the river delta. Millions of years later they lie there still, not far from the naturally preserved footprints of a three-toed dinosaur, exposed at low tide in the clay of Brook Bay.

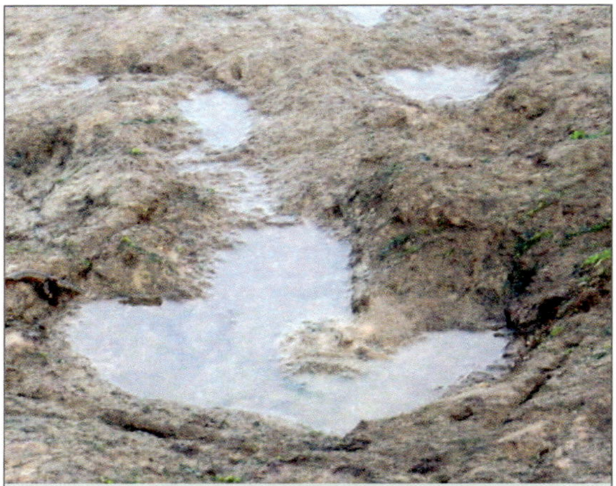

BROOK BAY, DINOSAUR FOOTPRINT 2005
ZZZ03988 (Matt Searle)

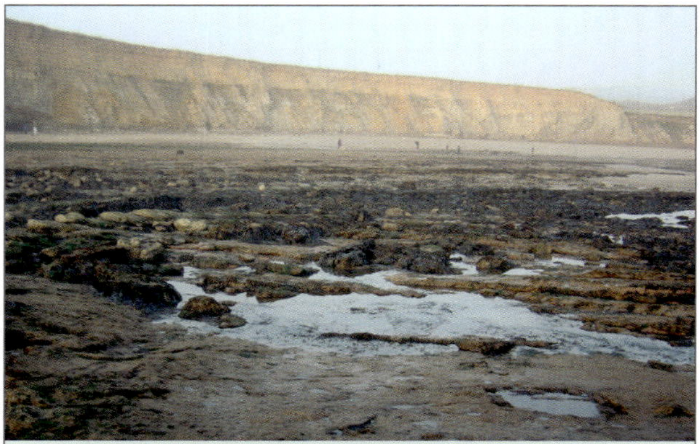

HANOVER, THE PINE RAFT 2005 H542701k (Matt Searle)

Dinosaur footprints (foreground) and the remains of the Island's fossil forest are seen here at Hanover Point.

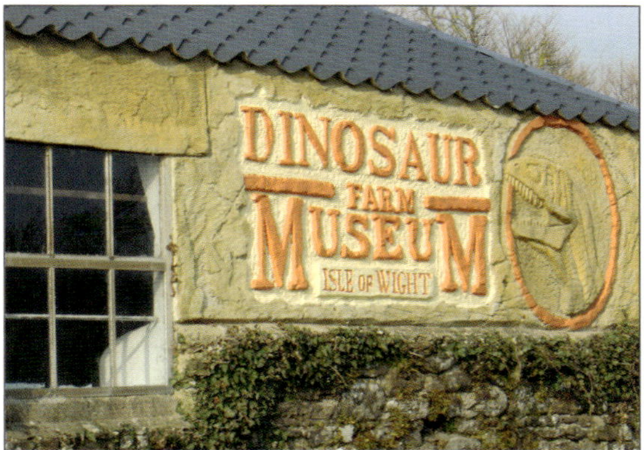

BRIGHSTONE, THE DINOSAUR FARM MUSEUM 2005
B543701k (Matt Searle)

To airbrush from the history of the Isle of Wight such extraordinary evidence of the primeval past is unthinkable.

It is only when you fast-forward through the best part of those 65 million years following the demise of the dinosaurs that you appreciate just how modern, in relative terms, the Island really is. The newly formed post-Ice Age offshore isle was the province of Stone Age men of the Mesolithic era. The contours of the land they surveyed were not much different to that of their 21st-century descendants. The Island would have been a little bigger, with the erosion of its coastline a subsequent process which is still ongoing, while its hills, the chalk downs which dominate the modern landscape, would have been a little higher than they appear today and the valleys between them a little less deep. Contours are one thing - but how was the Island's outline clothed back then?

The bleak, tundra-like landscape when the Ice Age was at its coolest, the coarse grass and stunted birch known to the hairy mammoth, whose teeth survive to confirm its former existence on Wight, had slowly evolved so that vegetation now covered the ground. Birch co-existed with pine, and later oak, as the Island's forests developed above thick undergrowth. Food was plentiful. Fish populated the sea and rivers; deer and wild boar were among the providers of meat roaming the land.

Initially - before and after the gradual final break with the mainland - those who lived off the land and waters of Wight were itinerants from nomadic communities. The Island's rivers, bays, harbours and beaches have yielded many clues to the lifestyle they pursued from their temporary low-level encampments, always close to the haunts of the animals and fish they hunted, snared and gathered. From arrowheads and fish-spears to scrapers, saws and axes - the relics of the craftsmen in flint have been found here.

When Neolithic farmers from the European continent began putting down roots in Britain some 3,000 years later, their arrival transformed the Island, its society and its economy, as dramatically as it did elsewhere in the south of England. These were the first true settlers, the first generations of Islanders, and the first to exercise a degree of control over the supply of food. Ample evidence of the animals, cultivation and trade that supported their domesticated life has re-surfaced on the Isle of Wight, though it is probable that there were no more than a few hundred at the most living there. How many of them were involved in lugging into place the Isle of Wight's one surviving man-made Neolithic monument, on the high ground

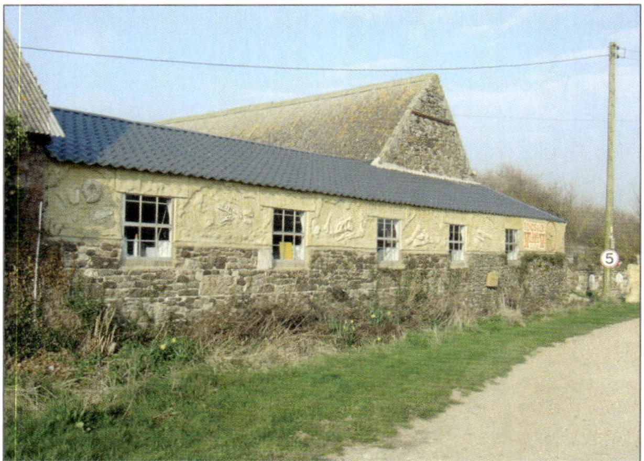

BRIGHSTONE, THE DINOSAUR FARM MUSEUM 2005 B543702k (Matt Searle)

The Dinosaur Farm Museum at Atherfield is close to the sites of many major prehistoric finds on the Back of the Wight.

above Mottistone in the rural south-west? It is an impossible question to answer, though fascinating to ponder.

More fascinating still is precisely what purpose drove those early Islanders to 'plant' around 5,000 years ago what later generations would call the Long Stone. Various theories have been put forward. Arguably the most plausible is the suggestion that the giant upright stone was one of a pair, possibly with the smaller stone that lies horizontally today at its base, carefully positioned to focus the light of the rising sun into an adjacent long barrow, where the ancestors of those who manoeuvred the stones into position lay

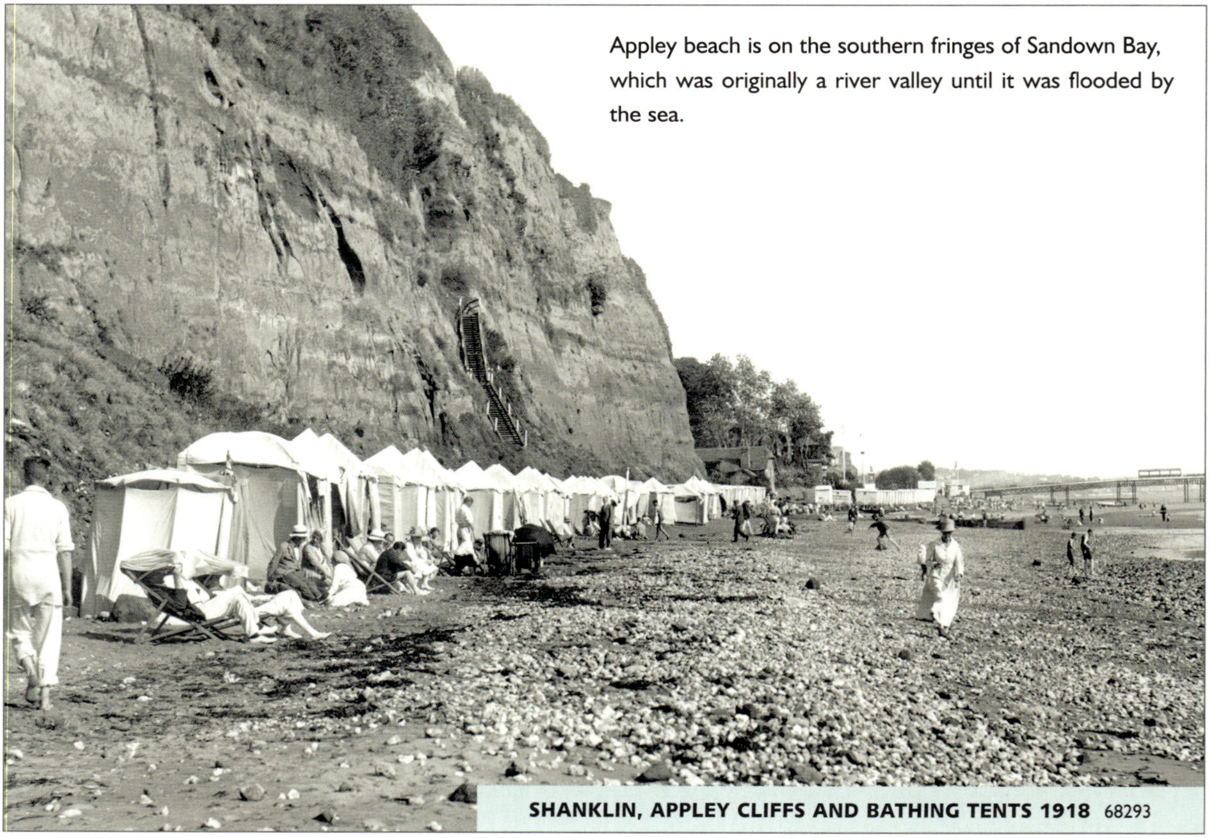

Appley beach is on the southern fringes of Sandown Bay, which was originally a river valley until it was flooded by the sea.

SHANKLIN, APPLEY CLIFFS AND BATHING TENTS 1918 68293

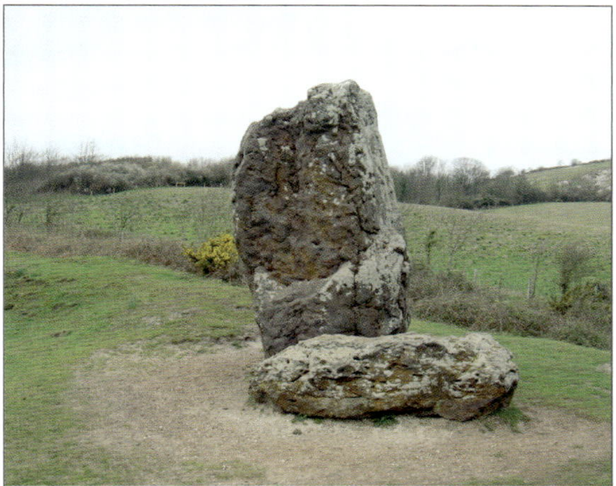

MOTTISTONE, THE LONG STONE 2005
M399702k (Matt Searle)

The Long Stone near Mottistone is the Island's oldest landmark relic of human activity.

buried, and whose spirits would hopefully be awakened by the warmth of the sun's rays. It is further suggested that this would have occurred only rarely, possibly on Midwinter's Day, adding further mystique to what is by far the oldest landmark relic of man's early occupation of the Island.

What, centuries later, the Anglo-Saxons made of it all, we can but guess. Yet it is probable that they recognised this as a site of spiritual importance. Arguably, at least, it was their elders who called men to solemn assembly here. It was, according to a widely accepted theory, their Moot (or Meeting) Stone, and it is a very short step from that to the name now borne by the nearby hamlet and manor house of Mottistone. But it is far, far too early in the tale of the Isle of Wight to be talking Saxons.

When Stone Age man finally gave way to the metal-workers of the Bronze Age, who moved to Britain from the culturally advanced central European regions in the early centuries of the 2nd millennium BC, the immigrant communities seem to have wasted relatively little time in taking up residence on the Island. Among the first to arrive, possibly as early as 1900 BC, were the Beaker people, who left behind examples of the distinctive pottery which, much later, would earn them their name. They buried other pottery artefacts alongside the dead in the chambers that have since been identified as theirs.

Wight holds many reminders of Bronze Age man. The profusion on the downland of their round barrows suggests a significantly increased local population, though whether this reached four figures is open to question. Sadly, the barrows have since proved irresistible magnets to a string of treasure-seeking grave-robbers as far back as medieval times, when barrow looting was often carried out by royal command.

Tramp along the coastal path across Headon Warren in the Island's far west for a good, and rare, example from the earlier Bronze Age, helpfully identified by information panels. The path has been diverted in recent years around the barrow to safeguard its own diminishing 'roundness' from further obliteration. Along with two smaller barrows in the field below, the Headon mound probably dates from around 1500 BC and, as the panels explain, was constructed above the graves of departed leaders. The looters holed it long before the walkers flattened it. Similarly desecrated, a few miles further

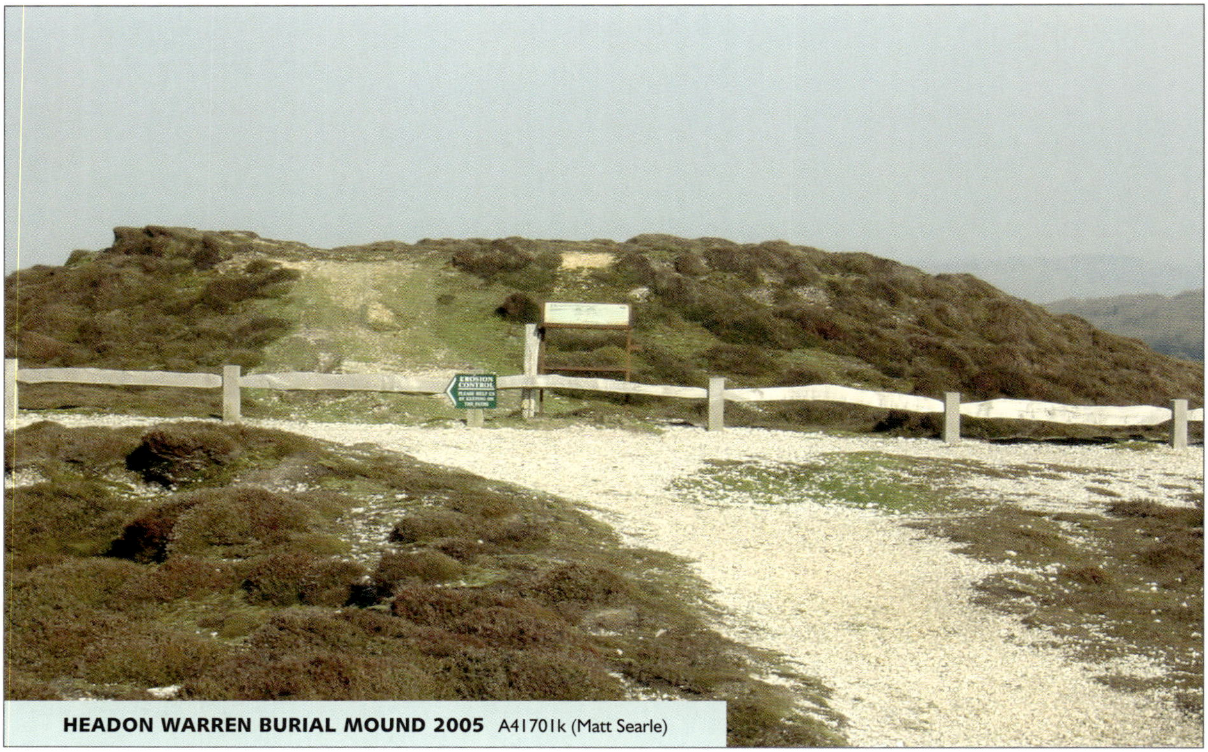

HEADON WARREN BURIAL MOUND 2005 A41701k (Matt Searle)

The footpath over Headon Warren has been diverted to prevent further damage to this rare example of an early Bronze Age mound.

east on Brook Down, are arguably the best surviving Bronze Age barrows - but not all the treasures buried with the Island's Bronze Age dead have been lost.

Probably the most spectacular collection of local Bronze Age finds was unearthed on the high ground in the east of the Island. Cleaned, catalogued and preserved, the spearheads, flanged axes, daggers and other metal implements which make up the Arreton Down Hoard were sufficiently important to be placed in the care of the British Museum. Along with the similar Moons Hill Hoard, which is still retained on the Island, these classic relics are also thought to date from around 1500 BC.

Three hundred or so years later, the gradual evolution of the Bronze Age into the Iron Age saw the arrival on the Island, and throughout southern England in general, of a fresh wave of 'incomers' who brought with them a more organised system of farming, in which crop rotation, the winter quartering of domestic animals and the first use of 'traction ploughing' were prominent features. These were the 'building blocks' for an economic and social system that, virtually unchanged, would extend into, and then through, the Iron Age right up to the time of the Roman occupation.

Celtic settlers in the Iron Age lived in somewhat cooler, wetter conditions than their predecessors. The use of iron opened up new horizons, almost literally as it provided them with the means to clear areas of forested land. It may be that a solitary tribal group occupied the Isle of Wight. This could explain why the remains of only one classic hilltop Iron Age fort have been positively identified there. The fort was built on Chillerton Down, close enough to the centre of the Island to suggest capital status. A single-rampart earthwork, complete with ditch, it seems to have been the sole defensive stronghold for a mainly peasant farmer population scattered around the Island, although mainly, it appears, in the southern half. The archaeological evidence tells us that they lived either in distinctive round houses at open sites - Sudmoor, near Brook, provides a good example - or within encampments enclosed by a system of banks and ditches, such as that identified at Knighton, near Newchurch.

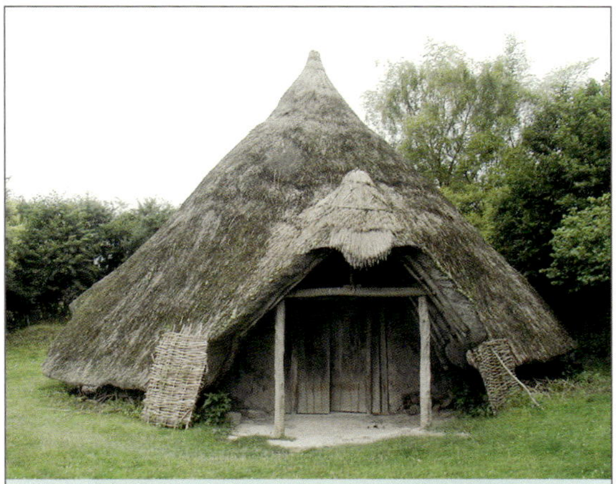

A RECONSTRUCTION OF AN IRON AGE ROUNDHOUSE ZZZ01297 (Reproduced by kind permission of the Ancient Technology Centre, Cranborne, Dorset)

The fort on Chillerton Down betrays evidence of an unfinished state. Maybe it was overrun before its builders had time to complete it. These were increasingly unsettled times. On the other hand, if only the one upland fort was required, as the archaeological evidence suggests, the very fact that Wight was an island might well have shielded its people from the worst excesses of inter-tribal warfare.

Its insularity could not, however, prevent the Isle of Wight from becoming part of the Roman Empire's conquest of Britain in AD 43 as the Emperor Claudius sought to impress the Roman masses with an early military victory soon after his elevation to the Imperial throne. The Island was taken by the 2nd Legion under the command of the inspirational 34-year-old Vespasian, but whether 'conquest' really is the correct term in the specific case of the Island's capture is very much open to question. By lumping it in with Vespasian's campaign heroics - his 30 battles on British soil, the taking of more than 20 'towns' (hill forts) and the subduing of two powerful Celtic tribes - the future Emperor's biographer, Suetonius, vaguely implied that force might have been employed when the isle 'near Britain,' as he described it, was 'brought under our rule', but his choice of words do not rule out peaceful diplomacy. There are several good reasons for doubting the use of force.

First, it is unlikely in the extreme that the semi-clothed Celtic population was sufficiently large, equipped or trained to defend - or even consider defending

- the Island from the highly disciplined, well turned-out, 5,000-strong 2nd Legion. Second, there is no archaeological evidence to suggest either a Roman military incursion or the building by the Imperial forces of a fort in the immediate aftermath of conquest (though one may well have been constructed at Carisbrooke much later) which might have been expected had Vespasian's troops encountered any meaningful resistance.

The third reason for doubting a forced surrender is the strong possibility that Islanders might actually have welcomed the Roman takeover. This rather depends on where their pre-invasion tribal sympathies lay. Did they support the Atrebates, a Belgic people who had crossed to Britain from north-west France and were strongly represented on the mainland, east of the River Avon? Or were they allied to the other major tribal group, the Durotriges, west of the Avon in Dorset? While the former enjoyed close links with the Roman Empire, the latter were openly hostile to the increasingly influential role taken by the Imperial power since Julius Caesar's conquest of France and initial foray into south-east England nearly a century earlier. Both tribes used coinage in their extensive trading activity, and coins from both have been discovered on the Isle of Wight, indicating that the Island's late-Iron Age community traded with Atrebates and Durotriges alike.

All of which means that it is impossible to be sure of the Island's tribal allegiance,

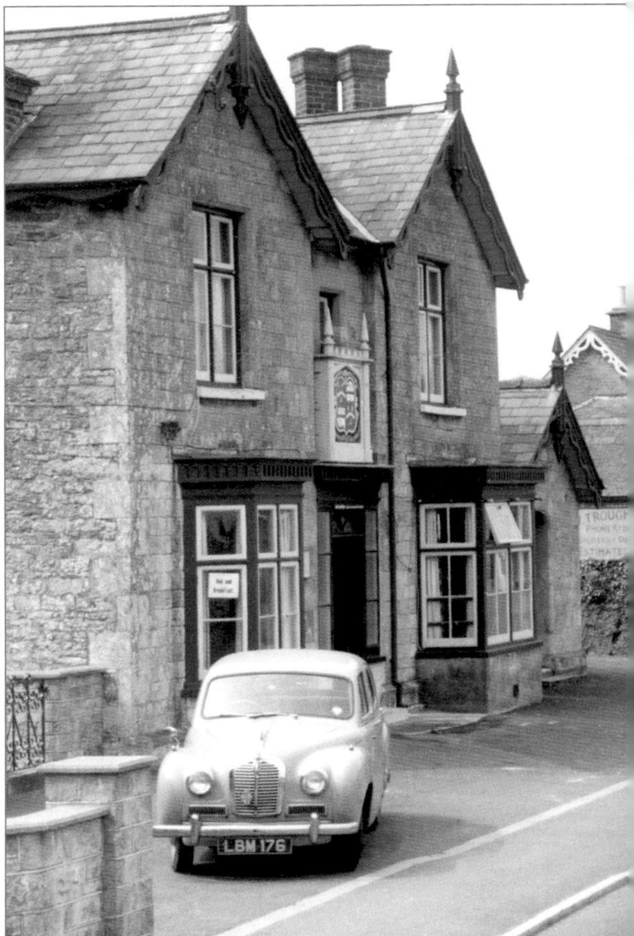

BINSTEAD, THE VILLAGE c1955 B772003

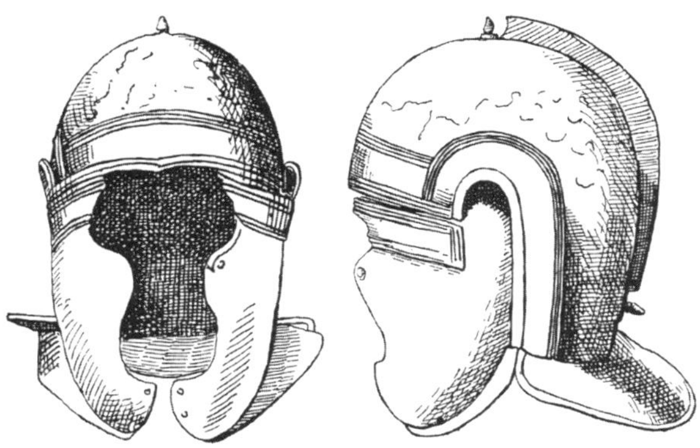
AN ARTIST'S IMPRESSION OF A ROMAN HELMET FOUND IN GERMANY ZZZ01293

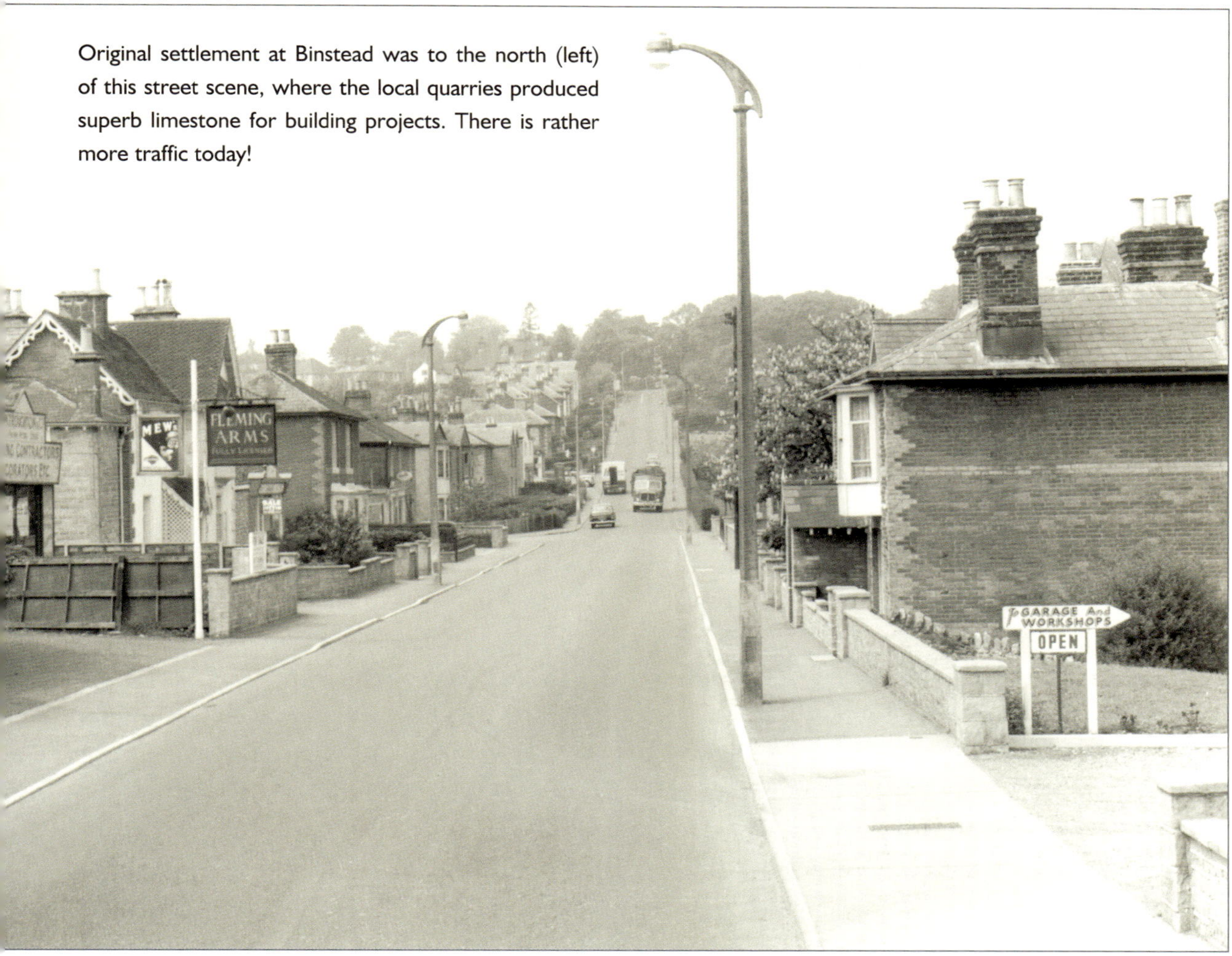

Original settlement at Binstead was to the north (left) of this street scene, where the local quarries produced superb limestone for building projects. There is rather more traffic today!

if allegiance there was, before the Romans came and equally impossible to state with any certainty how the Islanders reacted to the arrival of the 2nd Legion. Yet, it remains a strong possibility that Vespasian's 'conquest' was achieved without bloodshed or the use of military might, and with either local indifference or support.

Precisely where the 2nd Legion first set foot on the Island is another mystery, with few pointers, archaeological or historical, though the large expanse of land-locked tidal water which would later be known as Brading Haven (until its 19th-century reclamation) seems the most plausible landing site.

Suetonius's original Latin manuscript refers to the Island as insular Vectem or Vecta. From this is derived the word Vectis, the name by which the Island would be known throughout nearly 400 years of the Roman occupation. This was an altogether new name, but what it replaced is a matter for conjecture, and countless theories. Some have it that the pre-Roman name was 'Guith', a Celtic term denoting separation. Others suggest 'Ynys yr wyth' (a Celtic term for the Island of the Channel). If either of these two - or possibly both, at different times - is correct, then the origins of the word 'Wight' were seemingly established long before Vespasian's conquest and the Roman name both replaced, and was in turn replaced by, its derivatives.

However, it should be noted that an alternative theory holds firmly to the view that the present name derives from Wihtgar, the Saxon chieftain who ruled the Island in the 6th century, The origins of 'Vectis' are as clear as those of 'Wight' are muddied, and the old Roman name remains in fairly widespread use on the Island today, notably in the title of the local bus company, Southern Vectis.

Having in all probability been captured without a struggle, Vectis did not feature at all in the subsequent catalogue of rebellion, savagery and bloodshed which characterised so much of the early Roman presence in Britain. This sophisticated occupying power, culturally light years ahead of the indigenous Celtic population, left no evidence to suggest anything other than a peaceful, settled occupation of its offshore possession from start to finish. Initially, life in the Island seems to have been little changed by the invasion. The archaeological record confirms that its people continued to live in the same pre-conquest settlements, doing much the same things as they had done before Claudius sent in the legions. They had, for example, turned out pottery to meet local need before the Romans came, and they went on doing so afterwards, apparently unhindered by their new masters.

The most significant contribution made by Vectis to the occupation in the 1st century was the use of its quarried limestone in the construction of the magnificent Fishbourne Palace, just across the sea in present-day West Sussex. The Romans probably had the palace built for Cogidubnus, a noted Celtic tribal leader, to reward him for the unstinting support he gave to the Imperial cause. Did this mean, as some authorities have with good reason suggested, that Vectis was placed under the control of Cogidubnus following the division of the old tribal kingdom of the Atrebates into three Roman 'civitates'?

During their period of occupation, the Romans developed no towns on Vectis, and neither is there any firm evidence of a Roman road. What does survive, however, are the substantial remains of several villas - a villa is simply the Latin term for a farm - built to accommodate the households of the wealthy Romano-British. Perhaps the Island, much like today, was a favoured place of retirement, possibly for important former officials or military leaders, though it was only the rich who could afford the scale of retirement home provided by the villas unearthed to date. Whether they really did serve this secondary purpose or not, they certainly seem to have provided the hubs around which an intensive agricultural 'machine' thrived, involved with farming both crops and stock.

These elaborate homes, their rectangular design so markedly at odds with the Celtic

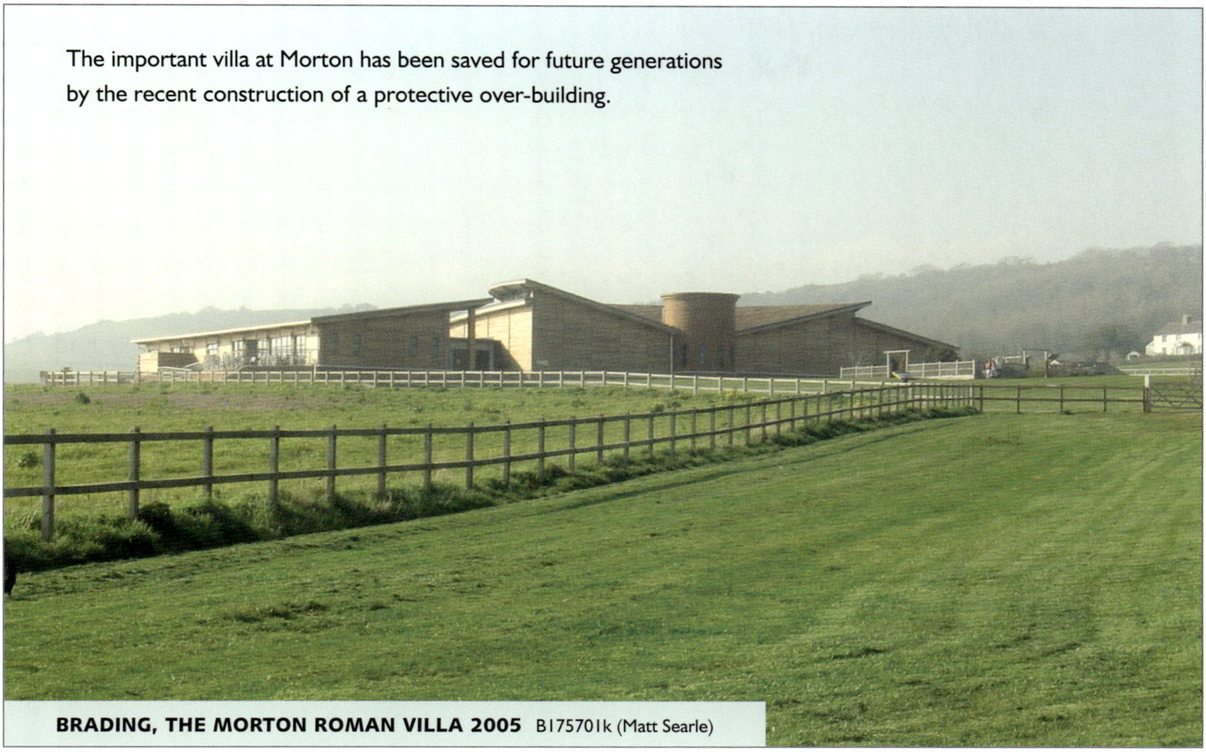

BRADING, THE MORTON ROMAN VILLA 2005 B175701k (Matt Searle)

roundhouse tradition, were isolated country retreats. The best known, overlooking the vast inland waters of Brading Haven at Morton, may have started out soon after the arrival of the Romans in the 1st century as something altogether more modest - the archaeological evidence suggests just a few simple timber buildings - but the site had certainly been dramatically transformed by the beginning of the 4th century. With its buildings grouped around a courtyard, this was now the location for a large, complex farmhouse, clearly the home of someone of considerable importance. It probably remained so until the Roman retreat from Britain in AD 410, and then retreated itself into ruin, disappearing beneath the rising ground over the centuries that followed until, finally, it was re-discovered in 1879.

The Morton villa's remains, including the bath block, the ingenious central heating system, frescoes depicting mythical scenes and the magnificent floor mosaics in the preserved west wing, are now among the Island's most famous tourist attractions, managed by the Oglander Roman Trust, which has just constructed a new protective 'over-building' and visitor centre, ending fears that the excavated remains might have to be re-buried in order to protect them from the ravages of exposure.

A second of the Island's Roman villas is also open to the public. Its discovery in 1926 changed the accepted wisdom surrounding

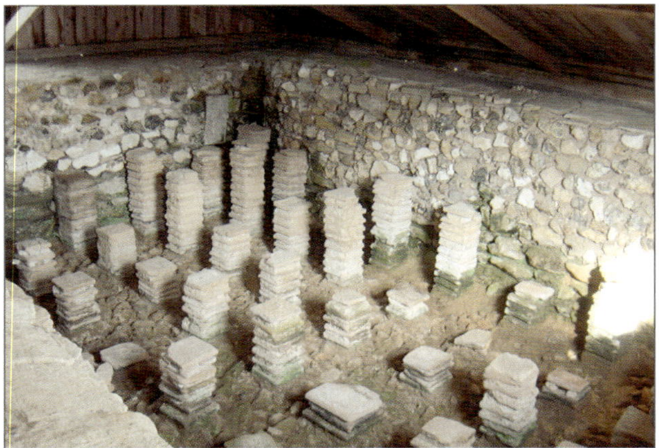

BRADING, THE MORTON ROMAN VILLA, THE HYPERCAUST 2005 B175702k (Matt Searle)

A close-up view of the ingenious underfloor heating system installed at the Brading Roman Villa.

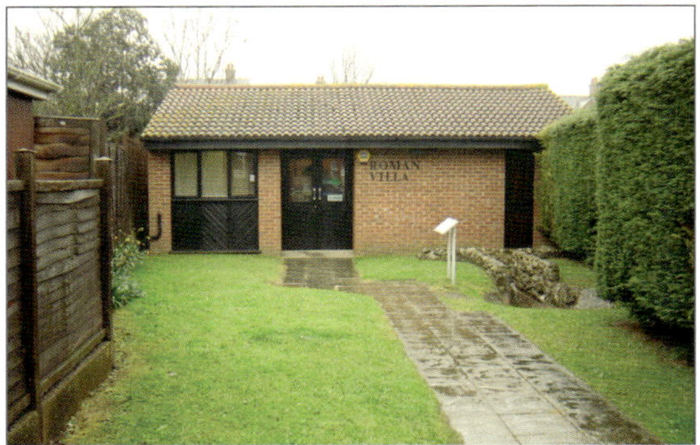

NEWPORT, THE ROMAN VILLA 2005
N247018 (Matt Searle)

The discovery of a Roman villa at Newport in 1926 led to a re-think on the origins of the town's capital.

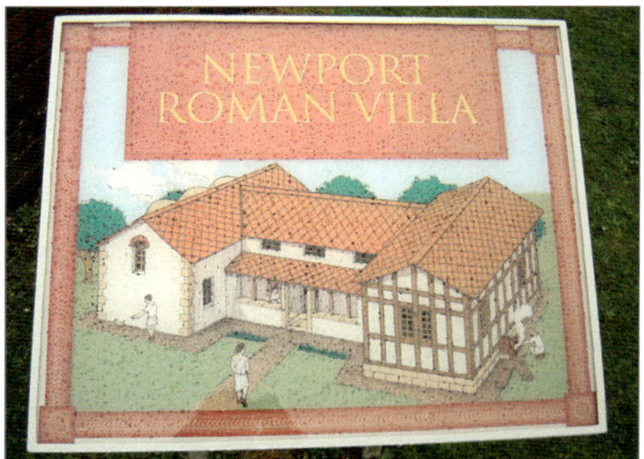

NEWPORT, THE ROMAN VILLA SIGN 2005
ZZZ03991 (Matt Searle)

The sign outside the Newport villa provides a good idea of how the building might have looked when occupied.

the origins of Newport, the Island's capital. Until then, there was nothing to seriously challenge the assumption that the town's easily traced medieval heritage represented the start of its development. In one sense, that remains the case today in that there is no suggestion Newport was a Roman township. Yet there was a Roman presence, before there was a town. The clues lay literally buried until the sinking of foundations for a garage at Cypress Road, in a residential area not far south of the town centre, revealed extensive remains of what is believed to be a Romano-British farmhouse dating from around AD 280. Back then, it would have stood at the centre of a substantial, isolated country estate in the heart of the Island, sloping down to the River Medina. There was no courtyard at Newport's villa; this was a building with corridors, and with a bath block and hypercaust system remarkably well preserved after more than 1,600 years beneath the ground.

Off the tourist maps can be found examples of the two remaining types of villa built during the Roman occupation of Britain. The remains of aisled farmhouses have been identified at Combley, south of Havenstreet, and in the vicarage garden at Carisbrooke, together with those of a 'cottage' style villa at

Rock, which lies to the north of Brighstone. Furthest north was the villa at Gurnard, excavated in 1866, but the opportunity for further archaeological investigations there was ended for good by the coastal erosion that long ago claimed it for the sea. Other villas await full excavation and examination at Bowcombe and nearby Clatterford, south-west of Newport. There may well be more. When it came to the raw materials for building villas, Roman Vectis had the lot, from the clay needed for bricks and tiles to the limestone and flint for the walls and the timber used in the floors and roofs.

All the evidence points to a comfortable co-existence for the primitive Britons on the Island and their Roman masters, whose presence ensured four centuries of peace and trade-fuelled prosperity on Vectis, where they got about as close as they could in cool Britannia to the climate of their homeland. It was certainly a very distinctive class system, but it seems to have worked. Then, ten years into the 5th century, the final curtain came down on this harmonious state of affairs with the recall from Britain of the occupying force to the heartland of its crumbling empire. The Dark Ages beckoned.

Not all the Romans left. For many, Britain was no far-flung outpost of empire, but the only home they knew. On the Isle of Wight, as elsewhere, some stayed behind and no doubt tried to galvanise the native population into some sort of cohesive shape to withstand the threatened invasion by the bloodthirsty, Rome-hating Germanic tribes who had begun attacking mainland Britain before the withdrawal of the empire. By the mid 5th century these tribes were approaching a state of dominance across the southern British kingdoms in the absence of the Imperial power. The Island stood no chance of effective resistance. For nearly 400 years its Celtic people had not been required to fight anyone, or even prepare for a fight; they had left it all to the Roman protectorate. Now the Roman protection was gone and the

The Roman Tin Trail

Although it may have originated as far back as 300 BC, the Island's role in the lucrative Cornish tin trade is most closely associated with the Roman occupation. Whether legend or fact, the story goes that the tin was brought overland from the West Country to Lepe, on the Hampshire coast, then transported across the Solent, possibly via a low tide causeway, to Gurnard, on Wight's northern shoreline.

From there, it was taken southwards across the Island to a tin mart at Niton, then on to Puckaster Cove, a fortified depot the Romans knew as Pudica Castra, for the start of a sea crossing to France and onwards, overland, to the Mediterranean port of Marseilles. The sea was then rejoined for the final part of a trading route that would eventually take the tin to Rome itself. This complex journey via the Island is explained by a fear of piracy on the sea south of Cornwall!

Island was ripe for capture. But who actually did the capturing?

Documented Isle of Wight history starts with the chronicles of the Venerable Bede, and runs immediately into controversy. If his account is believed, the Island was initially taken by Jutish warlords along with the land opposite, in southern Hampshire. Archaeological evidence - notably distinctive 'grave goods' at a number of sites - lends powerful support to this version of events. Yet, many historians have cast serious doubt on Bede's interpretation; indeed, on his account of Jutish intervention in the south of England generally. Some scholarly accounts of the Island's history ignore the Jutes altogether. This, of course, is the problem with the well-named Dark Ages; there is relatively little hard evidence to confirm anything conclusively. There is, however, consensus that the Island, despite its obvious vulnerability, was slow to fall into the hands of the Germanic barbarians.

There is also widespread agreement that, in AD 520, the Island was taken by Cerdic and his son, Cynric, who many sources describe as West Saxon chieftains, and who mercilessly slaughtered countless Islanders in the area of Carisbrooke in the process of annexing Wight to the sprawling kingdom of Wessex. Others are clear that the West Saxon takeover of Wight did not occur until the 7th century and there is much dispute about the true ancestry of Cerdic and Cynric. Were they actually descended from Angles rather than from Saxons? Would they be more accurately described as Jutish Saxons? Were they actually Germanic at all, as the names hint at a Celtic heritage?

West Saxons are recalled in history as Christian converts but, from the available evidence, it seems certain that Cerdic and Cynric were nothing of the sort. They arrived with their fearsome hordes on the Isle of Wight in 530 as true pagans, and the introduction of Christianity to the Island population would have to wait until well into the 7th century, long after it was embraced elsewhere in Britain.

Whatever the actual sequence of events, the dates and the origins of the key movers, the murky history seems to clear somewhat following the death of Cerdic four years after his conquest of the Island. Its control then passed to two of his relatives, Stuf and Wihtgar, whose name is widely accepted as the place-name origin for both Wight and Carisbrooke (via Wiht-gara-burh, the place of his burial in 544). Quite why Wihtgar's name, in its derived form, should have stuck in this way is another mystery. We know very little about him. In fact, we know very little at all about 'his' Island's history for the best part of the 120 years that followed his death.

It is hard to accept that Islanders basked in undisturbed calm while, on the mainland, bloody battles raged in an unceasing, and well documented, struggle for power. Yet the Isle of Wight is simply not mentioned in the chronicles until, in 661, it became the focus of attention for Wulfere, son of Penda, King of Mercia. He was every bit as merciless as Cerdic and Cynric had been 130 years earlier in laying the Island waste, wresting it from

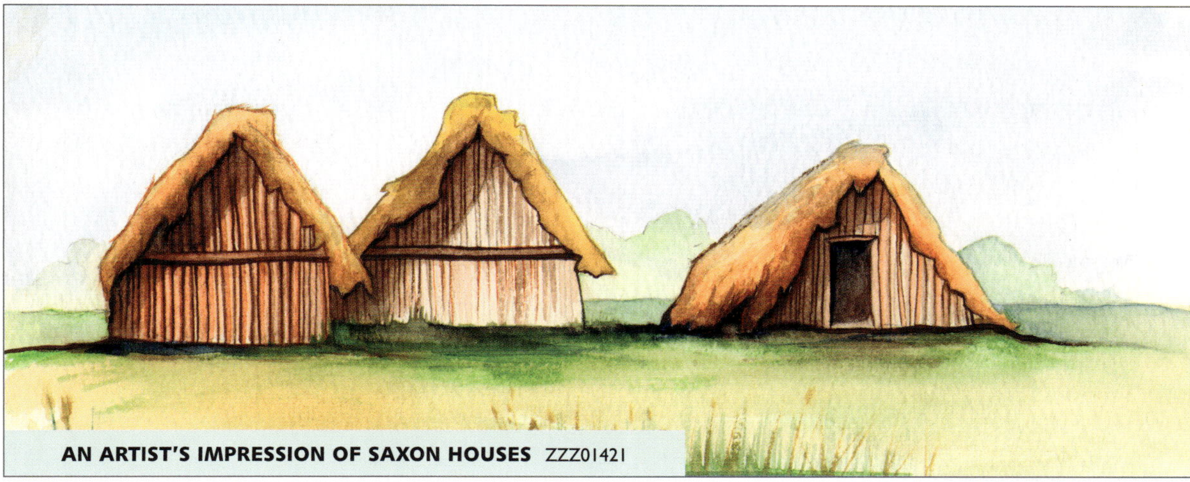
AN ARTIST'S IMPRESSION OF SAXON HOUSES ZZZ01421

Wessex and handing it over, for political and personal reasons, to Aldewach, King of Sussex.

The fruits of Wulfere's triumph in 661 went horribly sour 25 years later when the Island was wrenched back for Wessex by King Caedwalla, shortly after he had killed Aldewach in battle. Caedwalla's campaign was to have far-reaching consequences. The Wessex king had converted to Christianity. The suspicion is that he may have done so more with an eye on forging power alliances with other Christian rulers than for purely spiritual reasons, but Bede tells us he was so horrified at the evidence of idolatry he found among the still-pagan people on the Isle of Wight that he 'by cruel slaughter endeavoured to destroy all the inhabitants thereof and to place in their stead people from his own province ...' In other words, murder the pagans, and bring in the Christians.

Despite holding true to the old religious traditions for so long, Islanders had earlier been given a taste of Christianity with the arrival of the priest Eoppa, ordered to the offshore pagan outpost by Wilfrid, his bishop, and Wulfere in the wake of the latter's capture of Wight. As idolatry was still rife 25 years later, we must conclude that Eoppa had found it hard going.

Did you know?

Wulfere's Town

Wulfere's capture of the Isle of Wight in 661 is probably recalled in the names of the several Island settlements, some now disappeared, known as Woolverton (Wulfere's town).

Caedwalla's wrath changed all that. His initial resolve to slaughter the entire population mellowed into a directive that 300 of the Island's 1,200 families should be handed over for suitable treatment to the missionary bishop, Wilfrid of York (confusingly, this is a different Wilfrid to Eoppa's bishop), who happened to be on the Island at the time with his chaplains, Hiddila and Bernwin. So, what happened to the remaining Islanders not selected to receive Wilfrid's zeal? It is possible that they were sacrificed to satisfy Caedwalla's savage need to make examples of those who failed to follow the Christian creed. Perhaps they were replaced by an influx of Wessex Christians from the mainland. The new Island converts, we are told, were baptised by Bishop Wilfrid's team at Brading, where tradition asserts that the first of the Island's churches was constructed. And so, Bede recorded, 'last of all the provinces of Britain, the Isle of Wight accepted the faith of Christ.'

As well as being the *last* place to accept Christianity, according to some historical interpretations the Isle of Wight holds the dubious, and unlikely, distinction of being the *first* recorded location for a Danish attack on England. It appears to have been successfully repelled in AD 787 - which many sources would agree was the year Scandinavian savagery was initially unleashed on English shores. If it happened, the raid of 787 must have come as a very rude shock indeed for Islanders who, by all accounts (or the lack of them), had managed to live without serious fear of invasion or attack since the days of Caedwalla. There had been further changes of ownership for Wight, but these had been settled without the wholesale slaughter of its inhabitants.

Christianity had flourished and more churches had followed Wilfrid's establishment of the first church at Brading. Traces of later Saxon church-building can be found today on the Island, principally at Arreton and Freshwater, but nothing visibly remains of any of the churches said to have been founded by Wilfrid and his followers. Waves of rebuilding have washed them away.

After the initial excitement in 787, the Isle of Wight seems to have spent most of the following century largely undisturbed as the Danish invaders, the vicious Vikings whose sole purpose in life was to raid, fight and destroy just about everything they encountered, began their battering of the English mainland in earnest. The Viking raids were a periodic offensive that would extend well into the 11th century. It was always just a matter of time before the Island got involved. The Anglo-Saxon Chronicle records what may well have been the most famous involvement. In 897, three or so years before his death, Alfred the Great, King of Wessex, sent his new, speedy long galleys in pursuit of six Danish ships attacking England's south coast. The Chronicle tells us the Danes landed men on the Island 'and did much harm there.' It seems they came ashore at Brading, which was not the cleverest of moves as nine of Alfred's galleys proceeded to snare them within Brading Haven by mounting a blockade at its main entrance.

As the tide went out, both fleets became grounded. A fierce battle was then fought in the mud, the Saxons losing 62 men and the Danes, nearly twice that number. Three of the Viking ships managed to escape from the Haven but, badly damaged, at least two of them ran ashore off Selsey Bill in Sussex.

Their crew-members were rounded up and taken to Winchester to be hanged.

Not everyone goes along with the idea that Brading Haven was the setting for this battle; many prefer to locate it further west, in Poole Harbour. Be that as it may, Alfred's notable defeat of the Viking foe has given rise to a - literally - colourful legend on the Island, which maintains that the fighting extended as far inland as the area of a peaceful present-day copse, north-west of Brading. The copse and the once revered well inside it, that springs forth red-glint water, share the name of Bloodstone. Never mind the scientific reason for the water's redness, which is caused by algae growth on the pebbles, the legend insists this is actually the endless flow of blood from the Saxons and Danes who battled it out in 897.

There were to be no repeat performances - not on the Isle of Wight, at least - for more than a century. The death of Alfred the Great in 899 removed an outstanding Wessex monarch who was truly great in many ways beyond military prowess, not least in diplomacy, a sense of universal fair treatment and political acumen. He was the first sovereign who could be regarded, if unofficially, as a king to the English nation as a whole. Thanks to his astute planning, national kingship was developed over the next half century through the succeeding reign of Edward the Elder, who led the successful clawing-back of the bulk of the Danelaw, the substantial Danish territorial gains in Yorkshire, Leicestershire, Lincolnshire and East Anglia, and those of Athelstan and Edmund. Despite the on-off fighting with the Norse foe on the mainland, there is no evidence that any Dane set foot on the Isle of Wight again until the national situation was changed for the worse by the murder of Edward the Martyr in 979 and the arrival on the throne of the infamously unready Ethelred.

Ethelred's attempt to buy off the Danes backfired miserably when they pocketed the money and carried on raiding at every opportunity. From 981 onwards, they used the Island as a convenient base for launching attacks, usually with devastating effect, on the adjacent mainland coastal region. This did not mean that the Islanders themselves were spared - far from it. 'Nothing withstood them ... they never ceased from their evil doings,' reported the Anglo-Saxon Chronicle, looking back gravely on a typically savage, and clearly one-sided, encounter for the local population with the Viking hordes in 1001.

When the Danes were not actually raiding the Isle of Wight, they were very often occupying it, according to the documentary record, though archaeological evidence is distinctly lacking in support of this. There was certainly little hope of any Island settlements remaining settled when the Vikings were around.

They couldn't have been in residence during the Christmas of 1013, when Ethelred himself was on the Island, taking time off, it would seem, from the stressful business of holding onto his kingdom in the face of constant aggression from Sweyn, King of the Danes. Three years later, Ethelred died and was succeeded by his son, Edmund Ironsides. Following the death of his own father, Sweyn's son Cnut fought a bitter campaign against Edmund which resulted in them splitting the kingdom in half and ruling their separate areas. However, Edmund then died suddenly, and his half of the kingdom was taken over by Cnut, who thus became King of all England. He helped his cause by marrying Ethelred's widow and imposing a new system of national government based on the conversion of Northumbria, East Anglia, Mercia and Wessex into four constituent earldoms.

The Anglo-Saxon Chronicle tells us Cnut visited the Isle of Wight in 1022 'with all his ships.' Was this a bid to subdue a remnant of offshore resistance to his rule? It seems improbable, as the Island had been battered enough already. Danish rule, which would extend through the subsequent reigns of Cnut's sons, Harold and Harthacnut, was more likely to have been accepted with a shrug of resignation. The Chronicle offers nothing to explain Cnut's show of force.

Harthacnut's death in 1042 heralded the return of the Wessex line to the English throne through the accession of Ethelred's son, Edward, whose legendary, but probably over-stressed, piety and all-round goodness would ensure his elevated status in English history as 'the Confessor.' Unable to produce an heir of his own, did Edward, who had earlier spent 25 years exiled in the fast-developing Duchy of Normandy, really promise the English throne to William, Duke of Normandy, who became one of several claimants to Edward's legacy?

On the Isle of Wight in the mid 11th century, the finer points surrounding the English succession were lost in a haze of further unrest as Edward the Confessor's family conflict with Godwin, Earl of Wessex, turned nasty and a fresh batch of marauding Danes launched piratical raids against the impoverished Island population. Events took a decisive turn early in 1066 with the death of King Edward and the contested succession to the throne of Godwin's son, Harold, who had become Earl of Wessex on his father's death 13 years earlier. Soon afterwards, the Island appeared likely to suffer yet another violent takeover when Harold's half-brother,

WHIPPINGHAM, THE FOLLY INN c1955 W79003

The site of the Vikings' Island encampment is believed to have been on the west bank of the River Medina, opposite the Folly Inn.

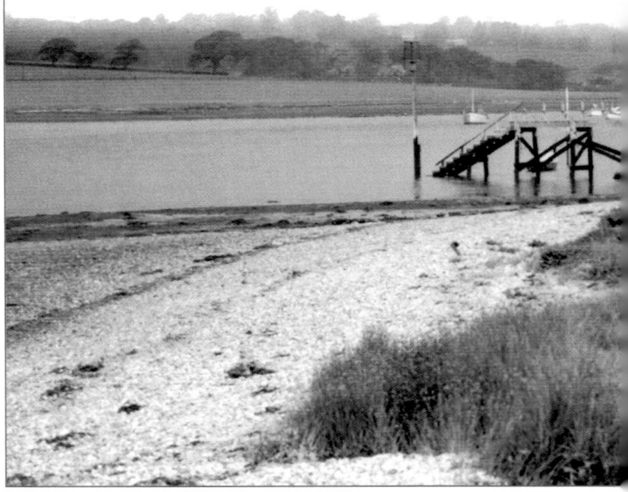

and sworn enemy, Tostig arrived off the coast from his Normandy exile with an invasion fleet, intending to take Wight prior to a full-scale onslaught on the English mainland.

In the event, Tostig was turned back before he could set foot on the Island. The next attempt at invading England from Normandy would prove altogether more successful. This time it would bring stability and security via the firm hand of law, and it probably couldn't have come too soon for the beleaguered people of the Isle of Wight.

Did you know?

A Haven for Vikings

The place most closely identified with the Vikings on the Isle of Wight is Werrar, on the River Medina's west bank, between Northwood and Parkhurst. It was probably used by them as winter quarters early in the 11th century. Some historians suggest they destroyed an existing village before taking over the site. That would have been entirely in character.

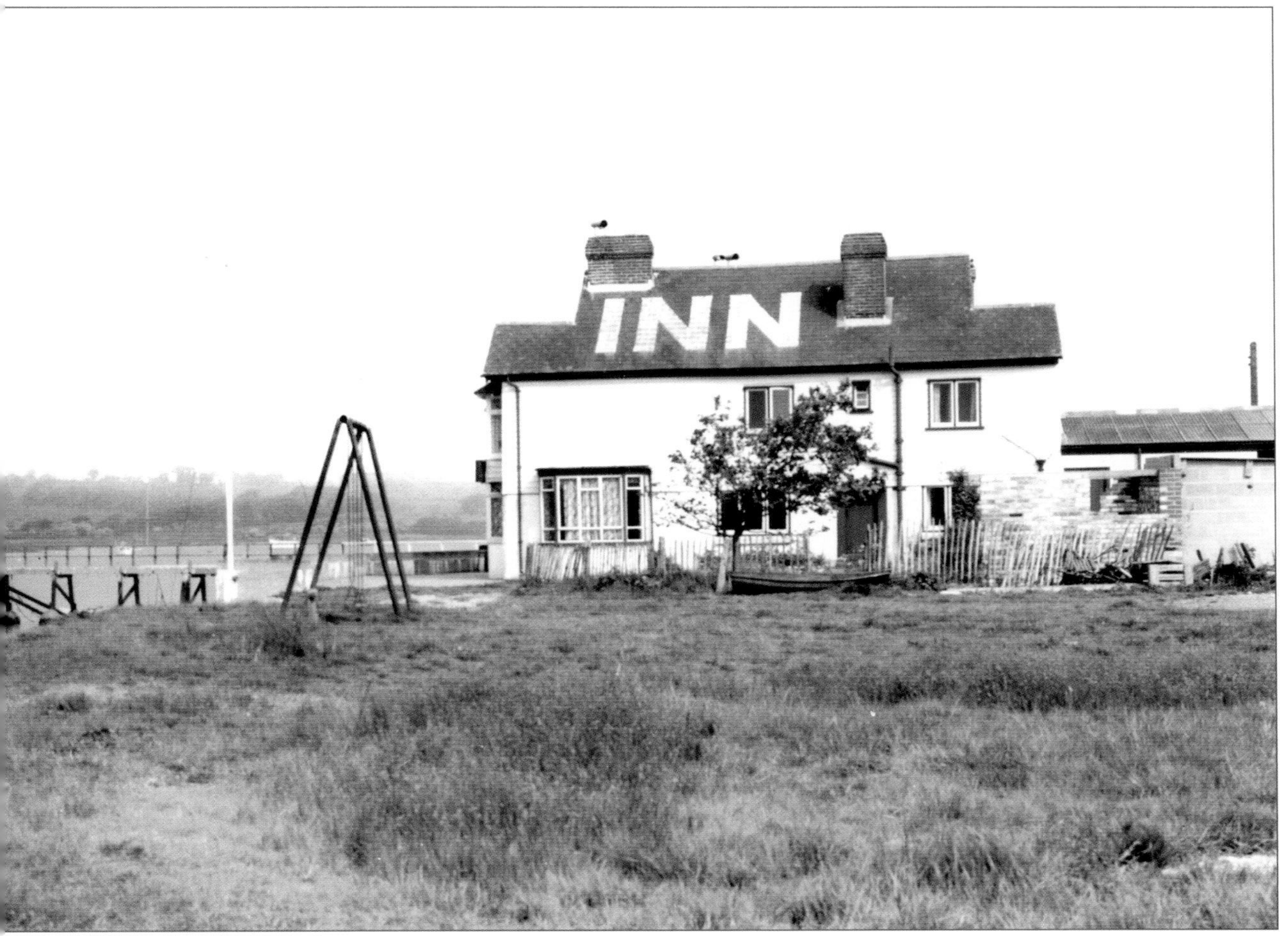

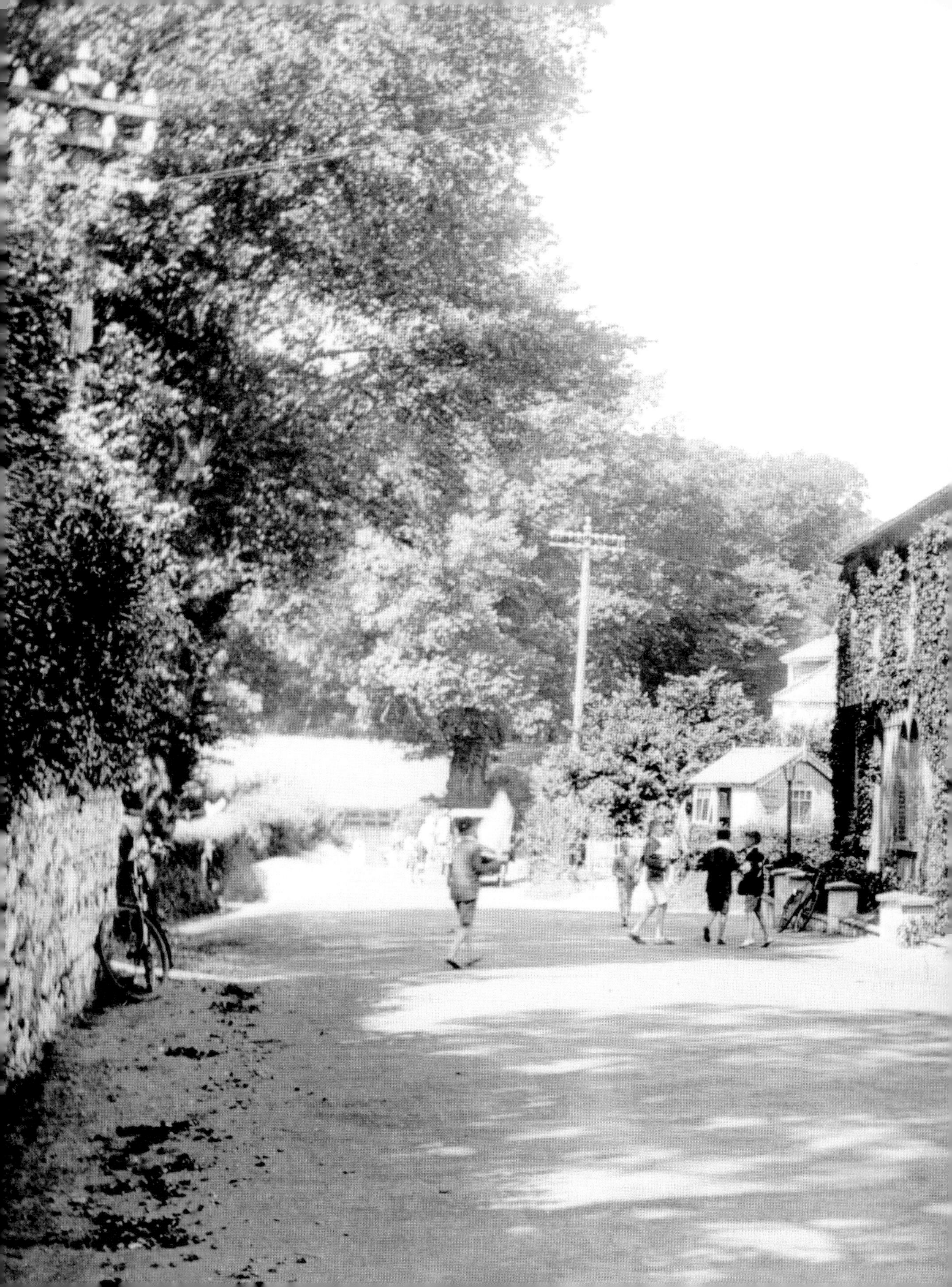

CHAPTER TWO

Norman Fiefdom – French Target

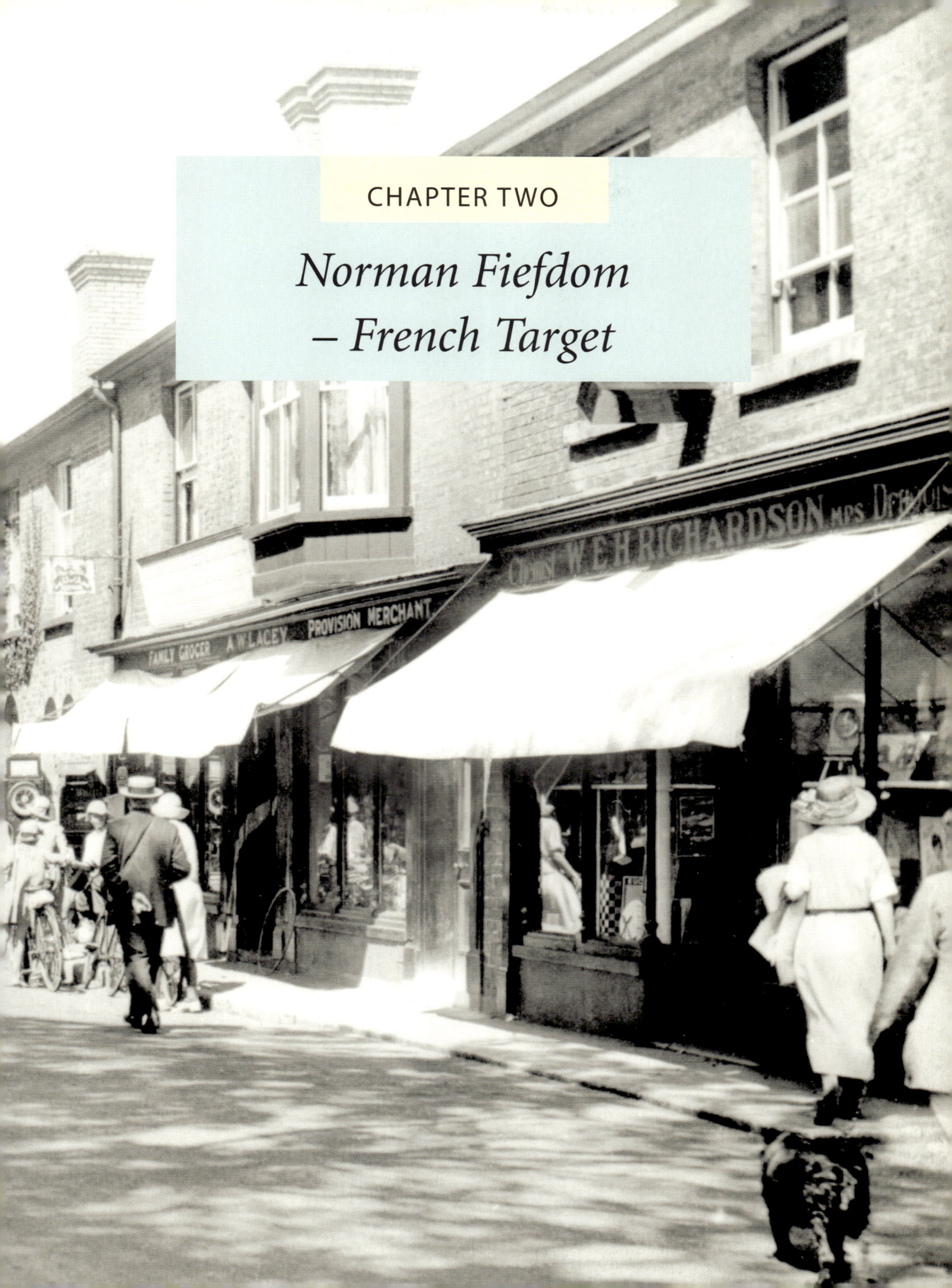

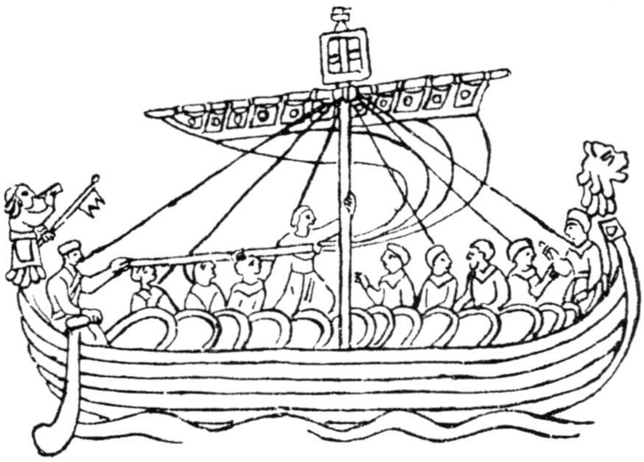

A NORMAN SHIP ZZZ01294

WHEN KING HAROLD'S exhausted army hurried southwards in the autumn of 1066 from defeating Harold Hardrada's Norwegian challenge to the English throne at Stamford Bridge, near York, a force led by two men named William prepared to inflict the decisive blow that would bring the Anglo-Saxon kingdom to a bloody end. William of Normandy's famous triumph over Harold at the Battle of Hastings on 14 October owed much to the military genius of his kinsman, lifelong friend and senior commander at the battle, William FitzOsbern, Grand Seneschal of Normandy, a man destined to play a major role in the development of the Isle of Wight under the firm grip of Norman rule.

The Conqueror, acclaimed King of England at Westminster Abbey on Christmas Day 1066, was generous in rewarding those who had helped deliver the kingdom into his grasp. Heading the list was FitzOsbern. His rewards were many, in the shape of titles and land, and they included the Isle of Wight. FitzOsbern was created Lord of the Island and that meant everything implied by the impressive title. In effect, he now owned the Island and, from the start, he was allowed to govern it as a semi-independent feudal state, answerable only to the Conqueror as his Norman overlord. It was a considerable gift.

This was a particularly strange turnaround for Wight which, according to some sources, only months earlier had hosted King Harold throughout the entire summer of 1066 as he awaited the expected invasion from Normandy, before being dragged northwards to meet the Norwegian threat.

FitzOsbern, all-powerful, was quick to impose the Norman imprint on Wight. Saxon landowners were ousted and replaced by his own followers, introducing Norman families whose descendants would feature prominently in Island affairs for centuries to come. Uniquely, they were obliged to swear allegiance to FitzOsbern as their Lord, rather than King William, and to dispense justice at the Cursa Militen, or Knights' Court, a peculiarly Isle of Wight institution which amazingly continued to sit as the Knighten Court, albeit in considerably watered-down form, right up until the mid 19th century. While the full breadth of the Court's early post-Conquest responsibilities are now unclear, it seems safe to assume that it was capable of handing down the most severe of punishments to the peasant population for a wide range of offences under the harsh Norman system of justice.

Holding a conquered, resentful population in check was vital, but of equal priority for FitzOsbern was the need to keep the Island as safe as possible from the threat of attack.

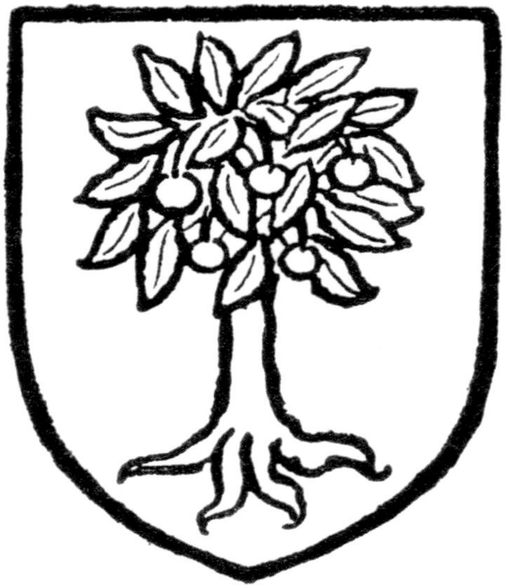

THE FITZSTUR FAMILY CREST
ZZZ03994 (Author's Collection)

The FitzSturs were among the great post-Conquest Norman families on the Isle of Wight. The Domesday Survey reveals that William FitzStur owned 21 of the 126 Island manor properties.

William the Conqueror's position on the English throne was far from secure in the years immediately following the Conquest, although the various rebellions against Norman rule up until 1070 largely bypassed the Island, and the fear of Danish raids had not yet dissolved. FitzOsbern needed a near impregnable defensive stronghold in his offshore domain. Happily for him, there was an obvious location for it, right at the heart of the Island, and the Saxons had already done the groundwork.

While debate continues over the possibility of an earlier Roman fort on the site, there is no doubt that the Norman castle at Carisbrooke was constructed above a Saxon 'burh' - one of the many fortified camps that sprung up to defend England's coastal regions against Viking violence. The Saxon builders had chosen easily the best available site for their fortress, high on a steep-sided ridge, south-west of

This shows an unusual view of the Norman castle of Carisbrooke, with the old mill in the foreground.

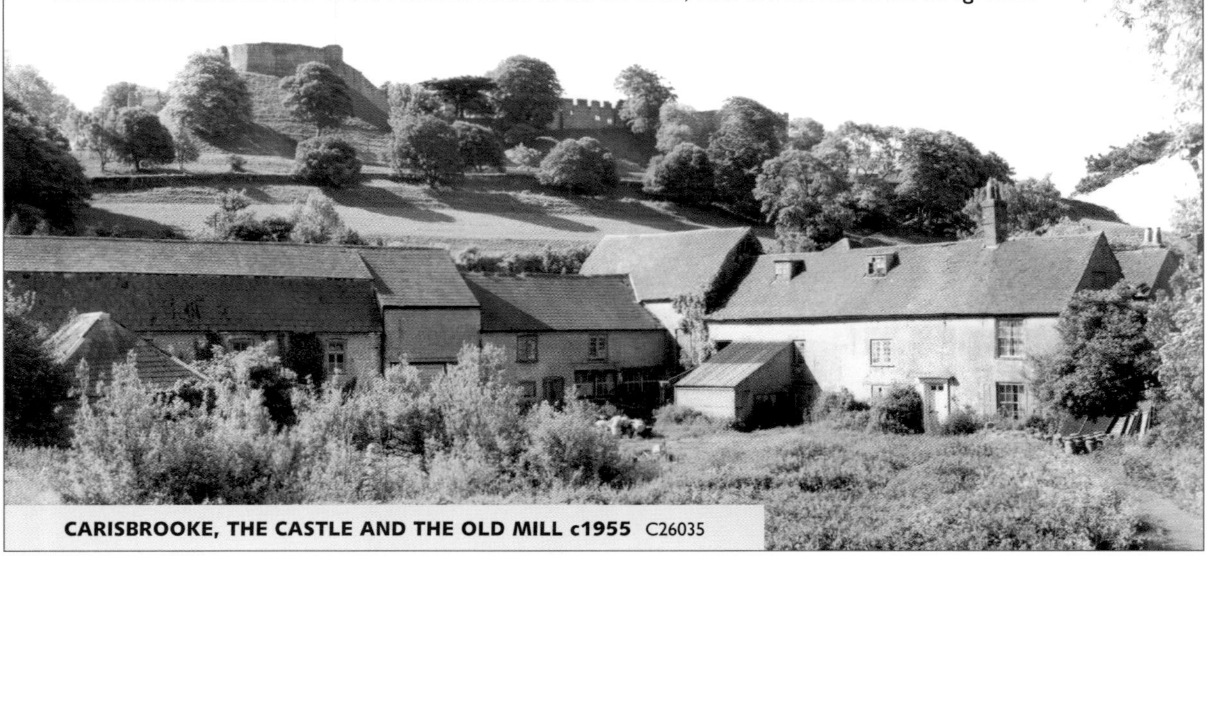

CARISBROOKE, THE CASTLE AND THE OLD MILL c1955 C26035

present-day Newport, which offered its defenders the luxury of spectacular, and strategically vital, panoramic views. FitzOsbern could have had no doubts that the stone-faced walls of the Saxon stronghold provided the ideal foundations for his own lofty fortress. The Norman castle's staged development would follow precisely the original lines of the Saxon burh. However, FitzOsbern's contribution to that development seems to have been confined to the building of an initial campaign fort in a corner of the site. It was left to his successors to finish the job.

The first Lord of the Island governed a town-less mini-state, with much of the land in the north and west still covered by forest. Carisbrooke is often described as the early Norman capital of the Island, but the settlement that developed beneath the castle mound was not planned, and did not really function, as a town. The people of Wight lived in village communities, grouped around the several churches constructed since the Island's late conversion to Christianity.

Seven original parishes stretched from the north coast to the south, their boundaries roughly parallel and their potential for prosperity, roughly equal. From east to west (using present-day place-names), the Saxon churches at Brading, Newchurch, Arreton, Carisbrooke, Calbourne, Shalfleet and Freshwater provided the focus in each case. Arreton parish, the largest, was later split into four following the creation of new, smaller parishes centred on Whippingham, Godshill and Niton churches, with Arreton in the middle.

Newchurch was one of the seven original Isle of Wight parishes, taking in present-day Ryde and Ventnor. William FitzOsbern may have built a 'new church' here to replace a Saxon original at nearby Alverstone.

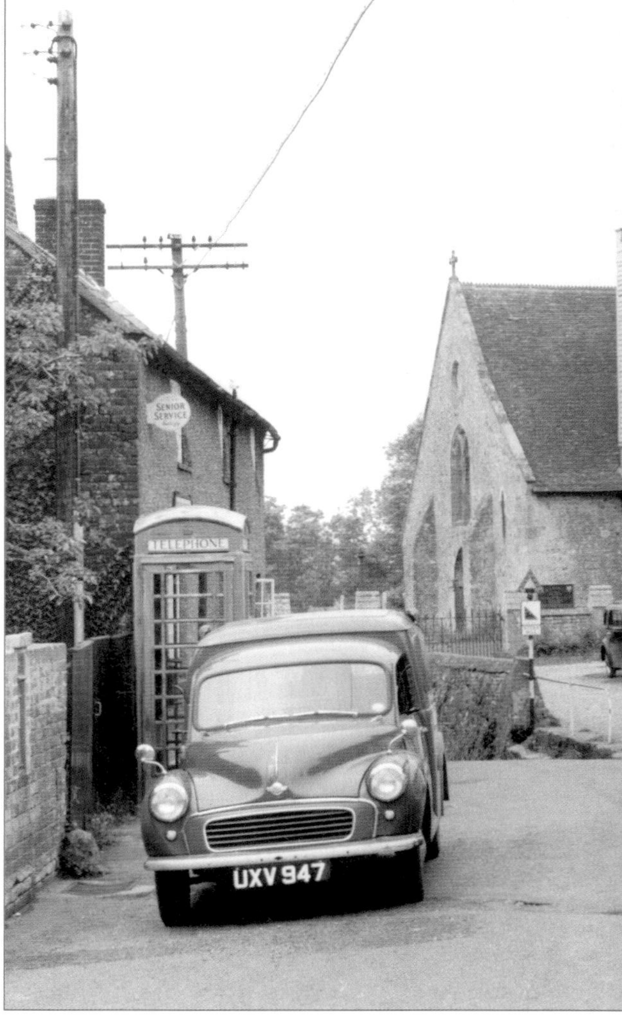

It was a remarkably substantial gesture when William FitzOsbern bestowed on the Normandy abbey of Lyre not only the spiritual management but also the proceeds - the tithes on agricultural produce and the rents - of no less than six of the Island's established churches. With a Norman

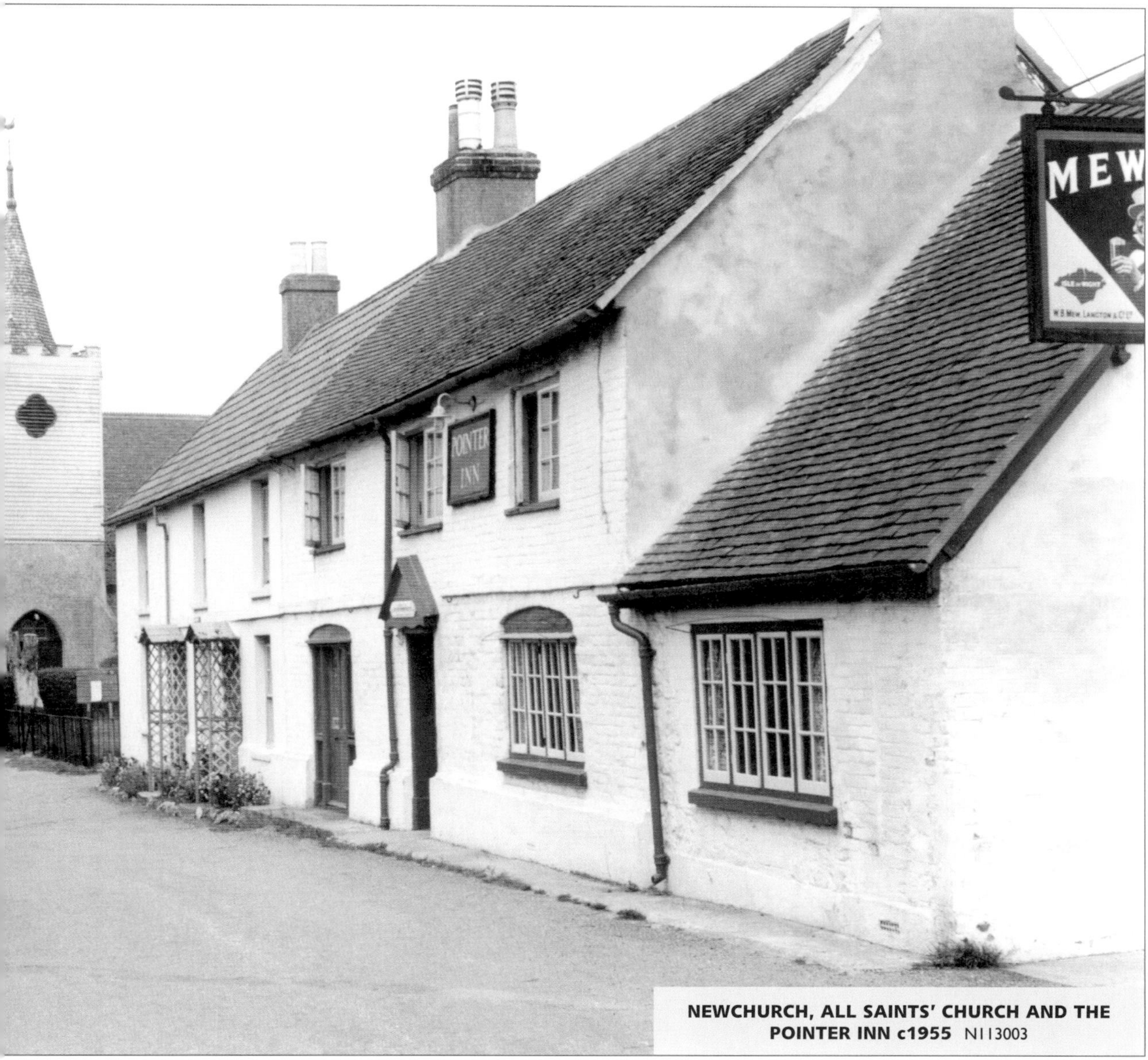

NEWCHURCH, ALL SAINTS' CHURCH AND THE POINTER INN c1955 NI13003

warlord's typical need for a demonstration of piety, thus erasing any guilt he may have felt over the shedding of so much blood in his military career, FitzOsbern had founded Lyre Abbey in 1045. Now, by guaranteeing it the income to maintain buildings and develop Christian ministry in the Isle of Wight parishes, he probably thought he had done more than enough to secure a safe passage to a heavenly afterlife. The churches were those at Arreton, Freshwater, Godshill, Newchurch, Niton and Whippingham. Together, the area of their parishes covered virtually half of the entire Island.

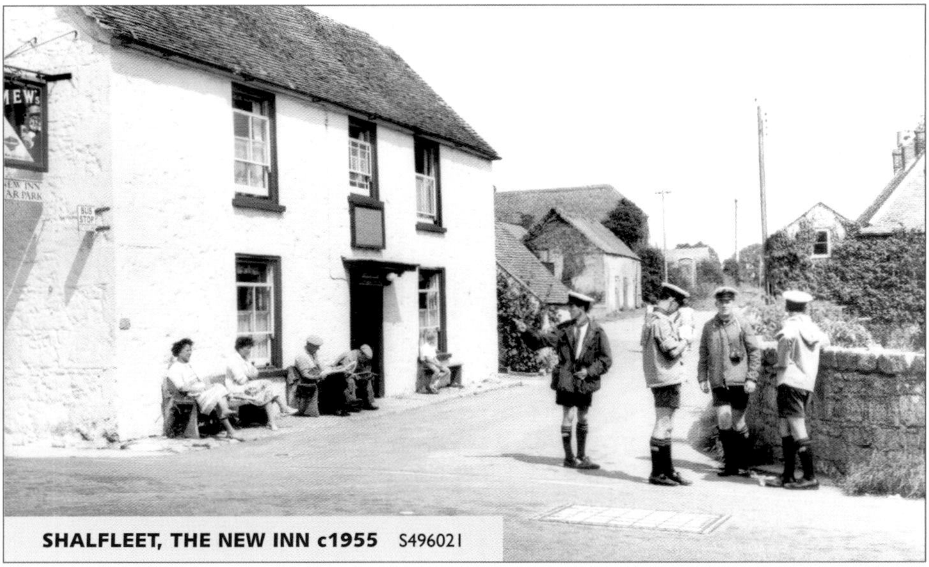

SHALFLEET, THE NEW INN c1955 S496021

Traffic is light-controlled in Shalfleet – another of the Island's original parishes - today, half a century after this picture was taken. The award-winning New Inn is still in business.

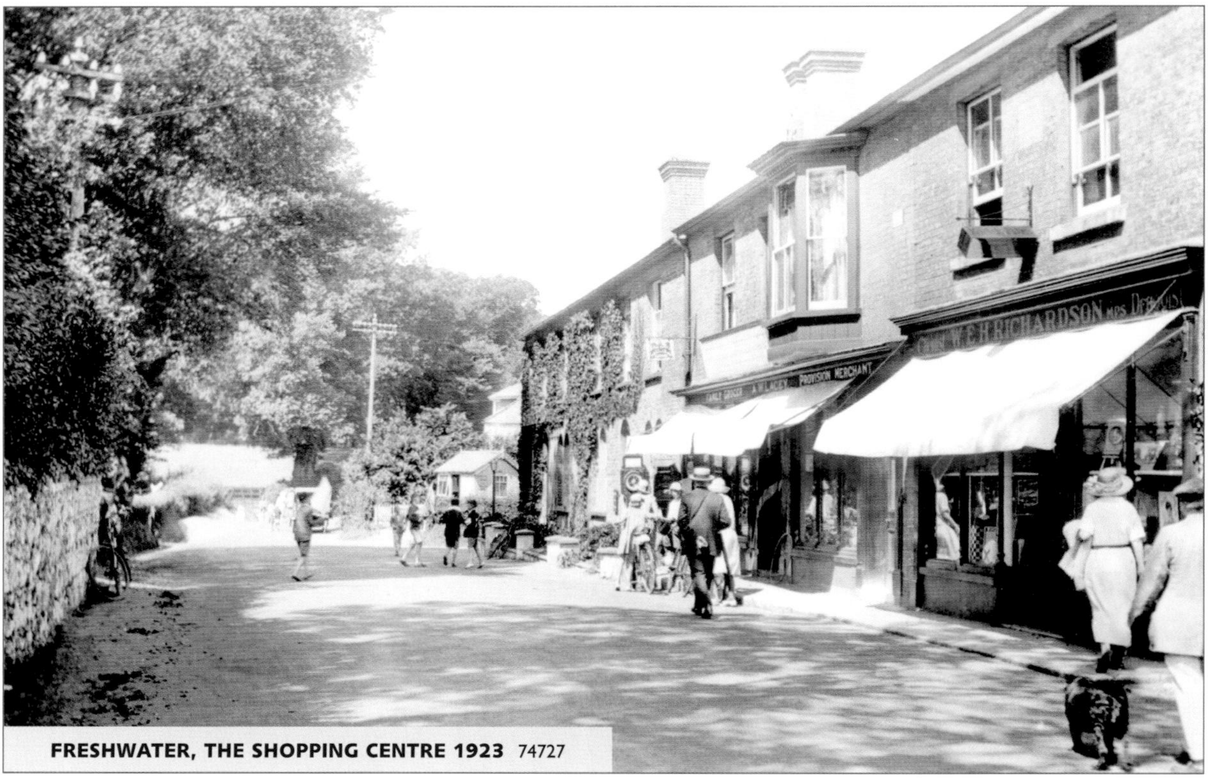

FRESHWATER, THE SHOPPING CENTRE 1923 74727

Freshwater was furthest west of the original parishes, but modern development has occurred some distance from the original village. Freshwater is now the largest commercial centre in West Wight.

FitzOsbern wasn't long in the Isle of Wight. Having successfully established Norman rule, he left England to fight - and eventually die fighting - in Flanders. The Island was then thrown once more into chaos when FitzOsbern's aggressive son Roger rebelled against the king in 1078, after taking over the Lordship. It cost him dearly, resulting in life imprisonment and the loss of the Island, which reverted to the Crown. William the Conqueror then underlined the new era of direct rule when he paid the Island a visit to put an end to another bit of treachery within his own family.

This time, the culprit was his half-brother Odo, Bishop of Bayeux (he had personally supervised the weaving of the famous tapestry) and Earl of Kent. Odo, it is said, had used the Island to organise an extraordinary expedition to Rome behind the king's back in a bid to become Pope. Enraged, William had him intercepted in the Channel and Odo was hauled back to the Isle of Wight to face the wrath of the Conqueror in the 'great hall', probably little more than a barn, at the fledgling Carisbrooke Castle. Odo soon found himself in mid-Channel again, this time heading for a dungeon in Rouen. No trace of that hall at Carisbrooke remains; the present great hall is a 13th-century replacement.

'He who holds Carisbrooke holds the Isle of Wight,' ran the traditional maxim and, for the remainder of the reign of William I, then through that of his successor, William Rufus, the castle and Isle remained with the Crown. The Lordship of the Island was revived by Henry I soon after his succession in 1100, again as reward for a trusted ally. It was granted to Richard de Redvers, who had supported Henry in seeing off the challenge of his elder brother, Duke Robert, to the king's titles, a quarrel finally settled on a Normandy battlefield. The powerful de Redvers family were destined to make an indelible imprint on the Isle of Wight as they held on to the Lordship for an unbroken period of virtually 200 years, enjoying the same near-absolute powers first granted to FitzOsbern in 1066.

Not that it was always enjoyable. The second in the de Redvers family line to hold the Lordship, Richard's son, Baldwin, Earl of Devon, notched up a series of good works during an eventful and far-reaching stewardship of the Island. But he scored a spectacular own-goal by siding with the Empress Maud (the daughter of Henry I) in her dispute with her cousin King Stephen over the accession in the wake of Henry's death in 1135. A year later, Carisbrooke Castle was given its first taste of military action when an angry Stephen besieged and captured it from Baldwin, who was promptly sent into exile by the triumphant monarch. Nobody was appointed to fill the void he left behind on Wight, and Baldwin eventually returned, reinstated as Lord of the Island, where he died in 1153. Remarkably perhaps, his great castle at Carisbrooke has come under attack only once more during its entire history, in 1377.

The castle begun by William FitzOsbern had acquired under Baldwin's father its characteristic motte and bailey (mound and courtyard) outline, and it was probably

Baldwin himself who saw to it that stone walls had been added to both by the time of his inglorious spat with King Stephen in 1136.

It was fortunate for the Island that the leadership qualities of the first Baldwin de Redvers - three later family members who held the Lordship were also known as Baldwin - was not permanently sacrificed. Many important developments occurred during his tenure at Carisbrooke. Among them, the Island at last began to develop proper towns. First in line was Yarmouth, the port of what Islanders now call the West Wight. Baldwin granted its first town charter around 1135. While this clearly makes Yarmouth the oldest of all the Island's towns, its origins as a place probably pre-date that first charter by less than 150 years. Much older is Thorley, a mile or so inland, which enjoyed port status under the Roman occupation and may even have been known to the Celts before that, fulfilling the same function. Thorley holds the key to Yarmouth's eventual arrival as a town.

It sat snugly on the estuary of what is now the Western Yar. Over many years, silt claimed the estuarine waters, leaving the port progressively more difficult to reach by ship. It was obvious a new landing place was required, nearer the coast at the mouth of the river. With Thorley left to slumber on

YARMOUTH, THE BUGLE INN 1923 74740

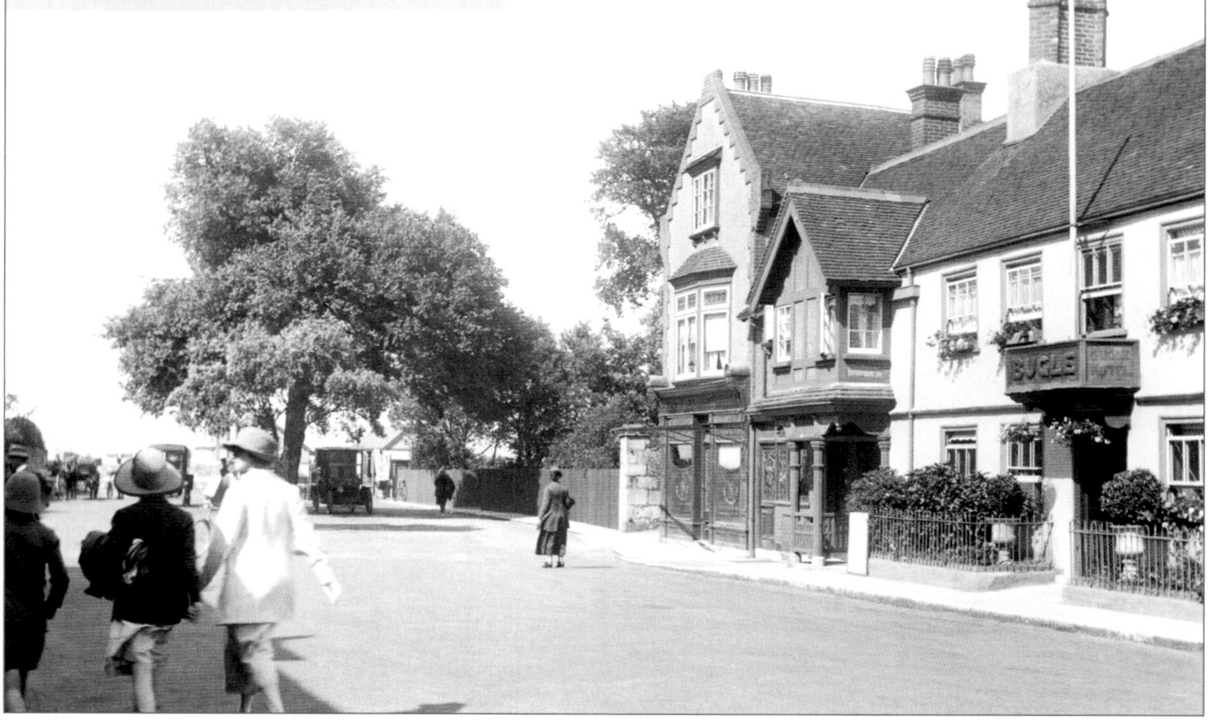

Yarmouth is the oldest, and least changed, of the Island's towns. This view of the Square features the Bugle, one of several of the name on Wight. The word is an Island term for a young bull.

QUARR ABBEY c1875 8144

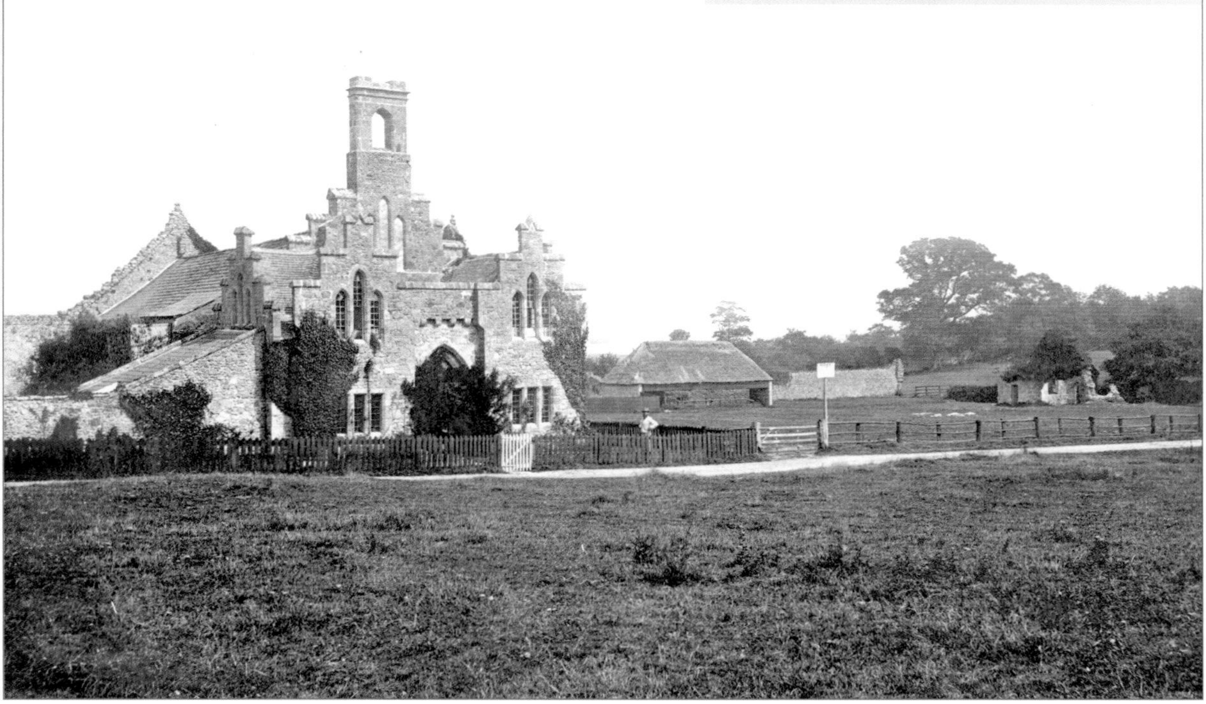

The remains of the great Cistercian abbey are seen here 340 years after it was suppressed. Originally from Savigny, Normandy, the monks once owned farming land throughout the island. This photograph shows the view north.

through the centuries as an inland village, the port at the river mouth inevitably spawned the emergence and growth of a completely new settlement around it. By 991, the year of its first recorded mention, it was known as Ermud, which later evolved into Eremuth and, finally, Yarmouth. This was the first of only three Island towns that were actually planned as such from the onset. High Street, the original trackway from Thorley, running parallel with the coast, provided the backbone; the 'ribs' joining it at right-angles are still recognisable in the streets and lanes of today.

Baldwin's 1132 founding of Quarr Abbey was a huge event. Earlier, Cluniac monks had established a priory at St Helen's towards the end of the 11th century (and built for use as their chapel a stone replacement near the shoreline for a wooden church said to date from the 8th-century activity of Bishop Wilfrid's missionaries). Soon after that, the Normandy abbey of Monteburg had followed suit with a modest second priory at Appuldurcombe and this, in turn, was followed by the building in Newport of the Priory of St Cross, a foundation of yet another French abbey, Tiron, which pre-dated the building of Newport itself by some 60 years. Historians differ in their accounts of the founding of the much larger Carisbrooke

WOOTTON BRIDGE, THE BRIDGE c1955 W282003

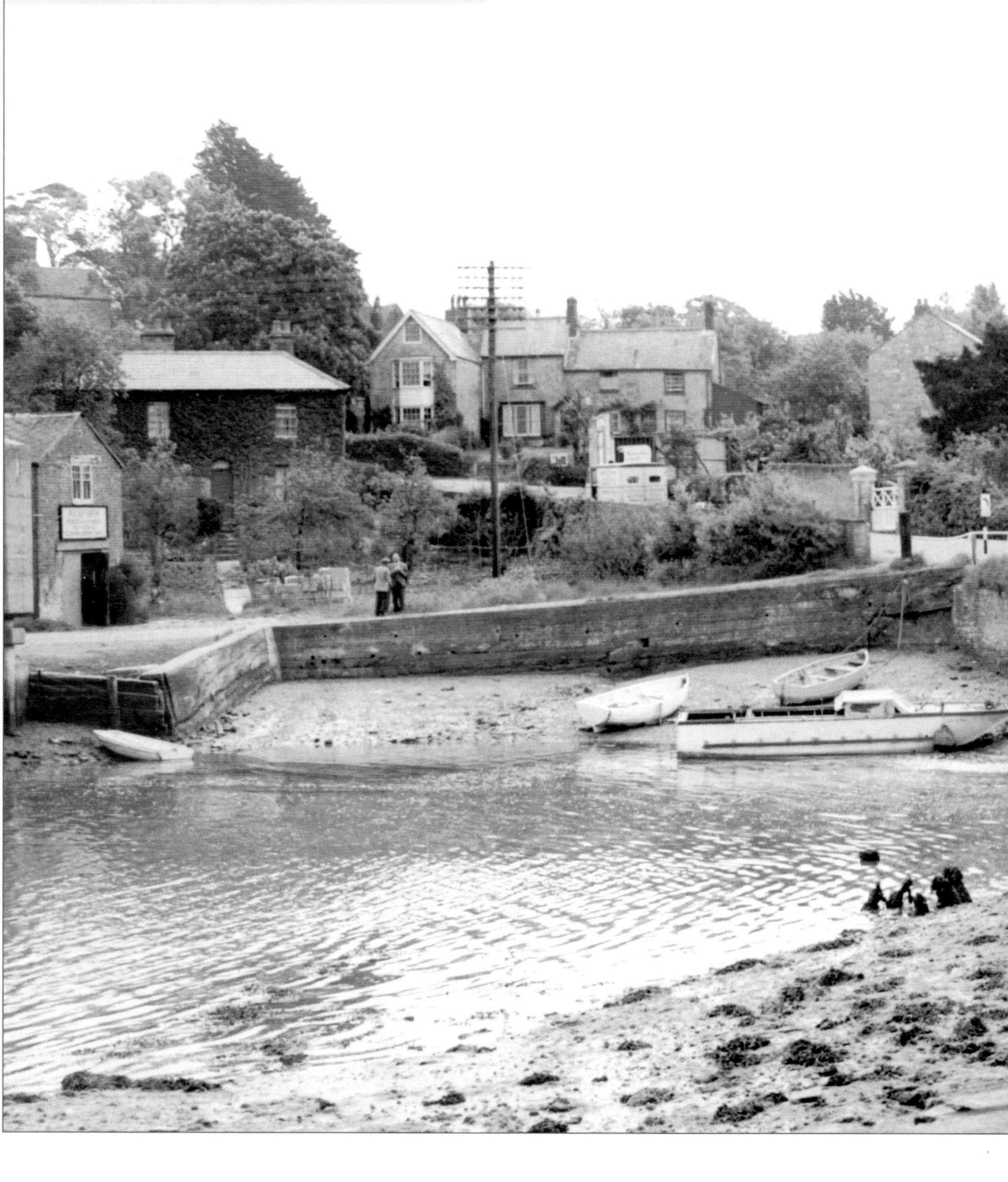

A view taken looking north-west, of the bridge and creek, which flows into the sea at Fishbourne - so called because old Quarr Abbey maintained a fish store there.

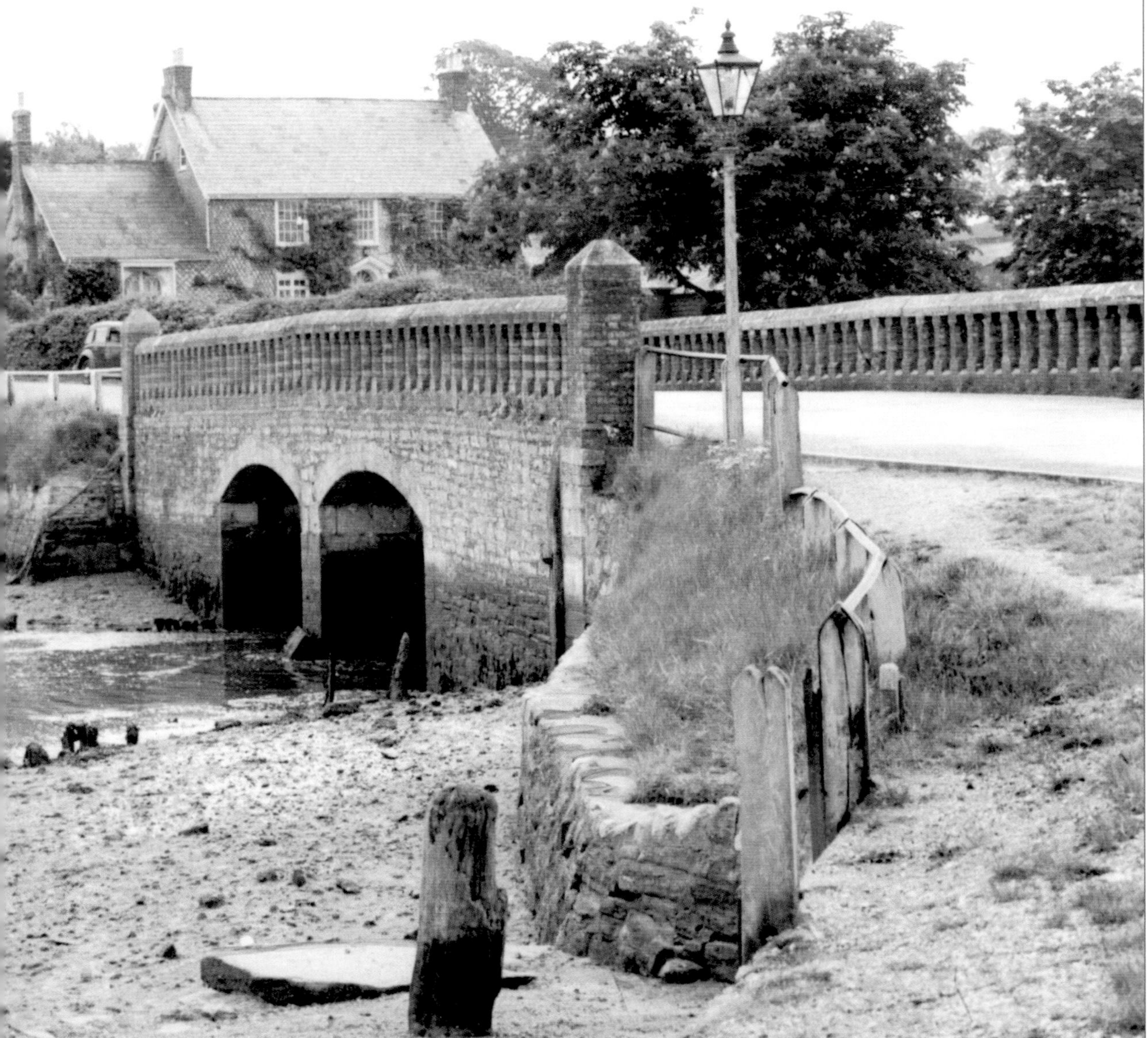

Priory. Several sources say it happened during William FitzOsbern's period; others claim it was not until around 1114, and the latter is an unusually long time before the 1156 building date suggested by other accounts. Attached to the northern side of Carisbrooke Church, the priory essentially served to provide Lyre Abbey with a convenient Island base to manage the extensive financial interests acquired from William FitzOsbern's six-church donation.

However, Quarr Abbey was far and away the greatest of the Isle of Wight's religious houses, a different proposition altogether. The name is a derived short-form of the Abbey of Our Lady of the Quarry, and the quarry in question was on the western fringe of nearby Binstead (which the Normans knew as Benestite), a short distance from the abbey its limestone would be extracted to build. The hard Quarr-Binstead stone, quarried from the pits that can still be traced in woodland alongside today's Quarr footpath, was so successful a raw material that much of it it was shipped across the Solent for use in prestigious building, or rebuilding, projects. It may have been utilised by the Romans in their construction of Portchester Castle. It was certainly used in the 14th century for Winchester Cathedral's magnificent new nave. On the Island, its

ST HELENS, THE BEACH c1955 S514201

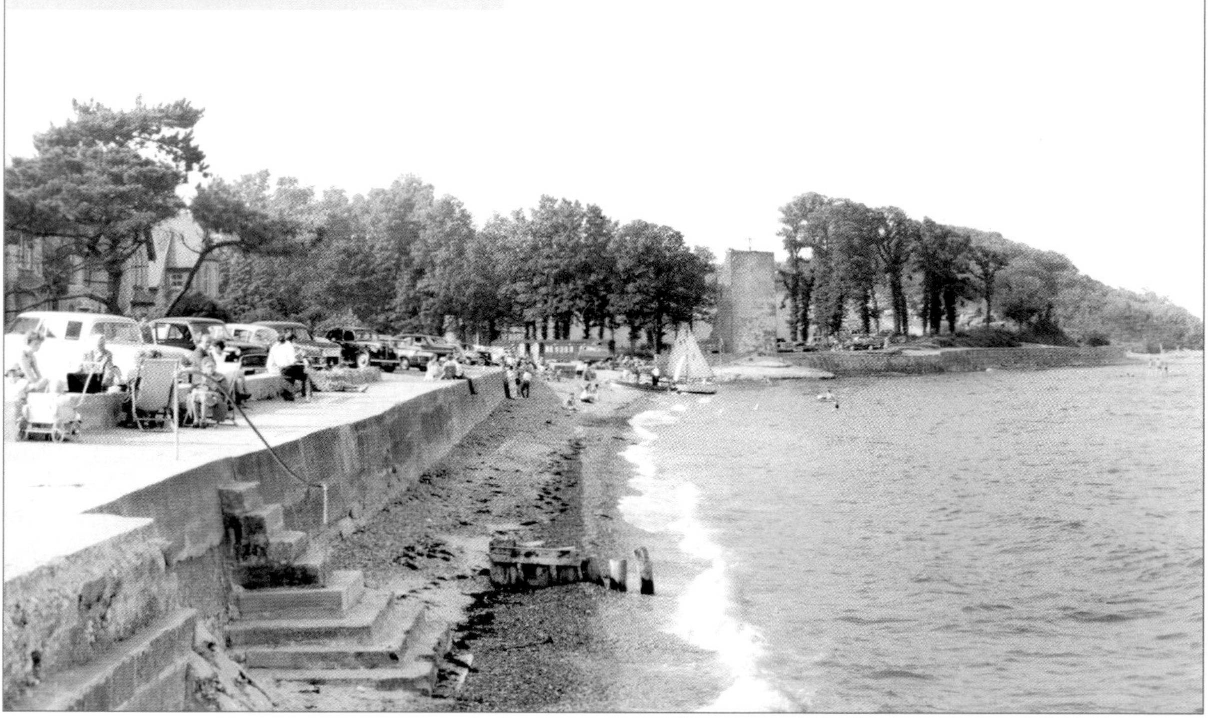

In the background are the ruins of the old St Helens 'Duver' Church, the origins of which date from the late 11th century, when it served as a chapel for the Cluniac monks at the nearby priory.

Eleanor of ... Quarr!

Local tradition suggests that Eleanor of Aquitaine, the rebellious queen of Henry II, was incarcerated at Quarr Abbey some time after 1173. This is not beyond the realms of possibility given the well-chronicled accounts of Eleanor's restricted movement at around this time in the south of England, following the support she gave her sons in rebellion against their father.

However, to further suggest, as does the legend, that she was buried amid woodland at Quarr, at the end of a secret underground passage, no less, is probably going too far, especially as the royal couple's 'official' coffins lay side-by-side at Fontevrault Abbey in France!

Who needs proof when you've got a legend as good as that one on your patch! Lack of evidence certainly failed to deter the Isle of Wight authorities from naming the section of the main Ryde-Newport road, which runs past the driveway entrance to modern-day Quarr Abbey, as Elenor's Grove. Did they deliberately misspell the name as a get-out? 'Oh no, we didn't mean THAT Eleanor!'

crowning glory was undoubtedly Quarr's original Cistercian abbey.

Many fine examples of ecclesiastical Norman architecture on the smaller scale survive on the Isle of Wight. Yaverland Church, dedicated to St John the Baptist, has been singled out as particularly special. Probably built around 1150, it served initially as a private chapel for the de Aula family, among those granted land on the Island in the wake of the Conquest, and did not become a parish church, freed from nearby Brading, until the 15th century. The chancel arch and south door are typical of their time, doorways to destiny for rich Normans and the congregations of centuries to come.

21st-century worshippers can still pass through Norman doorways at Carisbrooke, Wootton and the much-restored church at Northwood, among others. At Binstead's Church of the Holy Cross, the Norman entrance now provides access to the churchyard rather than the church itself. The latter is a 19th-century rebuild; the doorway is a remnant of an earlier church built for the use of local quarrymen and, no doubt, the servants and labourers who toiled at, or on the lands of, Quarr.

Were they familiar with the odd little sculpture which, badly weathered, adorns the apex? Grotesque in every sense, this work of indeterminate gender, sitting astride the head of indeterminate beast, is held to be a sheela-na-gig, an Irish term for the enigmatic effigies to which it apparently belongs. A rude Norman ornament, or a relic of fertility symbolism from the pre-Christian pagans?

There may have been an even earlier Saxon church at Binstead, and the same can be said of Bonchurch, on the margins of modern-day Ventnor. However, the older by far of Bonchurch's two surviving churches is resolutely Norman. Tradition asserts that monks from Lyre Abbey, arriving on the nearby coast from Normandy to collect the riches from their Isle of Wight possessions, discovered a Saxon church in a decrepit state and, fired by a combination of horror at what they saw and gratitude for their safe delivery from the English Channel, set about the task of rebuilding the church and dedicating it in memory of the revered Saxon Christian martyr, St Boniface.

The facts, judged on the physical evidence and what we learn from the Norman's great 11th-century Domesday land survey, confirm only that the church probably dates from that same early post-Conquest period. Its windows, square bell tower and porch are much later additions but, say the romantics, imagine those removed and you are left with a structure exactly as founded. This is possibly correct, although there is a counter-theory that the basic church is largely the result of a typical 13th-century stretch, if not a total rebuild. Whatever the truth of all that, many regard this enchantingly rustic, picturesque, idyllically located little church as the most decorative of all the many buildings the Normans left behind on the Isle of Wight. The tradition of its founding by the boat party from Normandy persists to this day in the name of their legendary landing place - Monks Bay.

During the two centuries that the de Redvers family and their de Vernon descendants held sway at Carisbrooke, right up until 1293, the Island witnessed not only a rash of church building and re-building, but also, following the lead of Yarmouth, the emergence of three other medieval towns, including the development of its modern capital in the shadow of the castle's always dominating presence.

To track that early development you need only to take the track! Originally, a trackway ran eastwards for roughly a mile from Carisbrooke down to the River Medina, thus providing the lofty, isolated castle with access northwards to the sea, its only route to the world beyond. As it neared the river, the track forked. Bearing left, one route carried on to reach the Medina's navigable limit, while the other veered right and continued as far as the first ford across the stream beyond the navigable river. The forked trackway remains in place. The left-hand route is now High Street; the route to the right is Pyle Street. Place-name theorists suggest 'pyle' may have been an early word for ford. The reason for

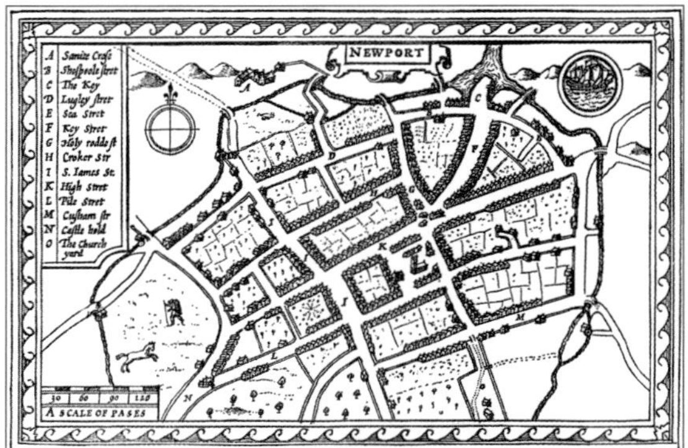

NEWPORT TOWN MAP 1611
ZZZ03996 (Author's Collection)

John Speed's map of the Island's capital shows clearly the medieval grid system used for his initial development.

NEWPORT, THE RIVER MEDINA 1955 N24008

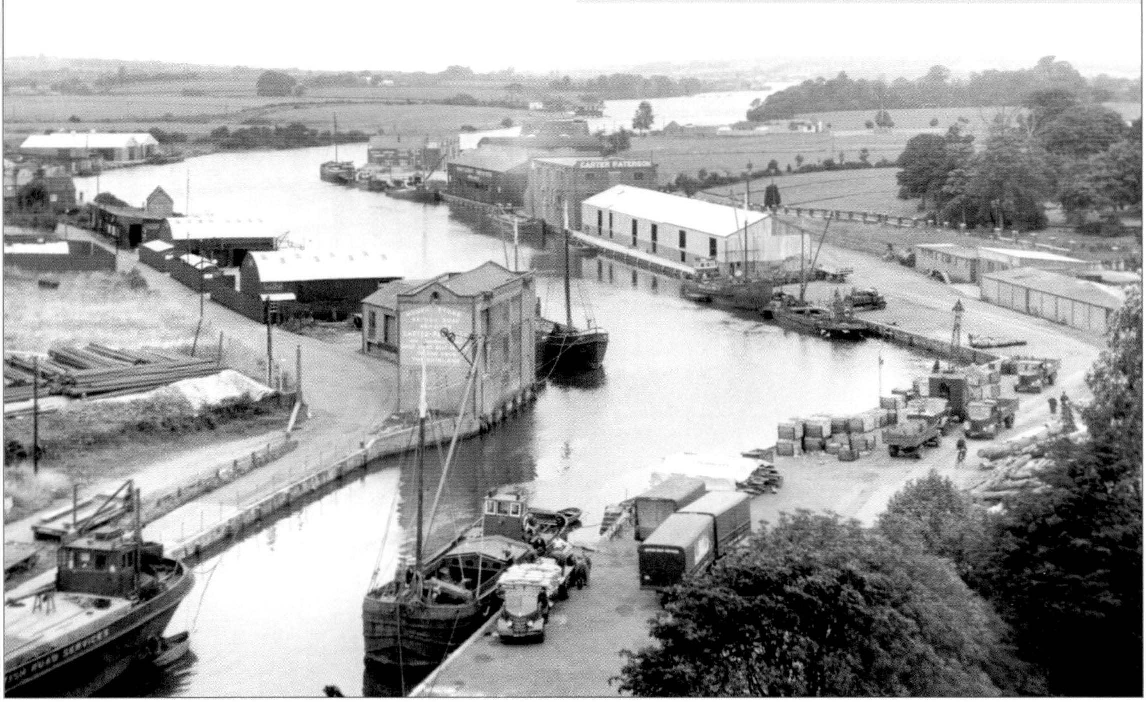

This view was taken looking north towards Cowes. It was the Medina's outlet to the sea that prompted the town's early development.

the naming of Carisbrooke's 'new port' on the Medina is rather more obvious.

Initially, the port would probably have amounted to little more than a crude landing stage. If there were any homes in the vicinity, they would more than likely have been the simple cottages of a few fisher-folk. Development would subsequently have occurred either side of the rough track from the castle, a mere extension of Carisbrooke village. Towards the end of the 12th century the Lord of the Island, Richard de Redvers, the third of that name, planned and developed the town of Newport on the grid system employed earlier in Yarmouth, with new streets at right-angles to High Street and Pyle Street, and others running parallel to those original trackway routes.

Included in the former category were the still identifiable St James's Street, Holyrood Street and Town Lane. The parallel roads to the north of High Street were, and are, Lugley Street and Crocker Street. Newport's first charter, the initial conferral of town privilege, was granted around 1180, a few years after Richard de Redvers had endowed it with its first church, dedicated to St Thomas à Becket, and arranged for the monks at Carisbrooke Priory to provide its spiritual ministry.

While the origins of both Yarmouth and Newport survive amid the modern townscapes, the former remains essentially the town it has always been, modest, compact and tidy, still recognisably medieval. The latter has long since outgrown the confines of the town plan of Richard de Redvers. The difference between the two could hardly be more marked - until you throw Newtown into the mix.

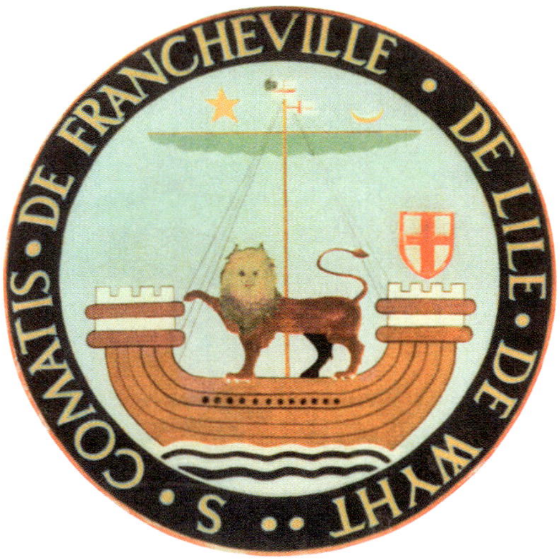

THE FRANCHEVILLE TOWN CREST
ZZZ03995 (Author's Collection)

The single-masted ship on the Francheville crest may have denoted former status as the capital of Wight.

That this quietest of Isle of Wight villages was ever once a town is, at first encounter, very hard to accept. There are no shops, few homes, and hardly any traffic. The place is a refuge for wild birds and stressed-out humans. Much of the evidence of former importance has been lost to wide grassy footpaths that were once the thoroughfares of commercial bustle, but the pub with no beer - it hasn't served any since 1916 - is a clue and, just up the road, the 17th-century Town Hall is a give-away. The Town Hall is not a dead one; council meetings are still held there, even though the former municipality is now merely part of Calbourne parish, and the building houses a fascinating little museum. But that's it. The old town of Newtown is no more, long since dwindled away. The question is, was it really there in the first place? Or was it a rebuild of the original town, the Francheville of the coat of arms defiantly displayed on the front of the old pub? That was the name on the first charter of which any record survives. This was granted in 1256 by Aymer de Valence, Bishop of Winchester. It fell to Aymer, rather than the Lord of the Island, to confer the privilege because this area of Wight, on the north-west coast between Yarmouth and present-day Cowes, had long been part of the manor of Swainston, and the manor had been granted by King Egbert of Wessex to the then Bishop of Winchester around the year 826. Whether there was a settlement of any sort at Francheville during the bulk of the next 400 years is impossible to say, as no real evidence has ever come to light, but it is safe to conclude that, by the time Aymer granted the first charter, a community thrived around its deep-water harbour

The name Francheville indicated a 'free town' where land and tenements were held at a fixed rent and the people were mostly free of the usual obligations to perform

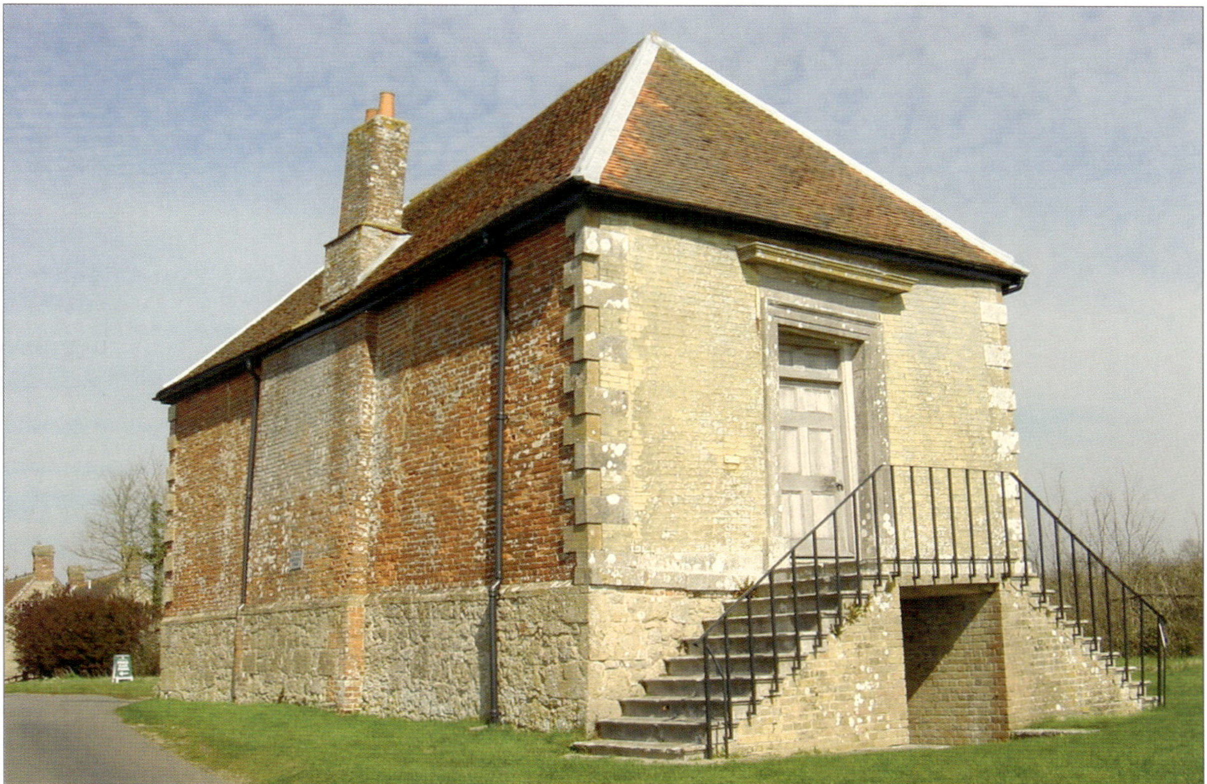

NEWTOWN, THE OLD TOWN HALL, SOUTH VIEW 2005 N271701k (Matt Searle)

The Town Hall at Newtown dates from 1699. MPs returned to Parliament from here included John Churchill, first Duke of Marlborough (1768) and George Canning (1804), who later became Prime Minister!

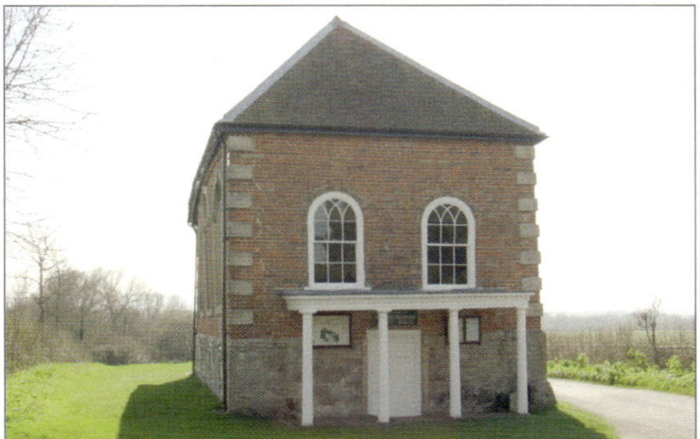

NEWTOWN, THE OLD TOWN HALL, NORTH VIEW 2005 N271702k (Matt Searle)

services for the Lord of the Manor. It was the proximity of the sea that led to the town's development and, it would seem, early prosperity. Its port rivalled those at Yarmouth and Newport and the single-masted ship dominating the old town crest suggests Francheville may actually have been the pre-eminent of the three. If so, there may be some merit in the theory that this dreamy, out-of-the-way spot was once the Isle of Wight's capital. We can be sure of one thing. Francheville was the third of the Island's quartet of incorporated medieval towns, and the last of the trio that were actually planned as such from scratch.

History is vague on precisely when it became known as Newtown. Both names (in one or other of their many forms) seem to have been used side-by-side for centuries. The most popular theory, that of the 'new town' emerging from the ashes of French massacre in 1377, is best left for later in the story.

Brading is both the oldest and the newest of the Island's four medieval towns! It is the oldest because its antiquity as a settlement, the probable site of the Island's first church, and a haven-side port, pre-dates the other three; it is the newest because it was almost certainly the last of the quartet to be granted a charter. That didn't happen until 1280, when Edward I conferred the privilege eight years into his reign. Brading thus acquired unique status as the only Island town to receive its first charter from the reigning monarch. This, and the fact that the land on which the town stood had earlier passed from private ownership into the hands of the Crown, led to it being known as 'The King's Town' and Brading, though long shorn of its corporate status, proudly hangs on to the regal sub-title today.

As a magnet for tourists, it also retains much of its former municipal 'furniture'; witness the old Town Hall with its stocks, whipping post and tiny lock-up, and pity the poor beasts that were once tied to the preserved, though recently re-located, bull

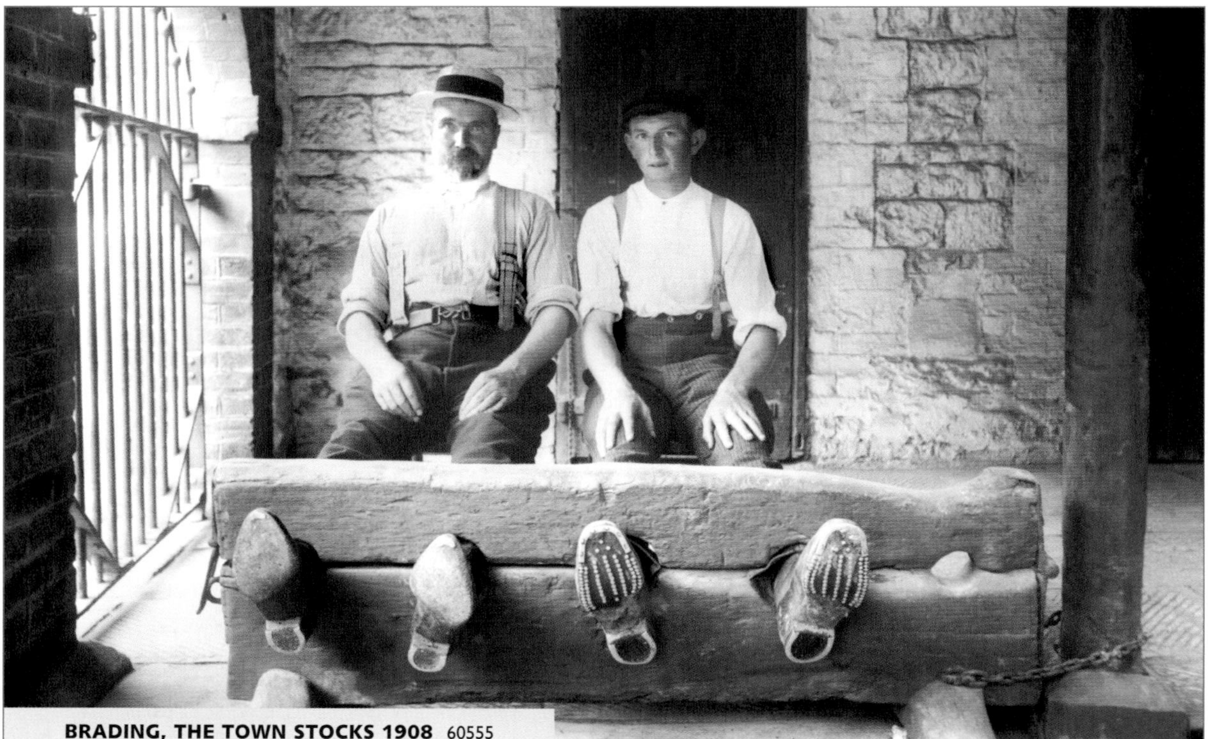

BRADING, THE TOWN STOCKS 1908 60555

Brading retains many of the features of its time as a corporate town. The stocks are preserved at the Old Town Hall.

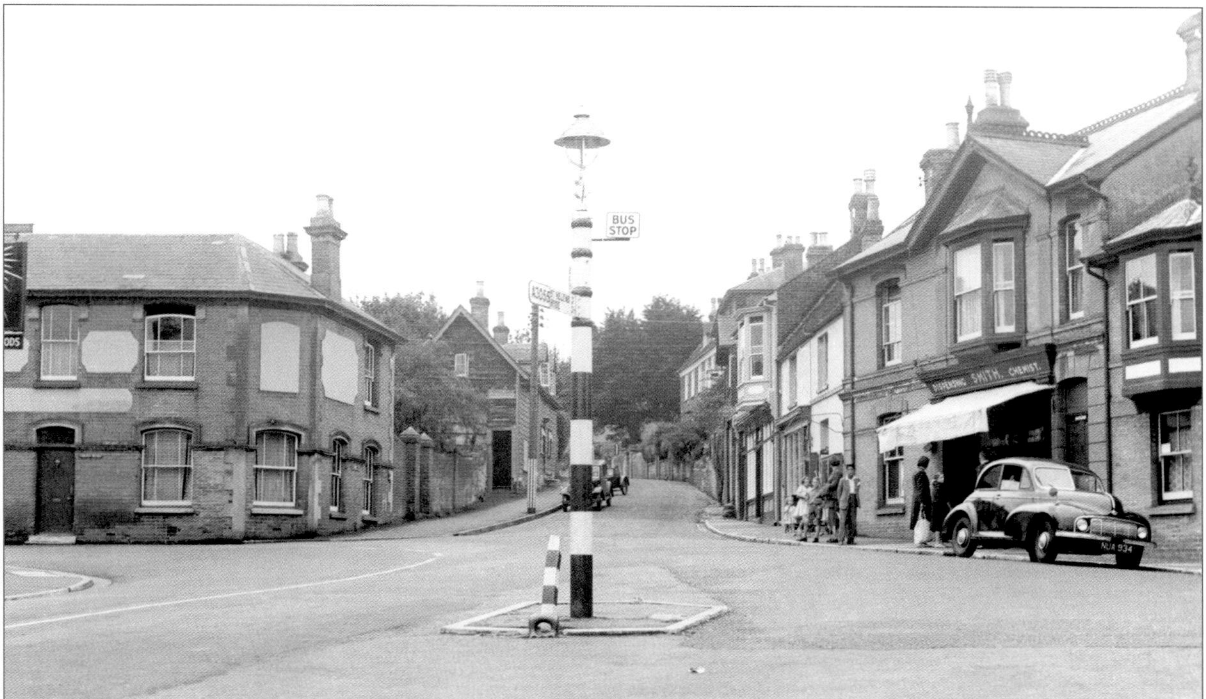

BRADING, THE BULL RING c1955 B175010

Brading's town centre is known as the Bull Ring but, unusually, the old ring itself is still there. It has been moved since this picture was taken to a safer location outside the New Town Hall (on a site behind the photographer).

ring. But Brading was never planned as a town. It simply grew from a port-village in the manor owned at the time of Domesday by William FitzAzor (one of the most prominent of the incoming Normans), when its former name of Brerdinge had strangely changed to Beradinz before resuming its convoluted route to the title used today.

Yarmouth was also a 'king's town' early in the 13th century, albeit briefly. King John made short visits in May 1206 and then in February 1214, *en route* to a catastrophic military defeat in France at the Battle of Bouvines. A third excursion by John to the Island in 1215, shortly after he had been forced to sign the Magna Carta at Runnymede, is more the stuff of legend. He spent three months on Wight, it is said, secretly plotting the downfall of his rebel barons. With the Island's Lordship held at that time by William de Vernon, a close ally of the treacherous John's late brother, Richard the Lionheart, it seems a foolhardy move, although this might explain why one version of the legend insists that John's time on the Island was spent with the king perpetually in disguise and never straying far from the coast. All sorts of - mostly unflattering - tales are thrown in for good measure about the king's legendary offshore sojourn: he lived as a merchant; he lived as a fisherman; he lived as a pirate; he fell hopelessly in love. All were probably invented by the many detractors of this lowly-regarded monarch. Yet, the Isle of Wight clings to the notion that he really was here in 1215. He landed, it is said, near present-day Wootton. The site is still known as King's Quay.

At the end of the 13th century the Isle of Wight's two-and-a-half centuries of semi-independence under private ownership was ended. The very final holder of the Lordship was actually a lady. Isabella de Fortibus was last of the ruling dynasty begun by the first Richard de Redvers. She has been described as beautiful, formidable, intelligent and energetic. A one-word summary would be - remarkable. She was widowed at the age of 23 and was just 25 when the death of her brother Baldwin propelled her to unexpected power at Carisbrooke as the Lady of the Wight.

Despite this unpromising start, the Countess Isabella ruled the Island with an astonishing degree of toughness for the next 30 years. She made enemies, largely by being over-fond of litigation, and, while granting freehold and privileges to the developing boroughs, she was in more or less constant dispute with abbeys, towns and other major institutions on either side of the Solent. Isabella was a woman alone in a society otherwise totally dominated by men, and her 30-year reign was no mean achievement.

But relationships between England and France were deteriorating. Edward I feared invasion and the Isle of Wight was an obvious stepping-stone for a full-scale onslaught against the mother country. Newtown's deep-water harbour might be a key factor in terms of both invasion and defence. Unsure of the support he might receive on the Island from Isabella de Fortibus, Edward snapped up the Manor of Swainston, of which Newtown still formed part, completing the purchase following a visit to the Island in 1285. It seems not to have been enough for the jittery monarch. So, when Isabella fell seriously ill, Edward seized his chance to act decisively. The Countess's son, Thomas, had died as a 16-year-old, leaving her without direct heirs.

On her deathbed in 1293, Isabella was persuaded by King Edward's officials to sign over the Isle of Wight, in exchange for a relatively paltry sum of money, to the English Crown, in whose hands it has remained ever since.

There was barely time for Islanders to draw breath following the sale of their homeland before the grim reality of being a fully paid-up part of the English state was rammed home to them. Within a year of Countess Isabella's death, England was at war with France, which soon afterwards formed an alliance with Scotland. Caught up in the rumpus, the Island was quickly on invasion alert, a timely 'dry run' for what was to follow. The Island resented the loss of its independence. Seven of its knights refused to fight the Scots and, later, there was successful opposition among landowners to the appointment, by royal command, of Edward II's favourite, Piers Gaveston, to the Lordship, now no longer

St Catherine's Pepper Pot

High on the table-top of the downs above St Catherine's Point, overlooking the English Channel in the Island's far south, stands the Pepper Pot, Britain's only surviving medieval lighthouse.

Officially St Catherine's Oratory, its origins date from a wild night in 1313, when a storm-tossed merchant ship carrying wine from Edward II's Duchy of Aquitaine ran aground on the treacherous rocks of Atherfield Ledge. Its cargo of 174 casks was salvaged, but a dispute arose over its ownership, with landowning Islanders in the vicinity claiming it by ancient right of salvage.

As the legal battles raged, the wine was dispersed. Much of it ended up with Walter de Godeton, who owned land in the manor of Chale. Before he could raise a glass to his success, de Godeton was charged with illegally receiving it. Not only was he ordered to pay a hefty financial penalty, he also found himself on the verge of excommunication from the Catholic Church for sacrilege as the ultimate owners of the wine had been the monastery of Livers in Picardy!

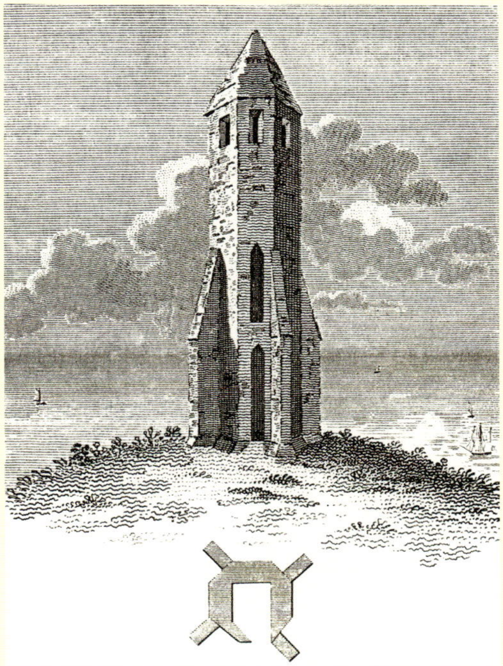

THE PEPPER POT ZZZ03997 (Author's Collection)
A sketch and plan of the medieval lighthouse at St Catherine's - minus the formerly attached oratory. The lighthouse is now an ancient monument.

To atone for his sin, de Godeton was ordered to build a lighthouse on the high ground above Chale and include an oratory for a priest to tend the light and pray for stricken mariners. The Pepper Pot was the result. Its oratory disappeared after it was suppressed by Henry VIII and the lighthouse itself proved less than successful as it was so often shrouded in mist. Today's lighthouse has been rather more effective.

determined by family succession. But there was no going back. The Isle of Wight had been snaffled up by the Crown and it was about to pay the real price for that unwanted absorption.

The reasons behind a youthful Edward III renewing hostilities with France in 1337 were many and complex. The protracted conflict would go down in history as the Hundred Years War and this would be the most wretched period in the recorded history of the Isle of Wight. The Island tasted the enemy's aggressive intent in early attacks before the French uncorked the full-on cocktail of sea-borne raids and onshore carnage in 1340 by spilling the blood of several defenders at St Helens, on the north-east coast. Theobald Russell, Lord of Yaverland, was among those killed, a significant scalp as he had been appointed to lead the local militia when the hitherto ill-defended isle, its population a scanty 5,000 at the most, had geared itself up for the inevitable onslaught in a state of frenzied emergency. Defensive strengthening would feature large on the Island throughout the long reign of Edward III against the backdrop of continued French aggression.

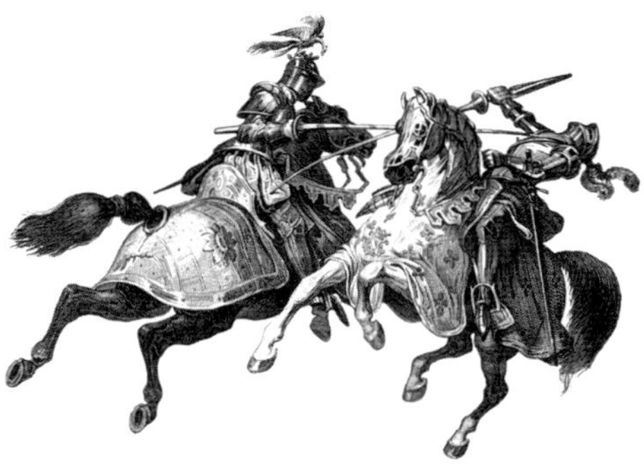

JOUSTING KNIGHTS ZZZ01296

Leaving the vulnerable isle, an option which must have been very tempting to many nervous landowners, was officially frowned upon and punished by confiscation of property. The lords of the various manors were each expected to provide the men to make up the militia, which was eventually organised under a district defence system as the call to arms became a requirement for all men aged from the mid-teens to 60. By this time, in response to the growing need to keep a constant lookout for the enemy, the Island had been equipped with an early warning network of signal beacons, 18 west of the Medina and 13 in the east. But nothing could save the Isle of Wight from the disaster of 1377, the year of the death of Edward III.

With its population and economy decimated by the horrors of plague - the Solent was no barrier to the Black Death - the Island constantly expected invasion and was knocked for six when it came in August 1377. The French, assisted by Continental allies, swarmed ashore on the north-west coast. Yarmouth and Francheville / Newtown were burnt to the ground as terrified women and children sought refuge from the wholesale slaughter. Many are said to have hidden in the massive square Norman tower at Shalfleet church, perilously close to Newtown.

The raiders moved menacingly inland towards Newport, now the established capital. It suffered the same fate as the coastal towns. Only the church was left standing by the French, who then advanced on Carisbrooke, where the Island's defensive forces were congregated. It was here that the tide at last turned against the invasion. Ably commanded by Sir Hugh Tyrell, Lord of the Island, the castle repelled the enemy's repeated attempts to storm it. French morale was weakened when part of the enemy force was cut to shreds in an ambush on the castle approaches, and then fatally wounded by the Lord of Stenbury, Peter de Heynoe, whose deadly accuracy with the crossbow felled the French commander. The slit from which he is said to have taken aim with his legendary 'silver bow' is still visible on the west wall of

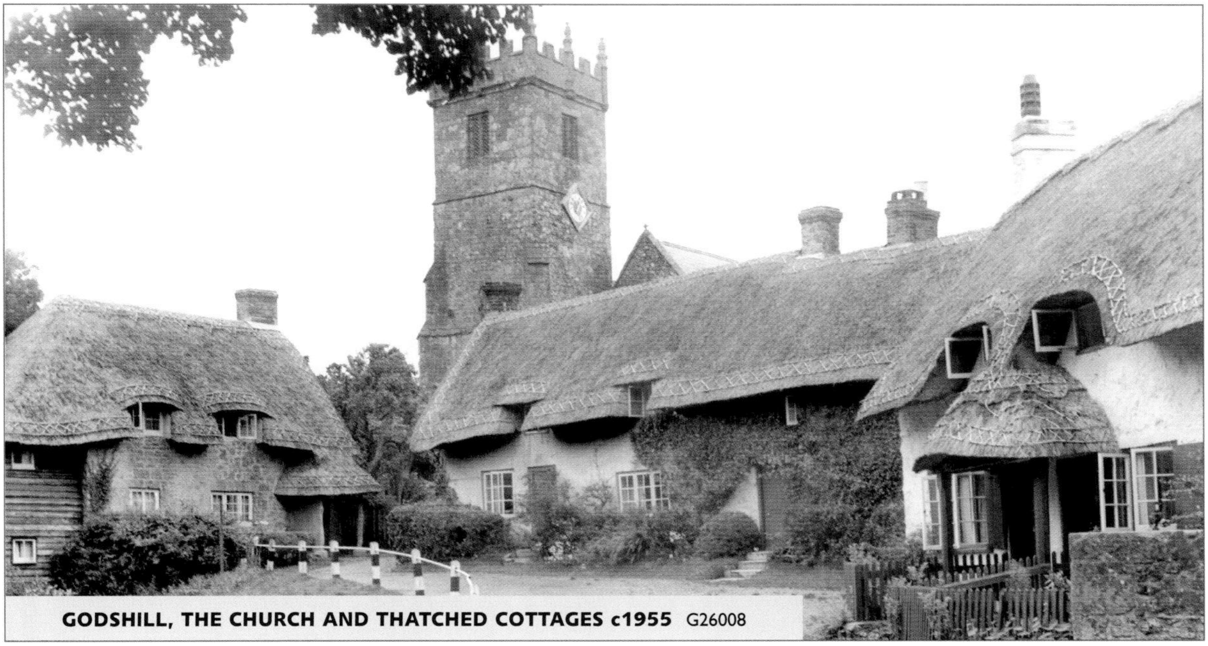

GODSHILL, THE CHURCH AND THATCHED COTTAGES c1955 G26008

Godshill's church is probably the most photographed on the Isle of Wight. It has the best examples of 14th-century 'decorated style' windows. The tower and transept arches are of the same period.

the castle, known as Heynoe's Loope, a relic of a true Island hero.

The result was stalemate. The castle could not be taken. The French could not be turned back. In the end, the dispute was settled by cash, the raiders agreeing to go home in exchange for a hefty lump sum, officially recorded as a fine. They left behind an island saved from long-term occupation, but smarting on its knees. A full 200 years would pass before Yarmouth and Newport - where nobody at all lived for the two years following the raid - could be said to have fully recovered from the devastation of 1377. In the case of Newtown, full recovery proved beyond reach. It was rebuilt, but never again truly prospered, clinging to its corporate status for centuries, but enduring a slow slide into obscurity.

Did you know?

The Fate of the Noddies

The track on which French soldiers were reputedly ambushed during the siege of Carisbrooke in 1377 became known as Deadman's Lane. Admiral Lord Nelson's victory at Trafalgar in 1805 led to its re-naming as Trafalgar Road. It is in the area of Newport known as Nodehill, which itself recalls the abusive term 'Noddies', used by 14th-century Islanders when referring to idiots - or Frenchmen!

The Isle of Wight post-1377 was demoralised, de-populated, and deprived. There could have been little enthusiasm or incentive for recovery as the war with France raged on. What was the point? The threat of invasion had been only temporarily lifted. Islanders had proved courageous and resilient in battle but their homeland remained weak and vulnerable, ripe for the taking. Leadership was notable by its absence - literally. The Crown-appointed Lords of the Island in this period were big names; they included Edward, Duke of York until his death in the mud of Agincourt, but they all had bigger fish to fry and were rarely, if ever, seen at Carisbrooke. As time wore on, and more people fled, the castle was under-defended and run-down. Petitions to the Crown for more men and weapons to aid security went unanswered. That the Island managed to resist being totally over-run by France, whose marauding forces were repelled in less significant raids several times more before the Hundred Years War had run its course, was remarkable.

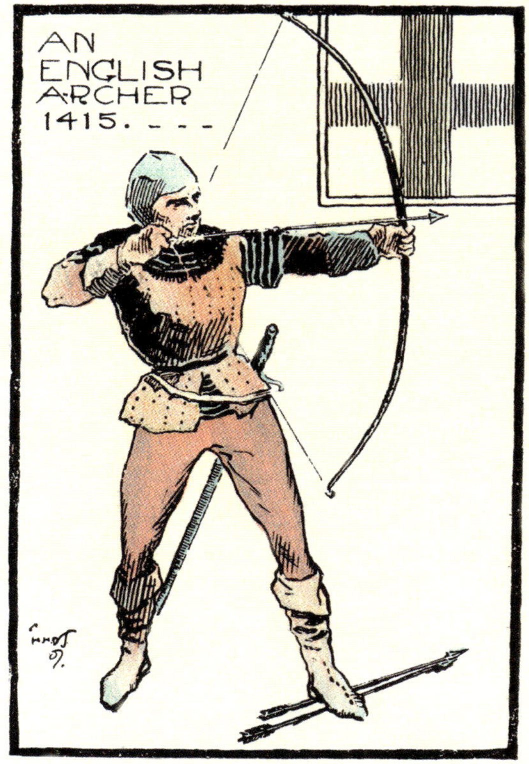

AN ENGLISH ARCHER OF c1415
ZZZ03998 (Author's Collection)

One of the characters of the Isle of Wight depicted in a lavish early 20th-century pageant at Carisbrooke Castle.

Did you know?

The King of the Wight

The Isle of Wight had a monarch all to itself in the mid 15th century when Henry Beauchamp, Duke of Warwick, was crowned King of the Wight by Henry VI of England. Apart from confirming Warwick's status as a favourite of the English king, it was a meaningless act. The Island's Lordship and government at the time was in the hands of Humphrey, Duke of Gloucester, the uncle of Henry VI, and it is highly unlikely that Warwick ever visited his offshore kingdom during a short reign of no more than four years, which ended with his death in 1446 at the age of 22.

With France temporarily out of the picture, the Isle of Wight was mercifully spared from taking sides and enduring further misery in the all-English Wars of the Roses that followed. Peace, extending into the early years of the 16th century, encouraged a wave of new building and re-construction on the Island, but the overdue provision of coastal fortifications had to wait until the reign of Henry VIII (1509-1547). The great Tudor monarch's fall-out with the Roman Catholic Church in the wake of his marriage to Anne Boleyn saw Quarr Abbey ripped to rubble as part of Henry's monastic vandalism - but the king was as concerned with construction as he was with destruction.

The reason was the periodic renewal of hostilities with France, which thrust the Isle of Wight, and the mainland coastline opposite, right back into the firing line. Apart from the need to safeguard potential landing places, Henry was also motivated by concern for the safety of the fledgling Royal Navy fleet in the Spithead anchorage off Portsmouth. This led to the building of several coastal forts either side of the Solent.

If the king needed reminding of how urgent a need this was, he got it in 1545. Seeking to tempt Henry's fleet away from the confines of Spithead and into the open sea after an inconclusive skirmish off Portsmouth, the French piled ashore on the Isle of Wight's eastern coast, destroying a small fort at the site of present-day Seaview. They ran into stiff resistance from an Island force, augmented by men and equipment from the mainland, in landings at Bembridge, Shanklin and, most notably, Bonchurch, where both sides lost a large number of men in a particularly bloody clash. The defenders made good use of the unusual amount of military hardware made available to them; farm carts strung out as barricades were also effectively employed. The French were outnumbered, outwitted, outfought and, after two days, out of sight. The result was a famous victory for the Isle of Wight.

Most significant of the defensive works that quickly followed on the Island was the stone-built square castle at Yarmouth (constructed along with nearby Sharpnode Blockhouse in 1547) and the twin forts guarding the mouth of the Medina in the far north of the Island at what was then known as Shamblord. Since the 14th century, Shamblord had been one of three recognised trading ports on Wight - the number had been deliberately restricted in the interests of security - along with Yarmouth, in the west, and La Riche (present-day Ryde) in the east. As the forts at Shamblord, constructed from stone recycled from the monastic ruins at Quarr and Beaulieu, in Hampshire, were built to frighten, or cow, enemy forces, this may well have been the origin for the names later adopted by the towns that developed either side of the river mouth - West and East Cowes - though an alternative theory suggests the name Cowes derives from a distinctively cow-shaped sandbank that lay offshore. The original name is recalled today at Shamblers Copse, on the west bank.

Henry VIII's fortifications can still be traced. Yarmouth Castle, surrounded on two sides by the sea, much modified from the Tudor original (see next chapter), is an ancient monument in the care of English Heritage, while West Cowes Castle, its origins barely recognisable, is now the home of the Royal Yacht Squadron. Nothing at all remains of East Cowes Castle, which is in no way connected with a much later building of the same name constructed as a home for the great Regency architect John Nash. Castle Street may provide a clue to the original fort's former whereabouts, now some distance inland of the present coast, because of subsequent reclamation.

Another of Henry VIII's Island forts was built on the east coast, guarding the other approach to the Solent, at Sandham, now part of Sandown. Richard Worsley, Captain of the Island (the term Captain was now used instead of the much grander-sounding Lord) organised its construction, but coastal erosion eventually claimed it for the sea. A 17th-century replacement fared little better. These misfortunes aside, the Island had at last been equipped to properly defend itself, and Spithead, from enemy attack. The coastal defences would be updated periodically right up to the 20th century. Despite many subsequent scares, the French raid of 1545 was the last full-scale invasion of Wight.

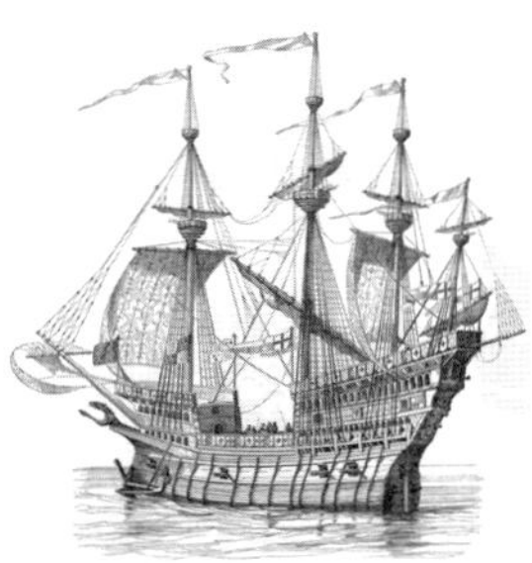

A TUDOR SHIP AFTER HOLBEIN ZZZ01290

The Squadron is based at Cowes Castle - Henry VIII's 'West Cow'.

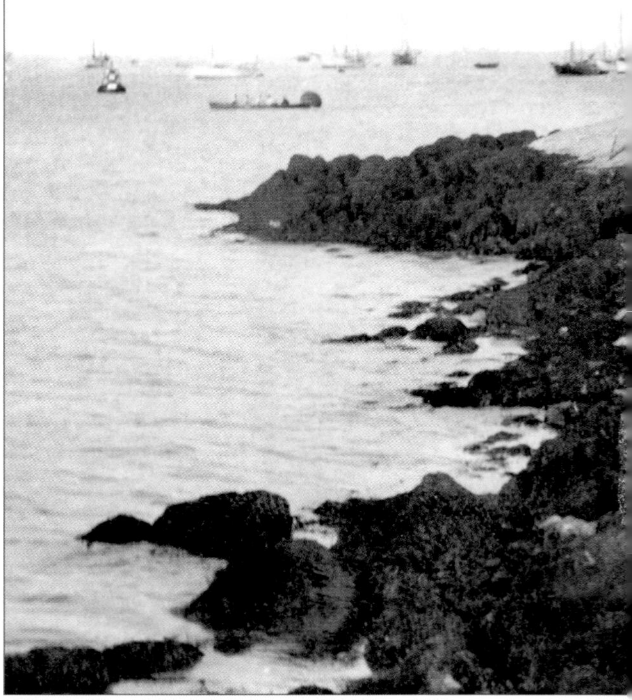

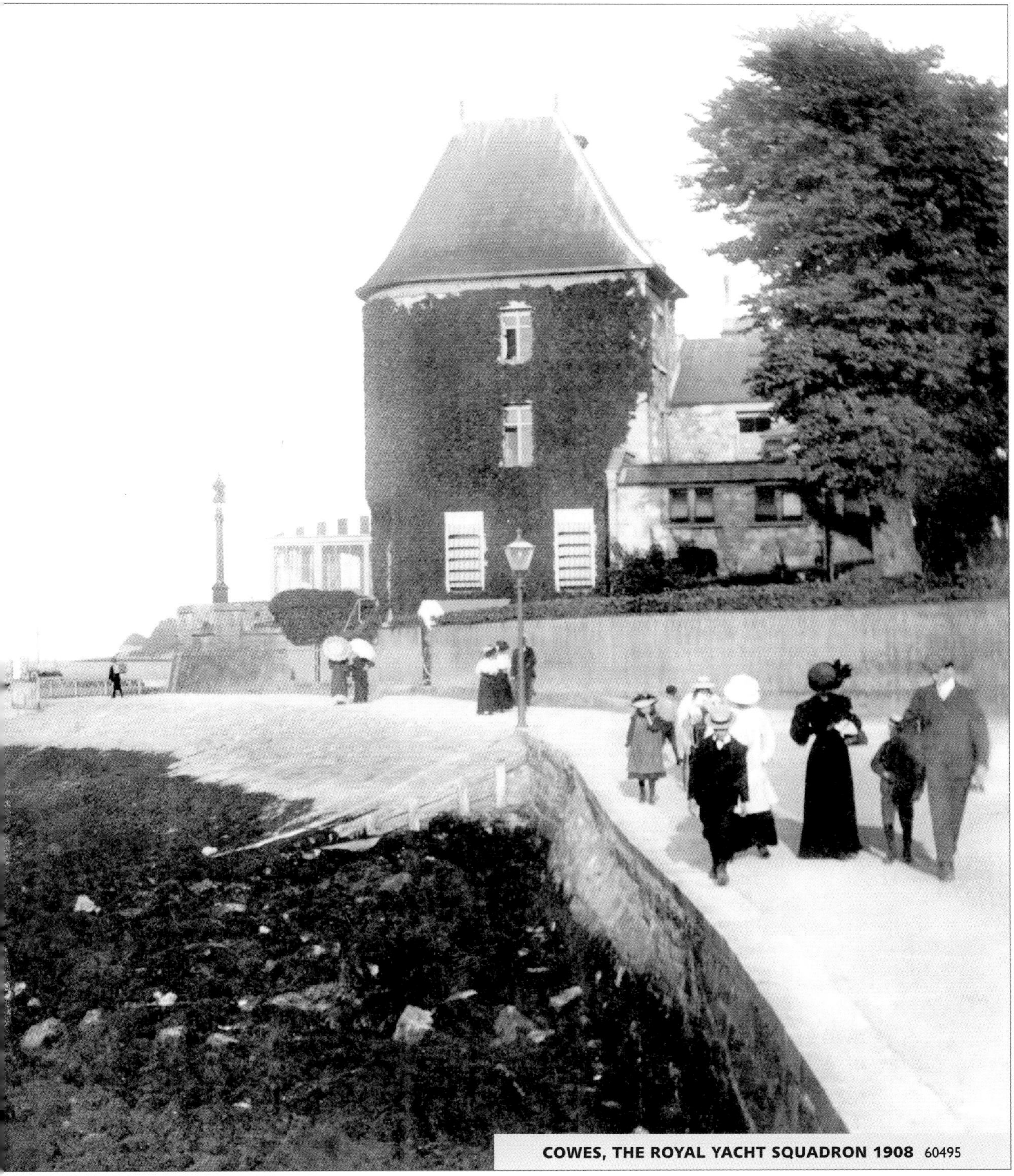

COWES, THE ROYAL YACHT SQUADRON 1908 60495

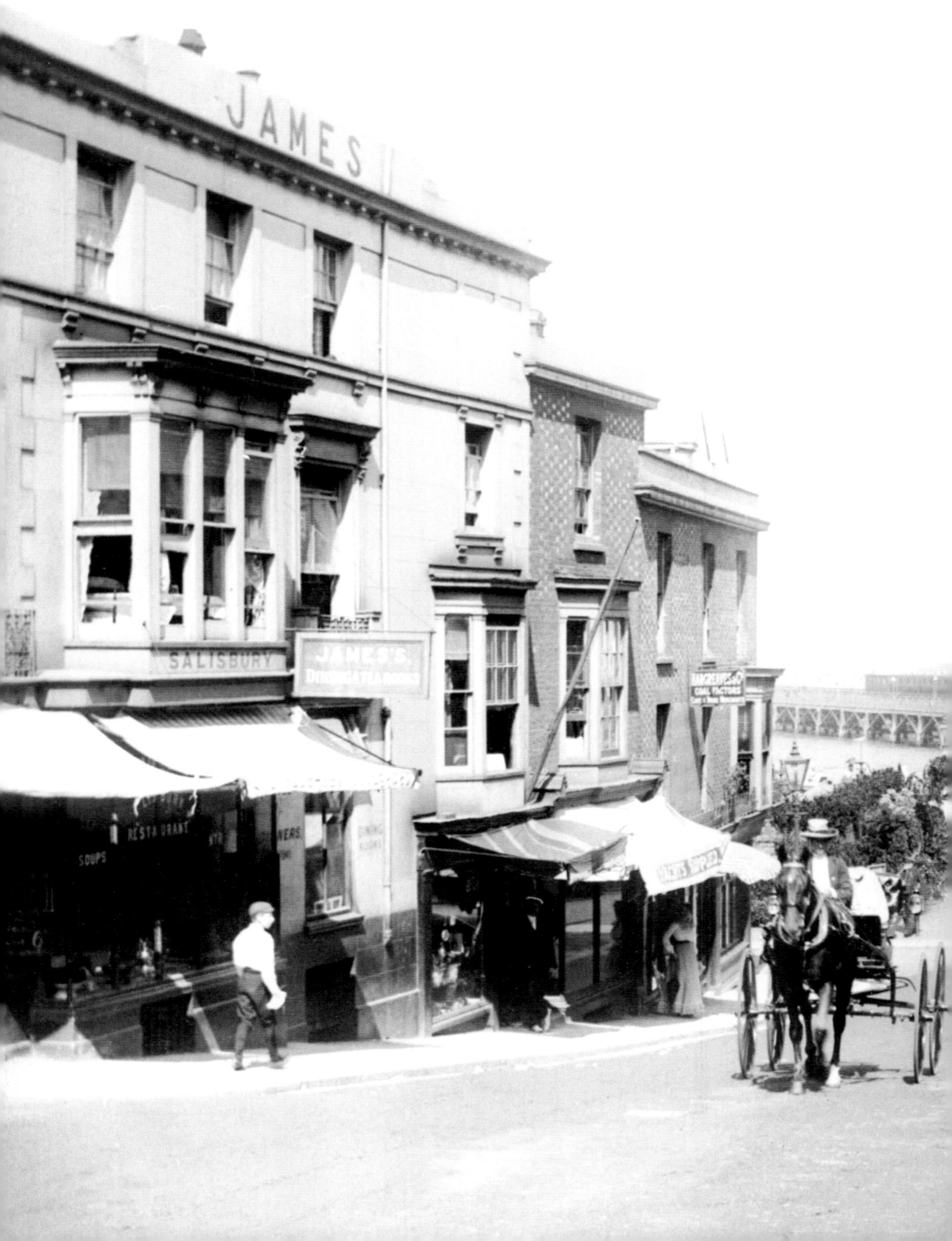
JAMES
SALISBURY
JAMES'S
RESTAURANT
SOUPS
COAL FACTORS

CHAPTER THREE

Pestilence, Politics and Prosperity

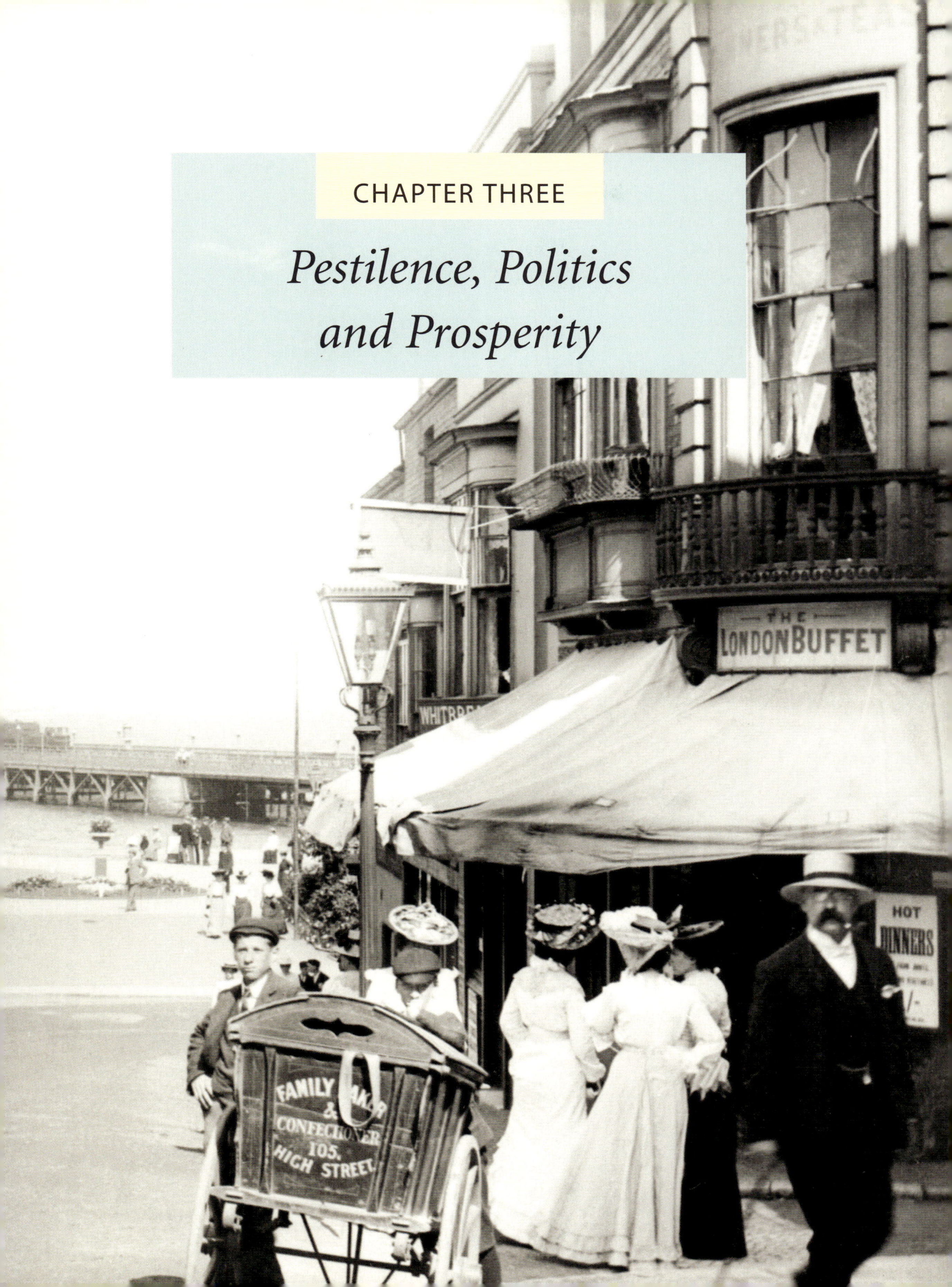

COASTAL DEFENCE CONTINUED to be an important consideration as the 16th century progressed on the Isle of Wight, but the real enemy lay within. The Island was in a bad state. The stabilising influence of the church had vanished, or at least diminished, following Henry VIII's Reformation. A demoralised population found itself without spiritual guidance owing to the absence in several parishes of a local priest. Guidance in general was missing from Carisbrooke Castle, which had fallen into a sad state of decay, and nowhere was this more apparent than in the Castlehold district of Newport. The castle's continuing hold on the area, formally, if not actually in practice, meant that it was outside the control of the borough. As a result, it descended into lawless chaos and virtual ruin. It was not much better within the confines of the borough boundaries. Contemporary accounts paint a sad picture of neglect and squalor, with rats in the houses and ruts in the roads.

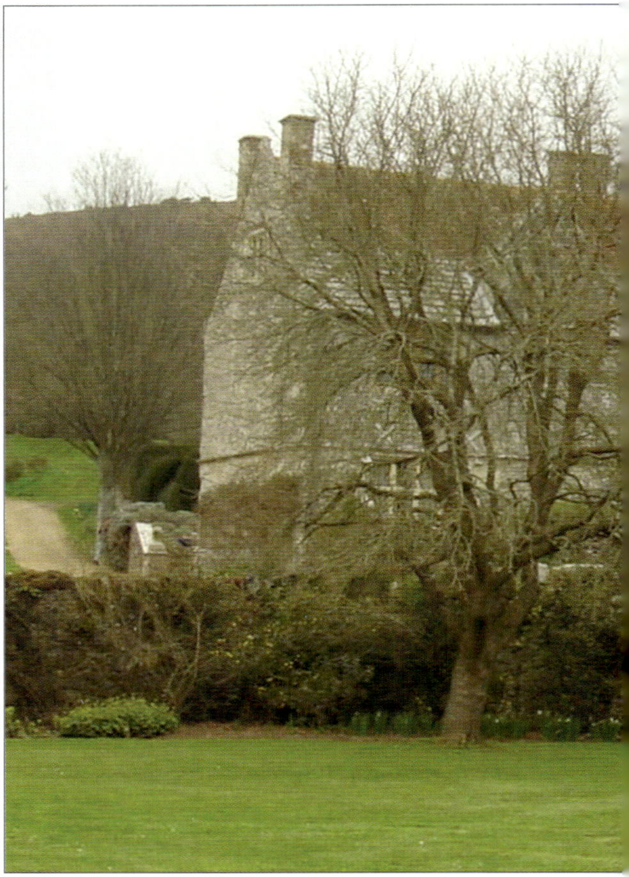

Did you know?

Castlehold's 'places'

In the late 13th century, Isabelle de Fortibus, last private owner of the Island, donated the freehold of virtually all the land on which Newport stood to its townspeople. She held on to just a small parcel of land at the junction of High Street and Pyle Street (the divergence of the original trackways from her seat of government at Carisbrooke Castle), which enclosed thirteen-and-a-half 'places' (building plots). The area became known as Castlehold for that reason, and retains the name today. Well into the 19th century, Castlehold held its own Court Leet, administering the equivalent of today's trading standards and environmental health functions, quite separate from the Court Leet covering the rest of the town.

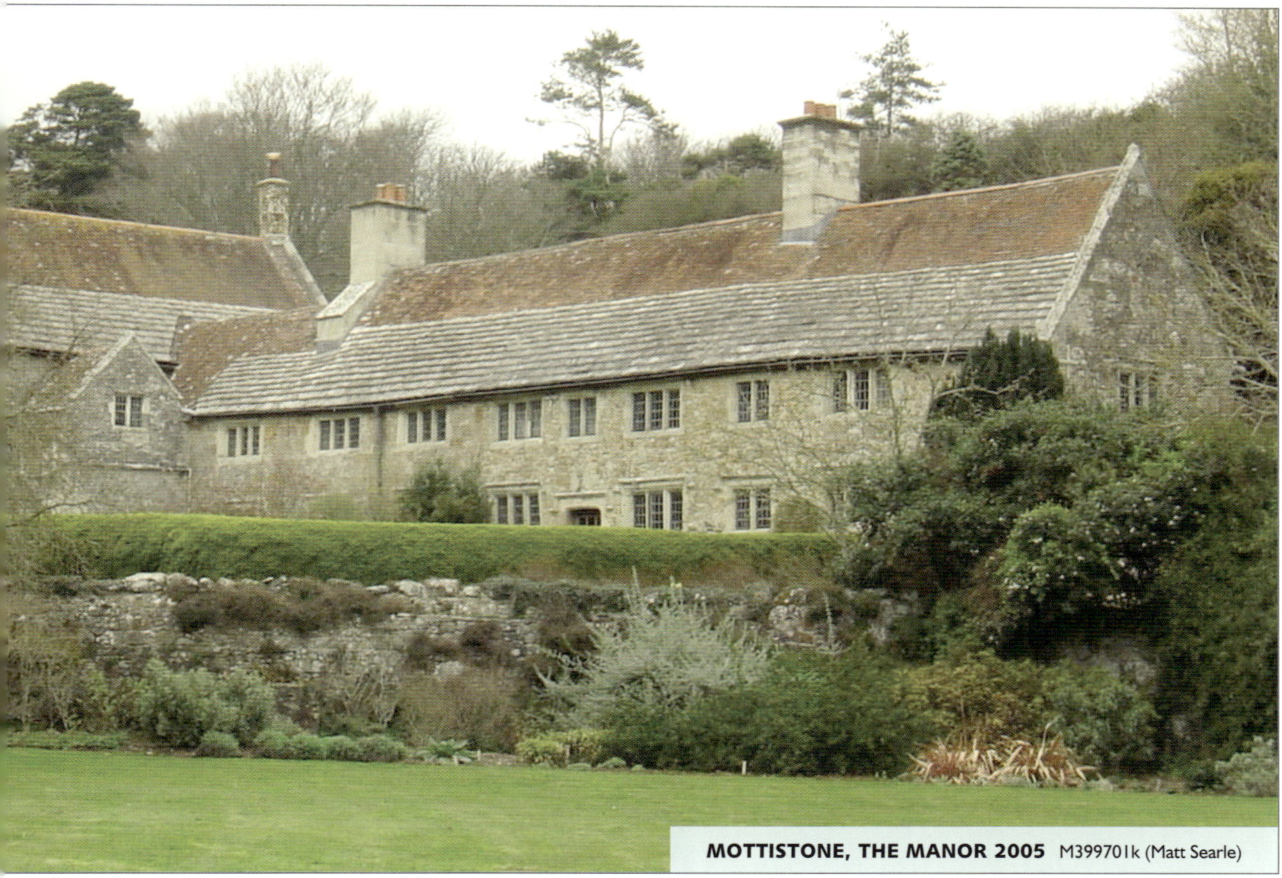

MOTTISTONE, THE MANOR 2005 M399701k (Matt Searle)

The present manor house dates from the 15th century and has been the home of many distinguished Island families. John Cheke, who lived here in Tudor times, was forced to leave Mottistone for the Tower of London after joining the unsuccessful attempt to put Lady Jane Grey on the English throne following the death of Edward VI.

Further north, at the mouth of the River Medina, things were more optimistic. The natural advantages of good geographical location, high water and an abundance of raw materials in Parkhurst Forest, which in those days still covered most of the Island's western half, made shipbuilding a logical development in the port of Cowes (the Shamblord of old), but overall the years of the Tudor succession from Henry VIII, Edward VI and Mary I through to the accession of Elizabeth I in 1558 were a struggle for the Island. Little else was being made and the traditional export goods of wool and corn were, by and large, staying put, victims of low demand. The return of plague was around the corner but at least there was the uplifting arrival of Sir Edward Horsey as Captain, who managed to put a collective smile back on the face of Wight.

Horsey took the job seriously. He had made his reputation for his no-nonsense methods of dealing with piracy and made sure the Island's coastal defences were maintained, but he was also a genial man who loved the good things in life. Horsey endeared himself to Islanders by his ready patronage of sport, hawking and bull-baiting, in particular, and country traditions. He also clearly endeared himself to the beautiful and equally extroverted Dowsabelle, North-country widow of George Mill, preferring the comforts of her manor house home at Haseley, near Arreton, as his seat of government to the crumbling, uninviting edifice at Carisbrooke.

The unofficial couple entertained lavishly at Haseley. Then, suddenly, the fun was over. Horsey died in 1582, a victim of plague, it was said. Oddly, he seems to have been Haseley's only casualty of the dreaded and highly infectious pestilence. Things would be different under the next Captain.

Haseley may have largely escaped the terror of bubonic plague, but it was rife in the towns. At Newport, the largest, the plague raged from late 1582, right through 1583 and well into the following year, claiming the lives of 200 townspeople, a statistic that led to the laying-out of the town's first burial ground at Church Litten. It is now a public park, retaining the distinctive stone archway which once provided access to the cemetery.

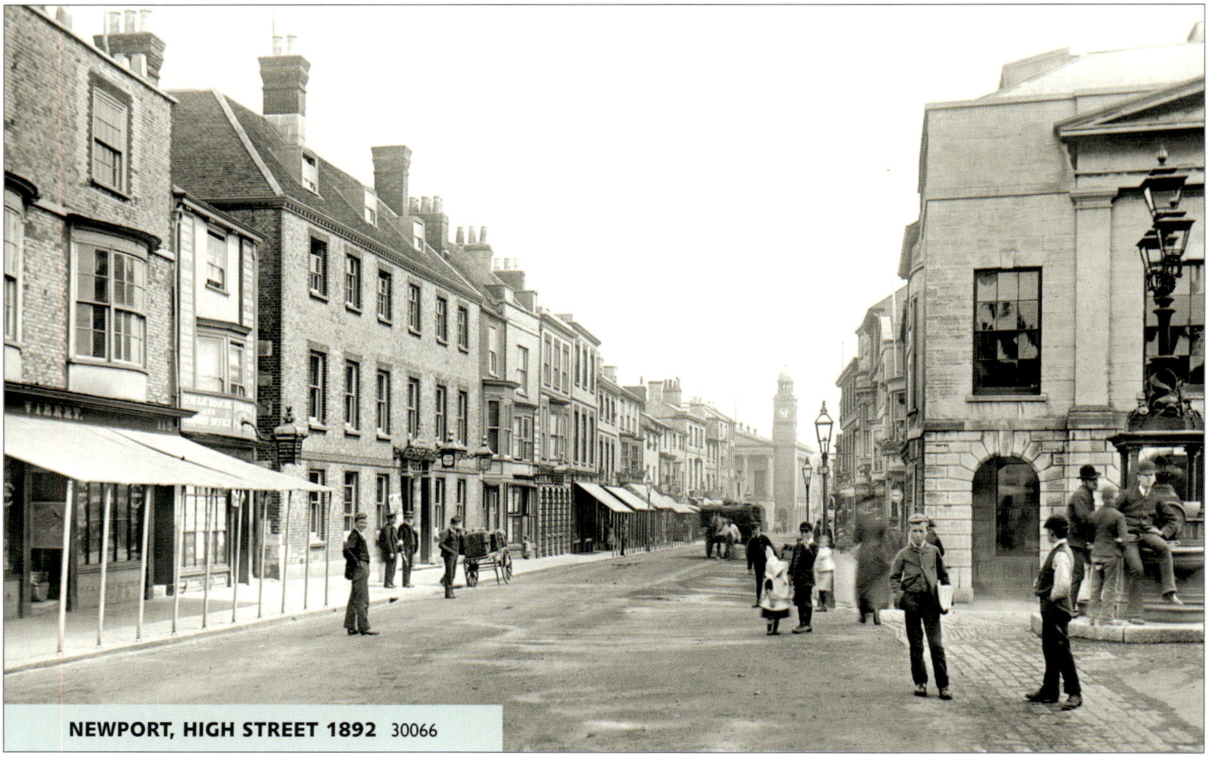

NEWPORT, HIGH STREET 1892 30066

Newport had to endure devastation from French attack and, later, bubonic plague on the road to the prosperity shown in this photograph, which was taken from St James's Square.

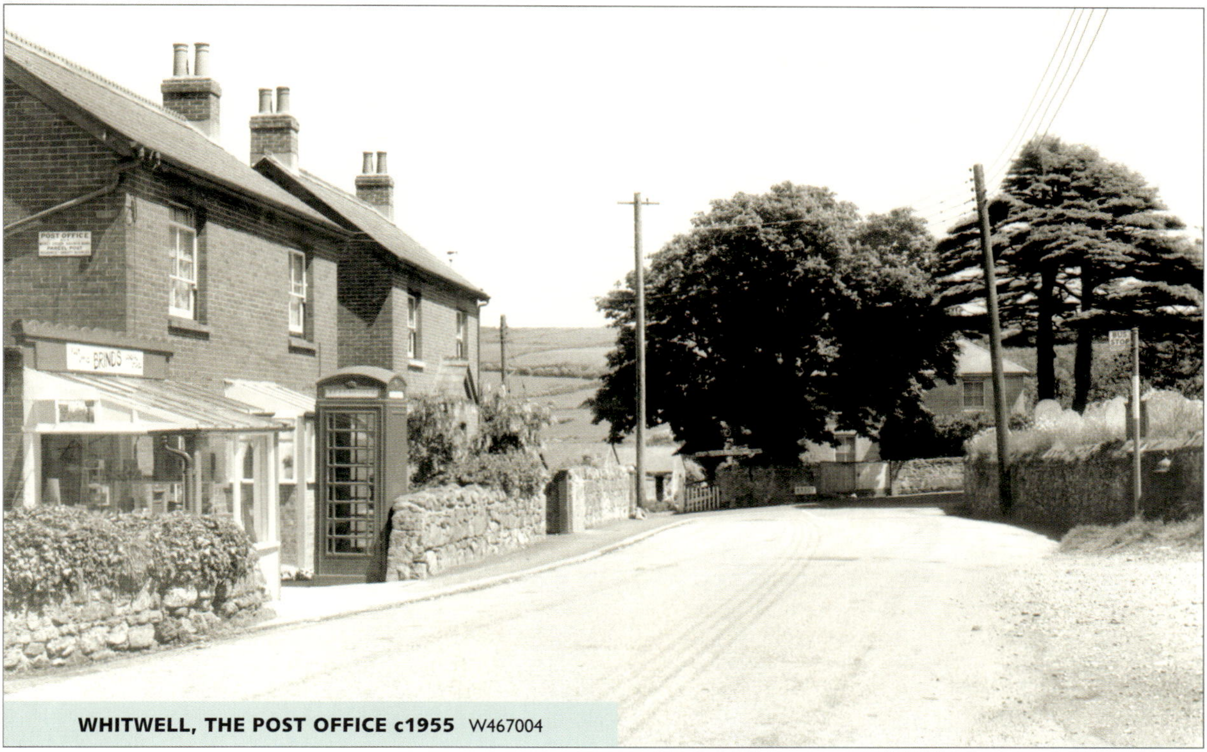

WHITWELL, THE POST OFFICE c1955 W467004

At the other end of the scale, Whitwell (meaning 'white spring') appears almost as quiet here as it would have been in the 16th century.

In nearby St Thomas's Square stands God's Providence House, now a restaurant but traditionally the site of the last house in Newport to yield a plague victim in 1574. Or perhaps, as some have suggested, it was one of the few - possibly the only - homes where nobody actually succumbed to the dreaded disease, 'by the providence of God.' The present building is a later rebuild of the original house, hence the date 1701 above the entrance.

As Newport buried the last of its plague victims, another pestilence lay in waiting - the Spanish. Horsey's successor, the much more austere Sir George Carey (a great-nephew of Anne Boleyn) had put the Island on invasion alert by ordering its young men to stop fooling around ('utterly leave the play at bowls, quoits and other unthrifty games') and get themselves fit and ready to meet the anticipated threat. The local gentry responded to Carey's hard-line leadership by raising the money for a team of conscripted workers to put Carisbrooke Castle, which Carey considered the only fit place from which to govern, into a more acceptable state of repair. But Sir George made himself highly unpopular by insisting that local tradesmen paid him for permission to export their goods. Carey may have acted out of a desire to ensure that as much food as possible was kept on the Island to guard against the possibility of war deprivation, but the tradesmen felt he was merely out to line his own pockets illegally.

Sir George probably felt vindicated, and equally nervous, when, in July 1588, the Spanish Armada was spotted off the Lizard in Cornwall. Armed to the teeth, 2,000 well-trained men, more than a fifth of the total population, awaited the enemy on the Isle of Wight. They had all heard the rumour that the Spaniards were intent on taking the Island. Some say it was the 'Rat of Wight', an early product of the Cowes shipyards, that first brought news into Portsmouth Harbour of the approaching 130-ship Spanish fleet.

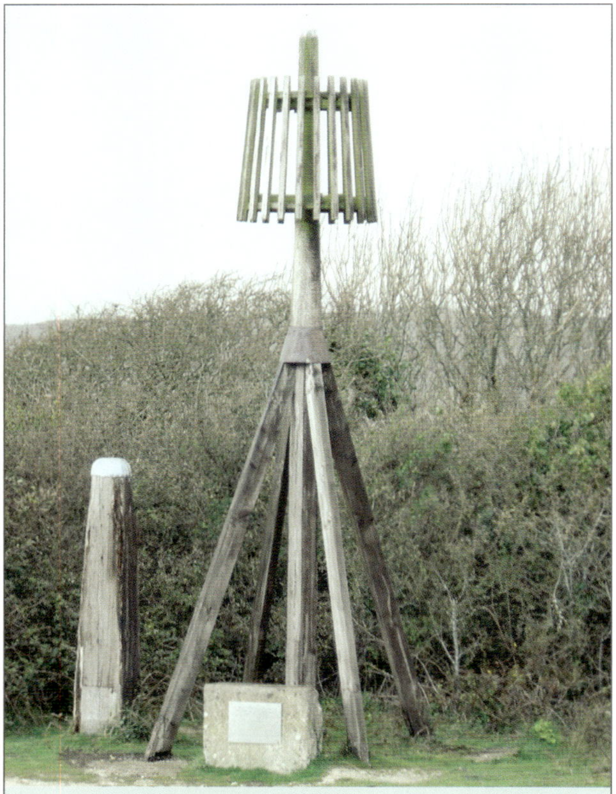

TENNYSON DOWN, THE SIGNAL BEACON 2005
F49701k (Matt Searle)

Armada alert! A scaled-down replica of a signal beacon, with the stump of the original, on Tennyson Down.

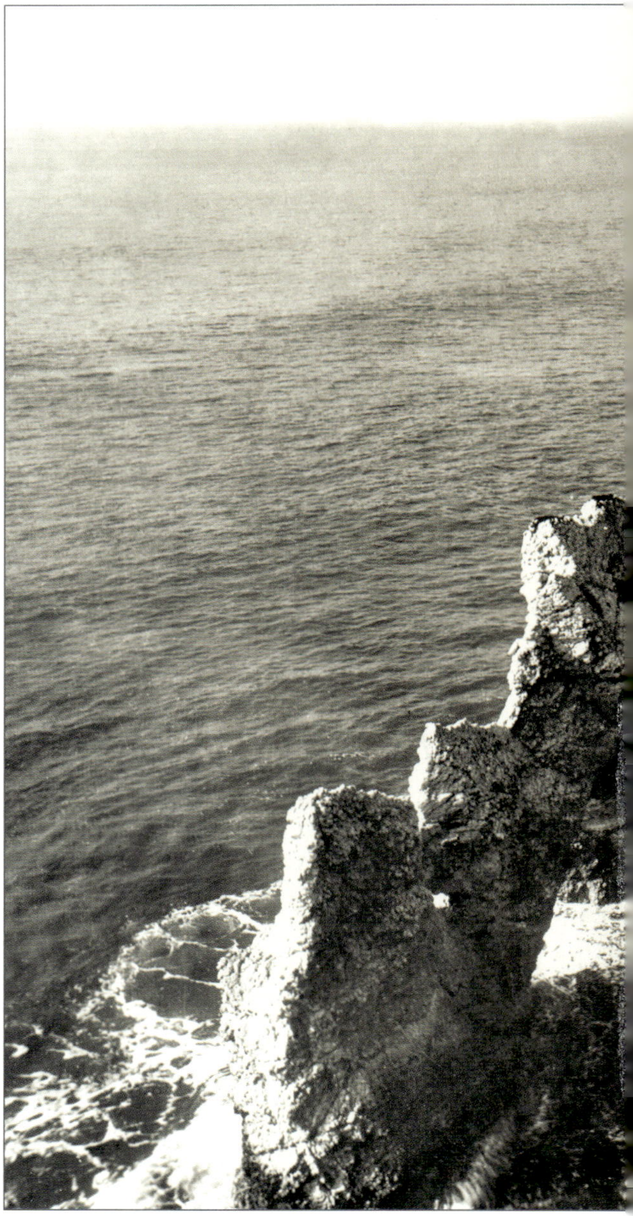

From each of the high downs on the Island, men kept a constant watch for the Armada. Below them, every conceivable landing place was guarded. Whether the Spanish really did plan to capture Wight remains arguable. In the event, harried by the nippy ships of the English fleet under Drake, beset by poor weather and let down by its lumbering galleons, the Armada failed to reach the Solent.

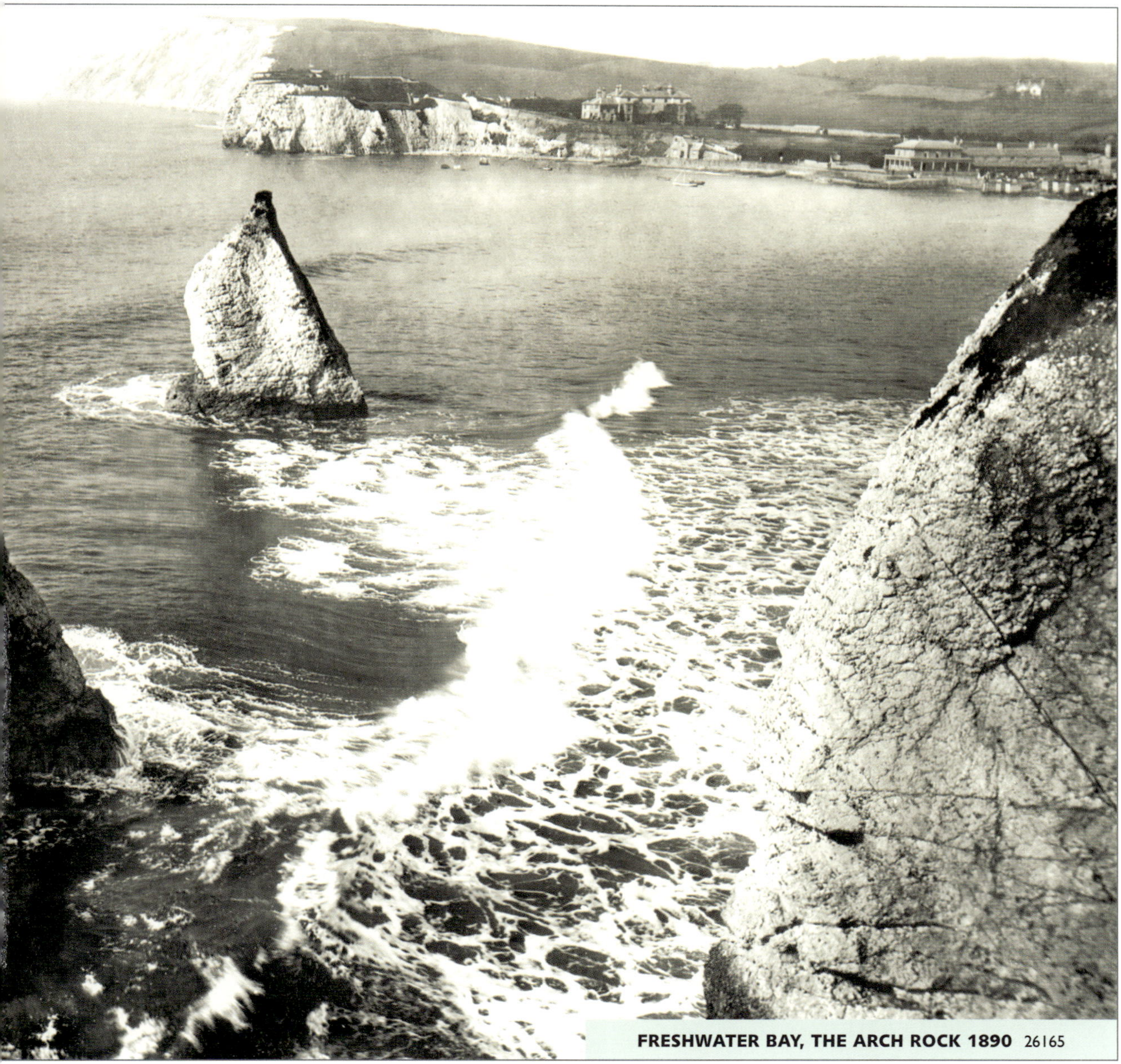

FRESHWATER BAY, THE ARCH ROCK 1890 26165

Tennyson Down provides the backdrop to the distinctive, but now-crumbled, rock.

Relief; celebration; optimism. The Islanders experienced all these following the rout of the Armada. Defence would still be taken seriously, officially, at least, but it would be the lot of future generations to prepare for the next threat to Wight from enemy forces. Instead of looking out to sea for signs of approaching danger, local people began scouring the land for suitable locations for building plots. Many of the Island's surviving manor houses date from this period, from Arreton and Yaverland in the east to Shalfleet in the west. Sturdy cottages, stone-built with thatched roofs and vegetable gardens, sprung up for the less well-off in a relaxed atmosphere. The Island had achieved a peaceful evolution at last.

Meanwhile, the evolution of the English monarchy saw Elizabeth, last of the Tudor rulers, succeeded in 1603 by the first of the Stuarts to occupy the throne, James I. When Charles I replaced him 23 years later, the Isle of Wight was on the brink of its most memorable period ever in the national spotlight.

The English Civil War saw no fighting on the Island, although the population was, more or less, equally divided between Royalist and Parliamentary sympathisers. Indeed, so peaceful was the Island during the war years that many people crossed the Solent from the mainland in search of an offshore haven. Charles I eventually joined them. Fleeing the uncertainties of life in London amid the victorious Commonwealth forces, the king left Hampton Court in 1647 and arrived on Wight, seeking sanctuary.

For Colonel Robert Hammond, who was governing the Island, this was awkward. Although a Parliamentarian, opposed to the monarchy, Hammond was also the brother of the king's chaplain. Initially, he welcomed Charles to accommodation at Carisbrooke Castle and the king was able to move around the Island unhindered as Hammond's guest. But the Isle of Wight was, and remains, an effective prison. Leaving it was not an option open to a king still insisting on his 'divine right' to rule.

An arch Royalist, Captain John Burley, did his best to get Charles out, but it was a botch-up as the king famously became stuck in the bars of the window in the Constable's lodgings, through which he was attempting to escape. Successive generations of the castle's guardians have metaphorically dined out on that story ever since!

The outcome was a Parliamentary clampdown. Charles now felt more fully the force of imprisonment. This didn't prevent two further attempts at rescuing him. The bars on the window again proved impenetrable before, in May 1648, a final bid for freedom was made from the room on the castle's north curtain wall to which he had been moved. Smuggled-in nitric acid might have helped him through the window bars, but the plot was foiled by an informer before the plan could be carried out.

In September, Charles was moved, under guard, to lodgings in Newport to negotiate a treaty with his captors. The town was swamped by supporters and officials of both sides. High Street inns, both now vanished, accommodated most of them - the Royalists in the George, on the south side, and the Parliamentarians in the Bugle, opposite, as they prepared to thrash out the terms of the treaty and, with it, the future course of English government. Precisely where the talks took place has long been the stuff of speculation. The 1619-built grammar school in Lower St James's Street, on the Lugley Street corner, now the town's youth centre, is a strong candidate, but it may have served as the king's presence chamber, with the negotiations actually taking place in the old Town Hall. In one sense, it matters little. After six weeks of talking, the Treaty of Newport was signed but, while it left Charles with his crown intact, there was little else in it for him and the whole process quickly became a waste of time when the massed army on the mainland lost patience.

Taking matters into their own hands at the end of November, they whisked the king away from Newport to a point west of Yarmouth, from where he was shipped across the Western Solent to the mainland at Hurst Castle. Resigned and melancholy, Charles Stuart then began his final overland journey back to London, and his appointment with the executioner at Whitehall on 20 January 1649.

Unlike her father, Princess Elizabeth, second daughter of Charles I, never left the Island once she had been taken there in August 1650. This extraordinarily gifted girl, who could read in French, Italian, Latin and Hebrew at just eight years old, was 14 when she arrived at Carisbrooke with her little brother, Henry, Duke of Gloucester, following initial banishment elsewhere, with Parliament fearing the continued presence of the children in London might re-ignite Royalist sympathies.

Their mother and elder sister had long since left the country for Holland and their brother, the future Charles II, had also escaped Cromwell's clutches. When the children reached Carisbrooke, they were effectively orphans. By all accounts, they were treated with respect and kindness at Carisbrooke, but Elizabeth's always fragile health failed her completely on the Island. Already suffering from rickets, she contracted pneumonia after being caught in a shower on the castle's bowling green. On the morning of 8 September, the young princess was found dead in her bed.

Her coffin was placed in a vault inside the original St Thomas's Church. A brass plate

Did you know?

A Rose for the Crown

Until recent years King Charles I's enforced stay on the Isle of Wight in 1647-48 as a prisoner of the Commonwealth was recalled in the name of the pub which formerly stood opposite the Wheatsheaf Hotel in Newport town centre. The story goes that the Rose & Crown earned its name because it was here that Frances Trattle, a young local girl, presented the doomed king with a damask rose.

made originally for a former minister was reversed, inscribed and fixed in place. And that, miserably, was that. Eventually, at the time of the present church's construction in the 19th century, an appalled Queen Victoria put right that final indignity by commissioning a magnificent sculptured monument above the re-located tomb. It stands at the head of the church's north aisle. Touchingly, Victoria ordered that the windows on the north wall near the monument should be fitted with stained glass so that only a gentle light should fall on the tragic princess's tomb.

Following the monarchy's restoration under Charles II in 1660, a somewhat disinterested Thomas, Lord Culpepper, was foisted on the Isle of Wight as its new Captain, or Governor, the term now more usually applied. Culpepper was eventually moved to bolster the defences when the king's wars with Holland and France renewed the threat of invasion but, while Dutch ships were twice sighted uncomfortably close to the Island coastline, the enemy on this occasion got no closer.

YARMOUTH, ISLE OF WIGHT.

PIER HOTEL.

King Charles II. stayed here 1671.

Entirely Re-Modelled, Enlarged, and Re-Furnished with every Modern Comfort, including Electric Light.
A Billiard Room has been added.
Ornamental Gardens to the Solent.
Three hours from Waterloo by Bournemouth Express.
Frequent Steamers to Lymington, Totland and Alum Bays, Cowes, Ryde, Portsmouth, and Bournemouth. Special facilities for Yachting men. Boating and Fishing. Tennis. Golf Links (near).
The peculiarly bracing influence of the "Western Wight" is unique.
Tariff on application to MANAGER.

AN ADVERTISEMENT FOR THE PIER HOTEL, FEATURING A ROYAL GUEST ZZZ04001 (Author's Collection)

Charles II had a happier time than his father during a visit to the Island in 1671, providing a useful bit of marketing centuries later for the Pier Hotel in Yarmouth!

It was clear by now that the Tudor fortifications were outmoded and not up to the job for which they were built. Yarmouth Castle was a case in point. The garrison may have reached its peak of 70 men during the Civil War but, just a year after the Restoration, in 1661, that swollen force had been disbanded. The swashbuckling Sir Robert Holmes, soldier of fortune, the man who renamed New Amsterdam as New York after snatching it from the Dutch, had the castle manned again when he succeeded Culpepper as Governor in 1669, but with only a token garrison of four gunners.

Later, Holmes undertook, on his own initiative, a general defensive reorganisation on the Island. At Yarmouth, he reduced the castle to a more manageable size by demolishing the earthworks, filling in the moat and building a house alongside it, which is now the George Hotel. The old castle entrance was blocked and replaced by the present access on the castle's south side (off Quay Street). The guns were sensibly concentrated on the seaward side, backed up by a new battery on the quay.

As it turned out, neither they, nor any of the weaponry installed elsewhere on the coast, were ever fired in anger. Free of threat, the Isle of Wight prospered anew, invaded now only by the first few tourists.

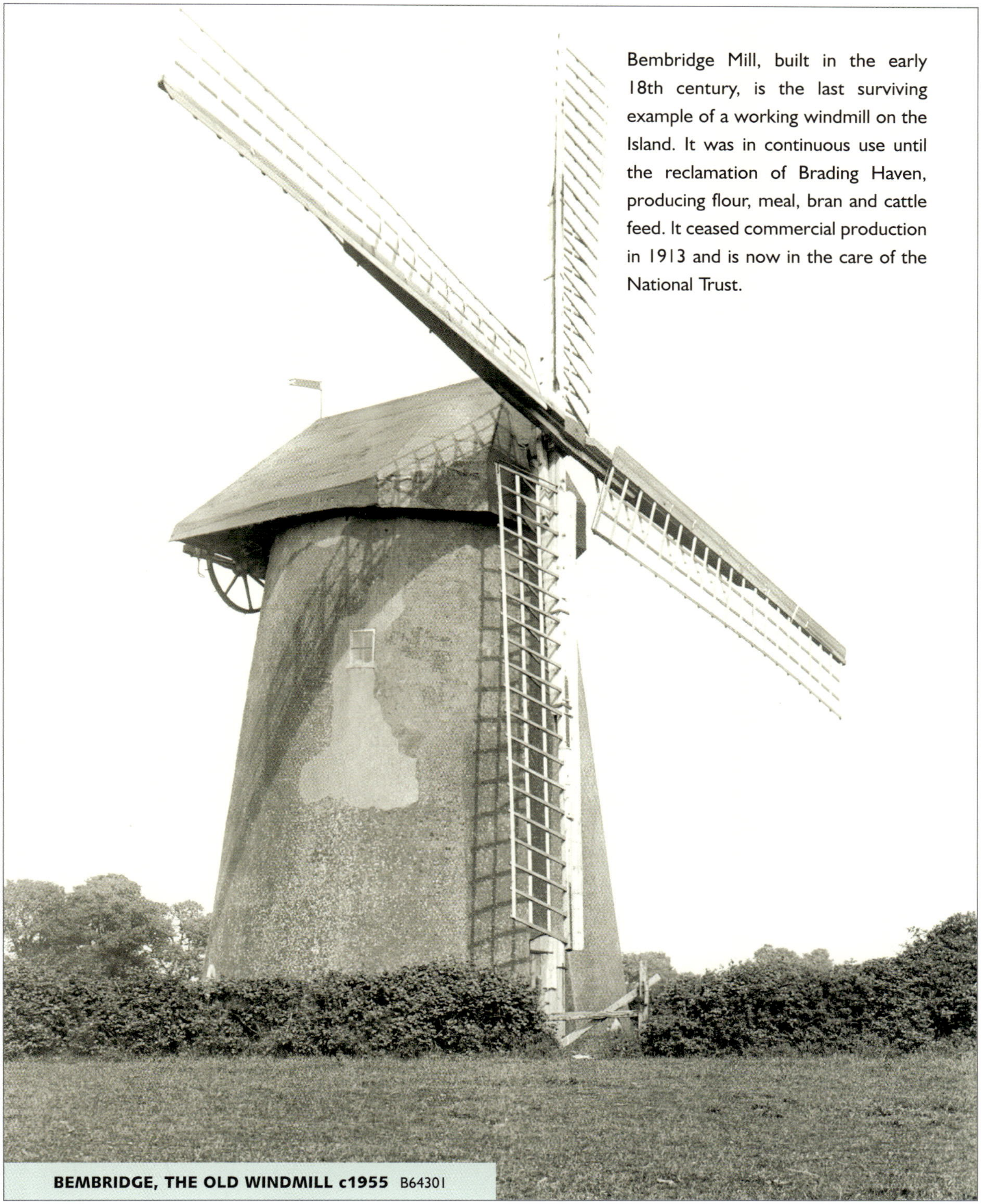

Bembridge Mill, built in the early 18th century, is the last surviving example of a working windmill on the Island. It was in continuous use until the reclamation of Brading Haven, producing flour, meal, bran and cattle feed. It ceased commercial production in 1913 and is now in the care of the National Trust.

BEMBRIDGE, THE OLD WINDMILL c1955 B64301

A 'snapshot' of the Island in the peaceful 18th century should probably start at Brading, where the drawn-out process of making the most significant change to the Wight landscape for centuries was under way. Work had begun as early as the 14th century to reclaim land from the sea in Brading Haven when Sir William Russell built a causeway and bridge between his manor house at Yaverland and Brading. This blocked the sea's encroachment, along the course of the River Yar, from Sandown Bay in the south-east, leaving only the north-east approach intact. It also ended the status of Yaverland, and of Bembridge beyond, as a self-contained tidal island - the 'Binbridge Isle' of early maps. The area of Sir William's 1338 scheme is still known as Yarbridge today.

A project to reclaim 126.5 acres of the Haven, in the area now known as North Marsh, had followed in the 16th century, a collaboration between the landowner, Sir George Oglander, of Nunwell, and Jermyn Richards, a Brading brewer who had cashed in on the demand for vast quantities of beer from the ships in the Haven and had used the proceeds to buy Yaverland Manor in 1553. Draining North Marsh eight years later did not threaten his beer sales. Richards's son, Edward, drained Mill Marsh and land in the Haven's south-west corner, between Yarbridge and Brading, in 1594, providing Brading with a new quay, east of High Street, in place of the former silted-up anchorage.

The plans of the 17th-century entrepreneur Sir Bevis Thelwell to reclaim the main expanses of Brading Haven, some 700 acres, and plant it with a mixture of wheat, barley, oats, cabbage and rape-seed were hotly controversial. King James I backed the

The City in the Copse

Prominent among a number of 'lost cities' on the Isle of Wight - old settlements of which little or no trace now remain - is Wolverton-in-Brading, in reality a medieval village which lay on the banks of Brading Haven centuries before its reclamation from the sea.

Wolverton's demise almost certainly came at the hands of French raiders in the 15th century, but legends dictate that it was doomed by the tainting by a pilgrim's blood of its revered spring water. He was stoned to death by the inhabitants, who had been warned that their town would crumble if the sacred water became impure. They had panicked when they saw the pilgrim kneeling at the water's edge. He turned out to be an innocent worshipper, so the people had unwittingly brought about Wolverton's destruction by their own actions.

The well was dedicated to St Urian, a 9th-century French churchman, as was the chapel built nearby. Today, the remains of the 'city' lie buried beneath St Urian's Copse - the Centurion's Copse of modern-day maps.

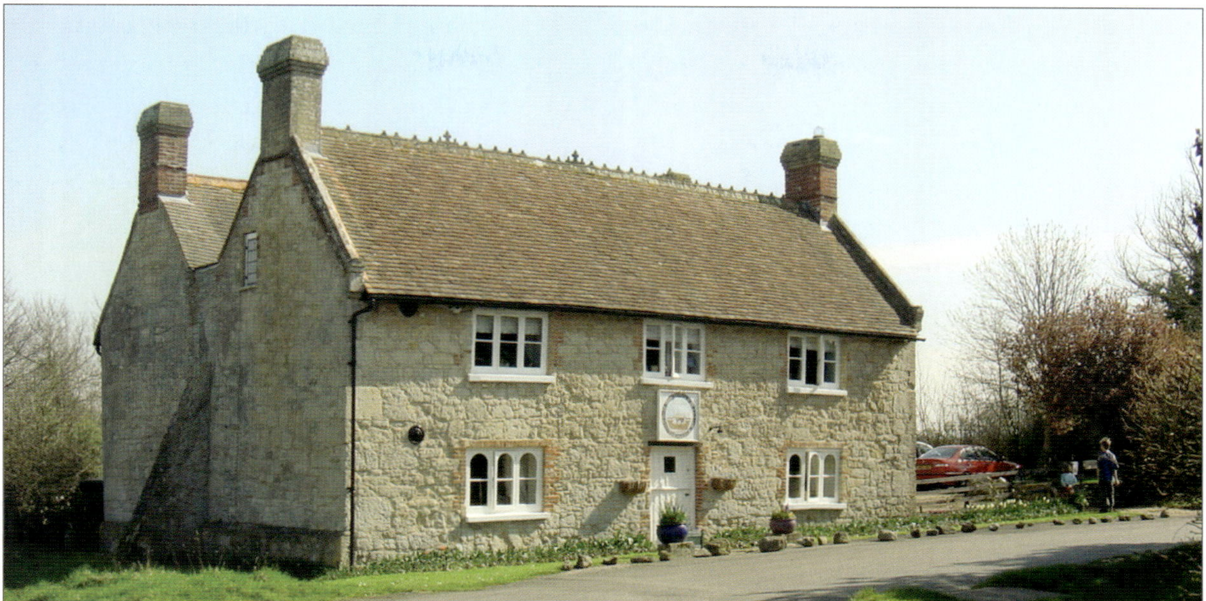

NEWTOWN, THE FORMER NOAH'S ARK PUB 2005 N271703k (Matt Searle)

Newtown was becoming something of a 'lost town' by the 18th century, but the pub - variously called the Noah's Ark or Francheville Arms - was still serving beer and would continue to do so up until the early 20th century.

scheme as a 'dry run' for the reclamation of Lincolnshire's Fens and Thelwell engaged Sir Hugh Myddleton, among the leading civil engineers of his time, to direct workmen from the Low Countries on the massive task in 1620. Two years later, the mouth of the Yar had been dammed at Bembridge. For the best part of the next decade, the Haven was dry.

But the experimental planting of crops proved a huge disappointment - only the rape flourished in the damp sand - and when the sea dramatically gained its revenge by smashing through the embankment in 1630, re-flooding the land, the scheme was dead. Houses, farm buildings and mills, built since the 'inning' works, were washed away. It had been an expensive let-down and, while small sections of the Haven were subsequently banked-off by various landowners, it would be late in the 19th century before renewed human endeavour finally saw the sea out of Brading Haven.

As the shallowing 18th-century waters lapped at the demise of Brading as a seaport, the fortunes of Cowes, the northern port at the Medina's river mouth, were heading towards the high water mark. Demand for Cowes-built ships had grown steadily since Tudor times. From the late 18th century, substantial men-o'-war were emerging for the Royal Navy from the former Nye yard during its periods of occupancy by Philemon Ewer and Robert Fabian, highly regarded shipbuilders from Hampshire, who made the most of the natural advantages - the abundance of high water and accessible raw materials - available at the port. Boats as well as fighting ships were turned out, notably the distinctive Cowes Ketch, which would be mass-produced throughout the 19th century and widely employed as a versatile workboat in the Solent and further afield.

Land settlement here seems to have been initially concentrated in the 13th century on the east bank, and it was at East Cowes that the port first developed international seaborne trade, and a Customs House to guard over it. From there, a constant battle was waged against the smugglers of contraband goods. Unsurprisingly, given the geographical location, the Isle of Wight and smuggling go hand-in-hand. For centuries before, and ever since, the establishment of formal Customs facilities at Cowes, smuggling has been a running feature of Island life. William Arnold, best-known of the Collectors of Customs at Cowes, did his best to stamp it out during a largely successful 23 years in the job from 1777. Arnold also had to contend with widespread corruption among his own officers. He must have been a busy man, but still found the time to produce an illustrious son in Dr Thomas Arnold, famous headmaster of Rugby School, whose own son was the poet, Matthew Arnold.

As William Arnold stamped his authority on Cowes, another of the Island's ports was taking the decisive step that would eventually make it the largest town on Wight. Ryde takes its name, via a series of earlier forms, from the old English 'rith' (pronounced 'rithe'), meaning a small stream, and the stream in question is today's Monktonmead Brook, which runs through the town, though mainly buried beneath it these days, to the sea. Centuries ago, its north-eastern location, directly opposite Portsmouth, made Ryde an obvious site for a ferry link with the mainland (see Did You Know? box: The Ryde Wherry).

Ashore, right up to the 18th century, there was very little. Ryde, originally part of the old manor of Ashey, began life as two hamlets, upper and lower, and neither amounted to much. Lower Ryde was a cluster of fishermen's cottages at the water's edge. Upper Ryde was focussed on St Thomas's Chapel, built by Thomas Player in 1719, soon after his arrival in the area from the mainland, to save local people a six-mile trek to the then parish church at Newchurch. 'A rude collection of huts on the brow of a hill' was the rather dismissive description of Upper Ryde in an early account of the town's history. Between the hill-divided Ryde hamlets, there was nothing but woodland and fields.

Then, in 1780, the two were linked by the construction of the appropriately-named Union Street, which today, and for many years, has been easily the grandest of all the Isle of Wight's shopping thoroughfares. The building of the eventually impressive Ryde Pier in 1814, twice extended beyond the low water mark, confirmed the status of passenger port. Before long, there was not only a town, its boundaries defined by the Ryde Improvement Act of 1854, but a 'watering place' which at one stage seemed set to rival Brighton as the most fashionable on England's south coast.

On the Island's east coast, Sandown's

Did you know?

The Ryde Wherry

Centuries before the building of Ryde Pier in 1814, cross-Solent travel from the port known variously as La Rye, La Riche and Ride was provided by the fishermen who lived on the coast. In the 17th century, regular services were operated by boats of the open-decked, two-masted Ryde Wherry type, specially designed for the job. They were replaced in 1796 by a larger vessel, known as 'The Packet'. Regular steam-powered services began in 1825 when, following an experimental service in 1817, the paddle steamer 'Union' was running two return trips a day between the pier and Portsmouth.

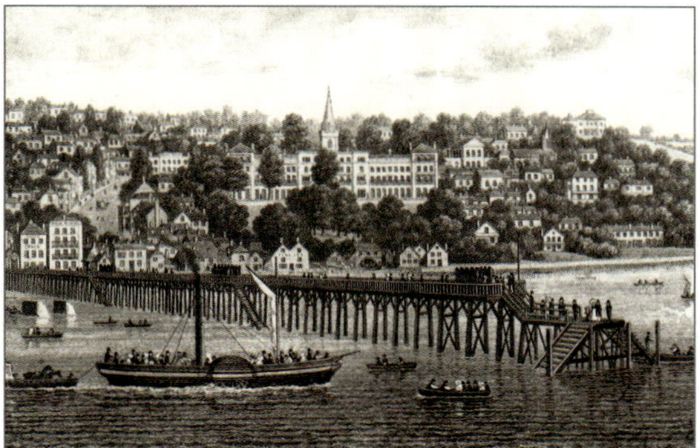

AN ENGRAVING OF EARLY RYDE c1825
ZZZ04002 (Author's Collection)

This shows the pier and the expanding town – the population grew from just 250 in 1700 to 10,000 by 1850.

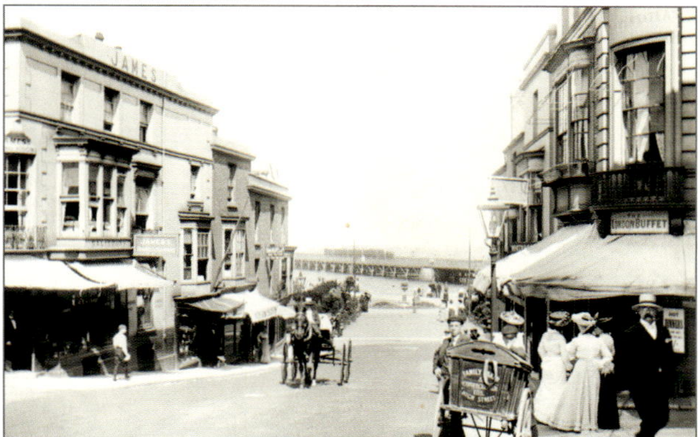

RYDE, UNION STREET 1904 53166

Union Street linked Lower and Upper Ryde in 1780, triggering the town's development.

'village by the sandy shore' was greeting its first notable resident at the end of the 18th century when the mischievous radical John Wilkes moved into his newly-built Sandham Cottage. No doubt he preferred his home by the sea to the Tower of London, where this eccentric product of what many historians call a wild, misspent youth had earlier been locked up.

The Isle of Wight's own establishment, its fashionable society, fizzed around the great houses of Appuldurcombe and Knighton Gorges. The former, newly-rebuilt on the site of its flattened Elizabethan predecessor near Wroxall, was the residence of Sir Richard Worsley, Governor of the Island between 1780 and 1782, military officer, politician and historian. The latter, an Elizabethan manor house perched prettily on a hillock near Newchurch, was home to George Maurice Bisset. Sir Joshua Reynolds, pre-eminent portrait painter of the period, and London theatre-land's Garrick family, were among the many illustrious personalities who passed between the two.

So did Bisset and Sir Richard's wife, the beautiful Seymour. George became one of Lady Worsley's innumerable male conquests. There was a tremendous scandal when they were found romantically entwined at a London hotel in 1781. Sir Richard sued Bisset for, among other things, 'carnally knowing' his wife, claiming a phenomenal £25,000 in damages. While the sizzling evidence proved the Governor's case, he was awarded just sixpence after it was shown that he had not only known all along about his wife's affairs but had actually encouraged them! The shamefaced Worsleys - Seymour admitted to 23 lovers in court! - were later divorced, but it was the end of Sir Richard's sparkling career in public life, and of Appuldurcombe's, too. After periods as a school and a temporary monastery for the Benedictine monks who later established the present Quarr Abbey, the great house had its roof ripped apart by a parachuted Luftwaffe land-mine in the Second World War. It is now a partially restored romantic ruin in the care of English Heritage.

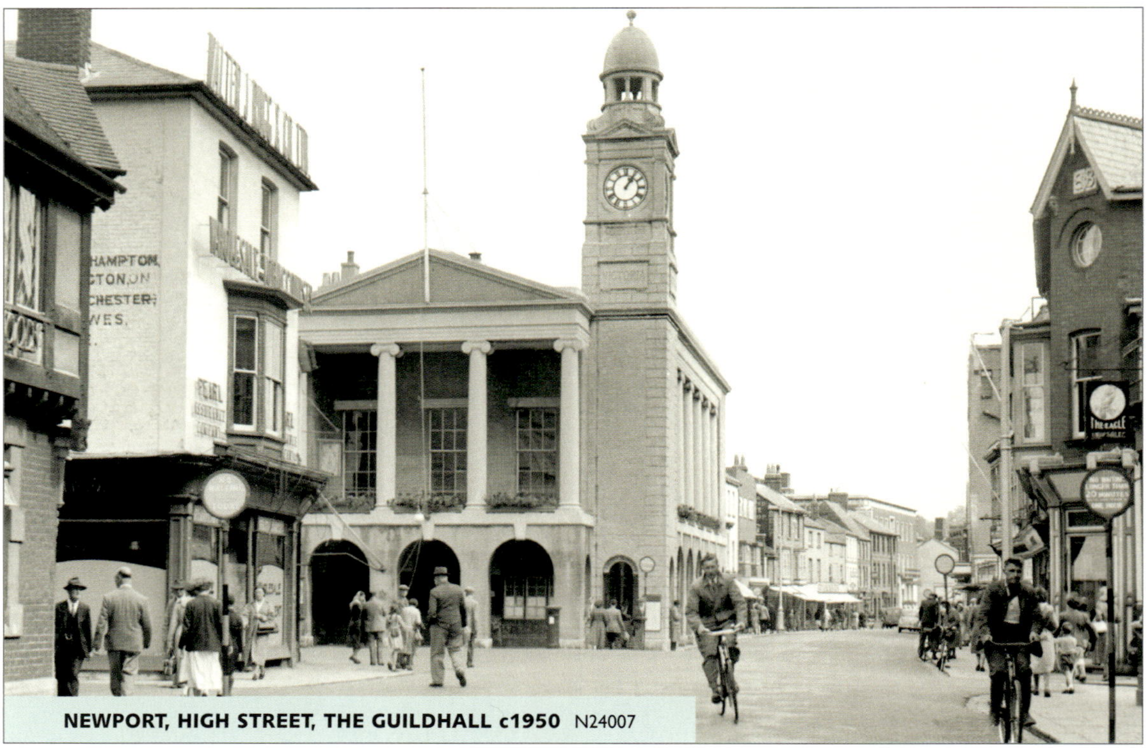

NEWPORT, HIGH STREET, THE GUILDHALL c1950 N24007

Now the Museum of Island History, the Guildhall was built by the great John Nash, who lived at East Cowes Castle. The clock tower was a Victorian addition.

All that is left of Bisset's house, Knighton Gorges, are the gateposts, supposedly haunted by the ill-starred Dillington family who lived there in earlier times. This splendid house, where John Wilkes had enjoyed the dubious delights of a Bisset-hosted Hellfire Club, met a tragic end. Following the scandalous 1782 trial Bisset was shunned by society. He became a reclusive figure over the next 20 years, slowly losing his sanity until, in a muddled state, he ordered the demolition of his own home brick by brick.

Generally, population and buildings were expanding as peace persisted. There was, however, very nearly a nasty sting in the tail when the Napoleonic Wars rekindled fears of enemy invasion. No less than 4,500 troops crossed to the Island to meet the threat. That was in addition to the 3,000 Islanders who had taken up arms, a startling ratio of one soldier to every three civilians! The French intercepted ships offshore and managed to capture intact one of the early Cowes-Southampton packet boats as a war prize. But they didn't use it, or anything else, to disembark on Wight.

Sir Richard Worsley's dramatic demise also brought down the curtain on the succession of Crown-appointed, salaried Isle of Wight Governors. From 1790, the post converted to purely honorary status. Thereafter, the Island's government was entirely entrusted to Justices of the Peace, sitting in Quarter Sessions, and, at the lower level, in the corporate towns, by locally-chosen representatives.

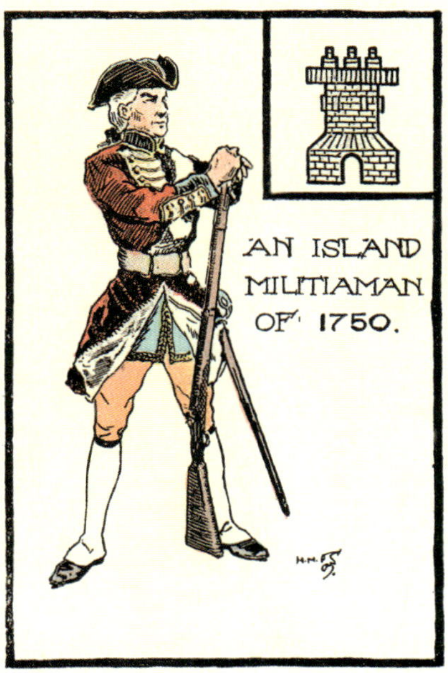

AN ISLAND MILITIAMAN OF 1750
ZZZ03999 (Author's Collection)

Another historical character depicted in the Carisbrooke Castle pageant.

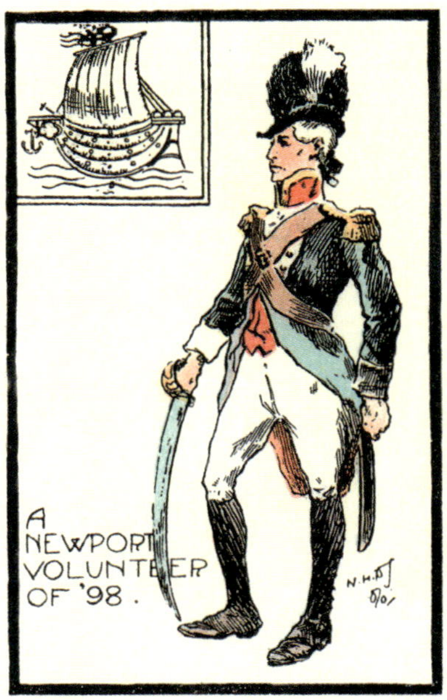

A NEWPORT VOLUNTEER OF 1798
ZZZ04000 (Author's Collection)

A final example of the castle-staged tribute to the Island's militia.

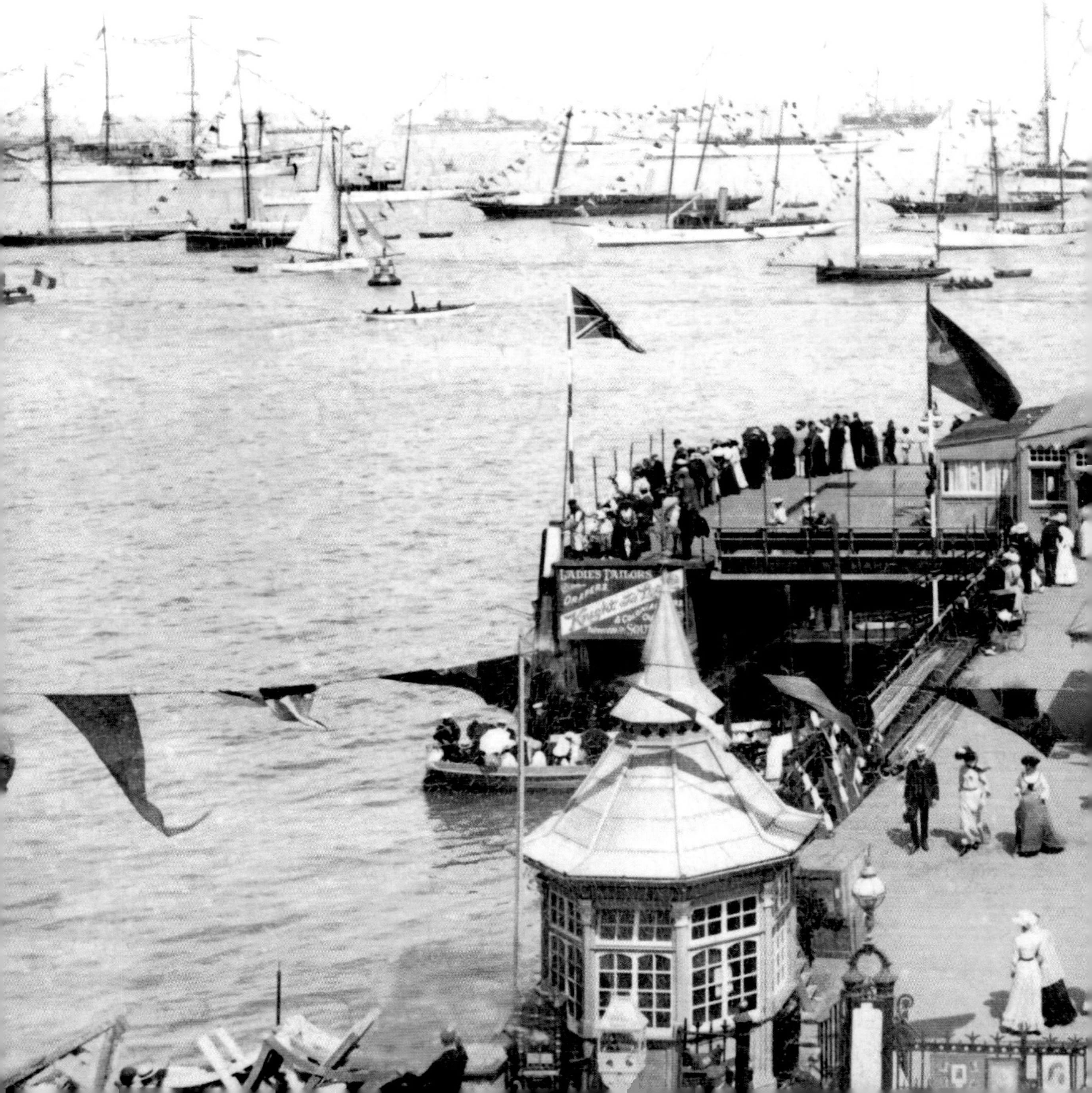
LADIES TAILORS
DRAPERS
Knight

CHAPTER FOUR

Victoria – The Icing on the Cake

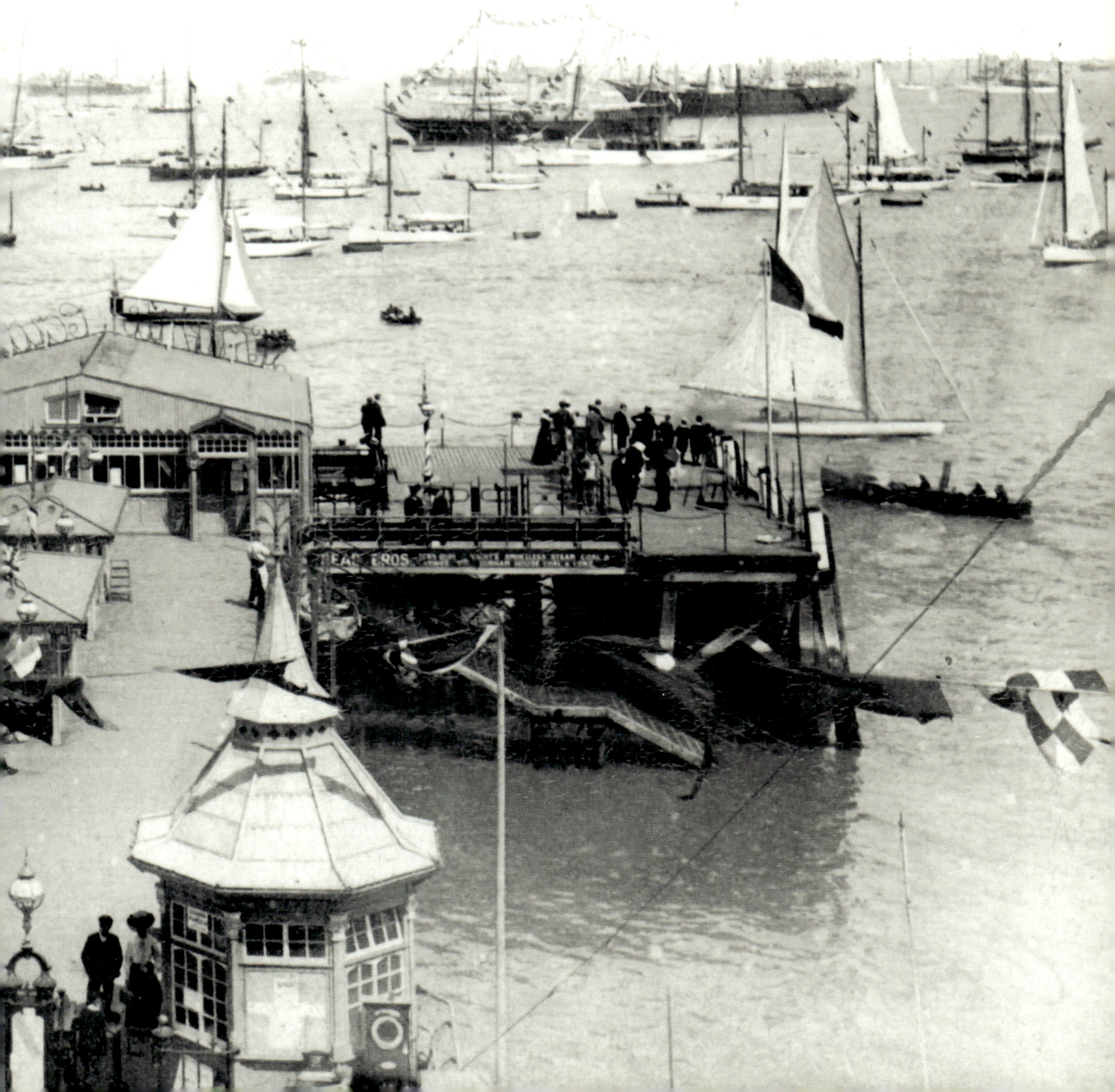

TOURISM. The word has been synonymous with the story of the Isle of Wight, previously an island dominated by agriculture, over the past two centuries. Shanklin, for example, may have been mentioned in Domesday but, as with close neighbour Sandown, most of its history has been condensed within the 19th and 20th centuries. It had the early benefit of a natural attraction, arguably the Island's first-ever tourist haunt, thanks to the existence of its chine, a dramatic natural cleft which once supported a spectacular wilderness. The chine gave Shanklin its name. It comes from the Anglo-Saxon words 'scenc' (the cup) and 'hlinc' (in the rising ground). John Keats was one of the first to appreciate it.

Keats Green, on the cliff path above the seafront, recalls the poet's second visit to the Island in the summer of 1819. His two-month stay at Eglantine Cottage saw him battling against failing health, but still producing 1,500 lines of verse. Some of his best-known works were part-finished here ('Hyperion', half of 'Lamia' and four acts of 'Otho the Great'). Less than two years later, he was dead, aged just 25. That was just 16 years before the start of Queen Victoria's long hold on the British throne, an era that would bring other literary giants flocking to the offshore isle, cementing its reputation among the nation's

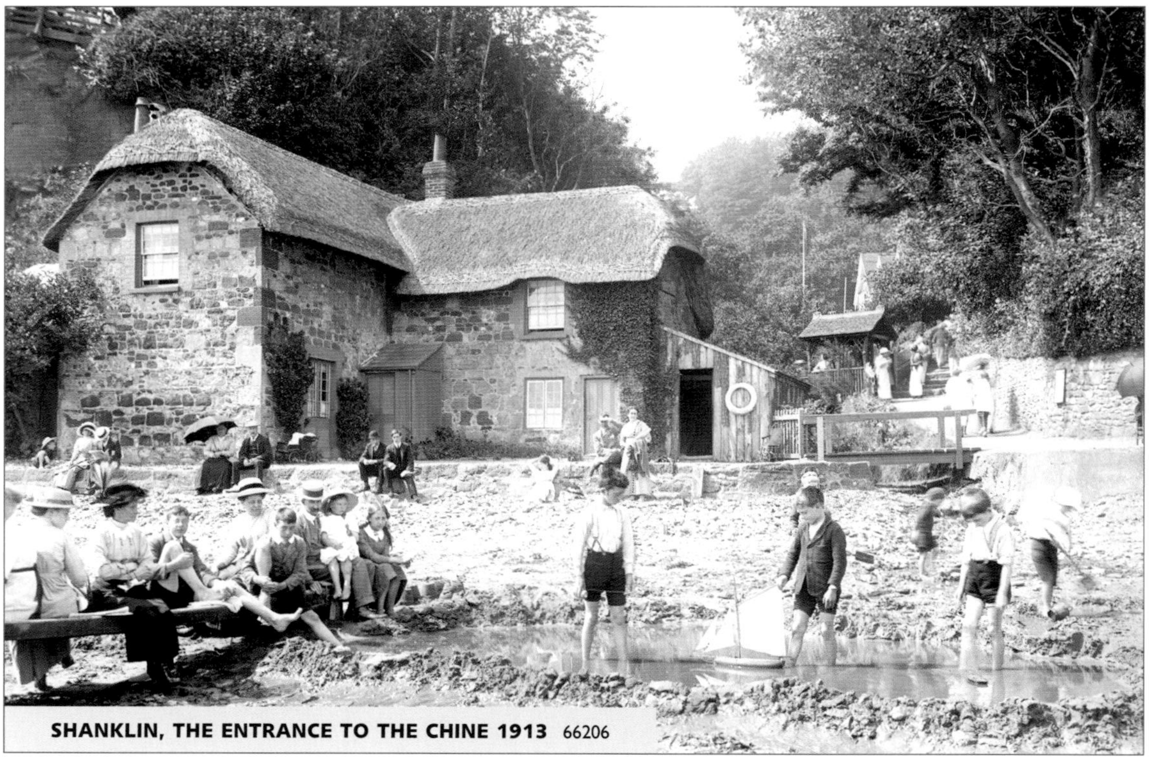

SHANKLIN, THE ENTRANCE TO THE CHINE 1913 66206

This shows the beach-side entrance to the chine, arguably the Island's oldest tourist attraction. Fisherman's Cottage (left) is still there today.

leading tourist destinations, and providing a home for the queen herself.

The mild Island climate has always been a plus factor. This is especially true of south-facing Ventnor, protected from harsher northern influences by the highest hills on the Isle of Wight. There was barely room in which to squeeze a town between them and the English Channel. As a result, development was, of necessity, strung out along a series of terraces, unique on the Island, connected by climbing roads of Alpine proportions. This unusual topography delayed the awakening of Ventnor from its lingering slumber as a secluded, barely visited fishing village. A few cottages, a solitary mill and the Crab & Lobster Inn was all there was when John Turner sketched on the shore and, in 1830, when Dr James Clark was immediately struck by the health-giving properties of the extraordinary local climate, reputedly the most equitable in England.

Equally impressed by the wild, romantic Undercliff just along the coast, Clark sat down to compose a treatise so full of praise for the place that it would change it forever. The eminent doctor had witnessed at first hand how hugely beneficial the conditions at Ventnor could prove to patients suffering from tuberculosis and other pulmonary disorders. His paper was widely read and his opinions respected. In no time at all, Ventnor was mushrooming out of Bonchurch parish into a fashionable health resort. Undeterred by the distinct absence of level ground, people built fine houses wherever they could find room on the terraces. From a few hundred in the first decade of the 19th century, Ventnor's population rocketed to more than 5,000 in a little over 30 years.

Ryde, meanwhile, had developed magnificent retreats for some of England's leading aristocratic families. Street names still recall the origins of the villas built for the Duke of Buckingham and Earl Spencer, although the still impressive houses themselves are now divided into flats. Newport, the bustling, thriving capital at the heart of Island affairs, had sprouted elegant town houses to accommodate the wealthier residents of Wight who increasingly sought a say in the politics of the place. Travelling periodically into the town from their country piles to exercise their influence was not a workable option, given the awful state of the Island's roads. With other towns also benefiting from the growing interest in the 'unexplored' isle, all it needed was the proverbial icing on the cake.

It came, of course, with the decision of the newly-married Queen Victoria and Prince Albert of Saxe-Coburg to adopt the Island as their home, a country retreat away from the formalities of presiding over the British Empire from Buckingham Palace and, they reasoned, better suited for the role than their other options of Windsor Castle and the Royal Pavilion in Brighton. Victoria's mother, the Duchess of Kent, had earlier paved the way by taking out a lease in 1831 on Norris Castle at East Cowes which, despite its Normanesque appearance, was actually a product of the late 18th century. On holiday there, the young Victoria fell in love with Norris Castle - and with the Isle of Wight.

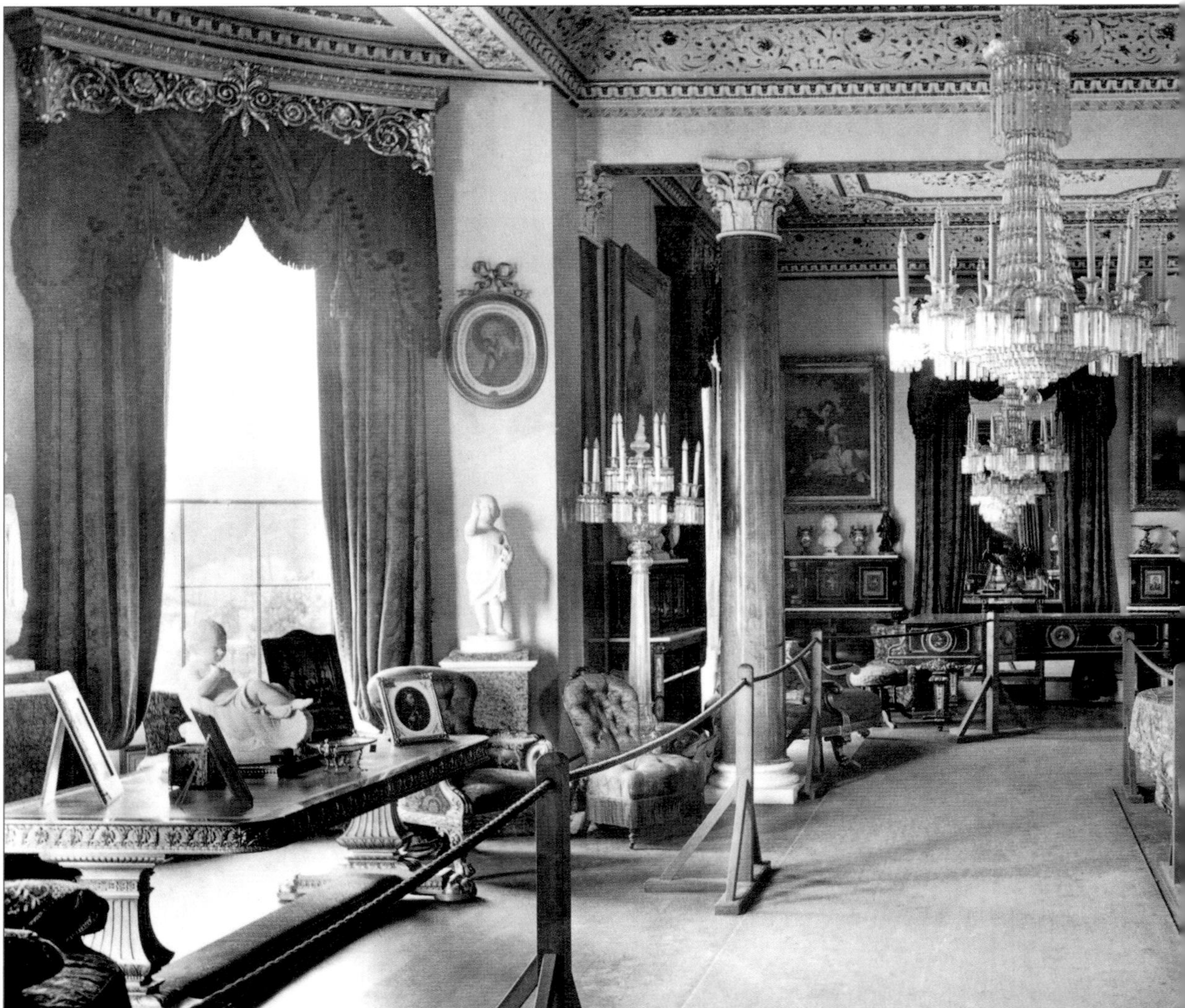

OSBORNE HOUSE, THE STATE APARTMENTS, THE DRAWING ROOM 1908 60586

The drawing room was pictured just four years after Queen Victoria's death.

Close to Norris stood the Osborne House estate. In 1845, five years into their marriage, Victoria and Albert snapped it up from Lady Isabella Blatchford. The original house fell victim to the royal couple's desire to build their own home. They had the site re-developed with a spacious, high-towered mansion which would not look out of place overlooking the Bay of Naples, the precise intention of Prince Albert, who had been struck by the similarity of the view over the Solent from Osborne with those he had encountered in Italy. Albert designed the house himself, though he leaned heavily on

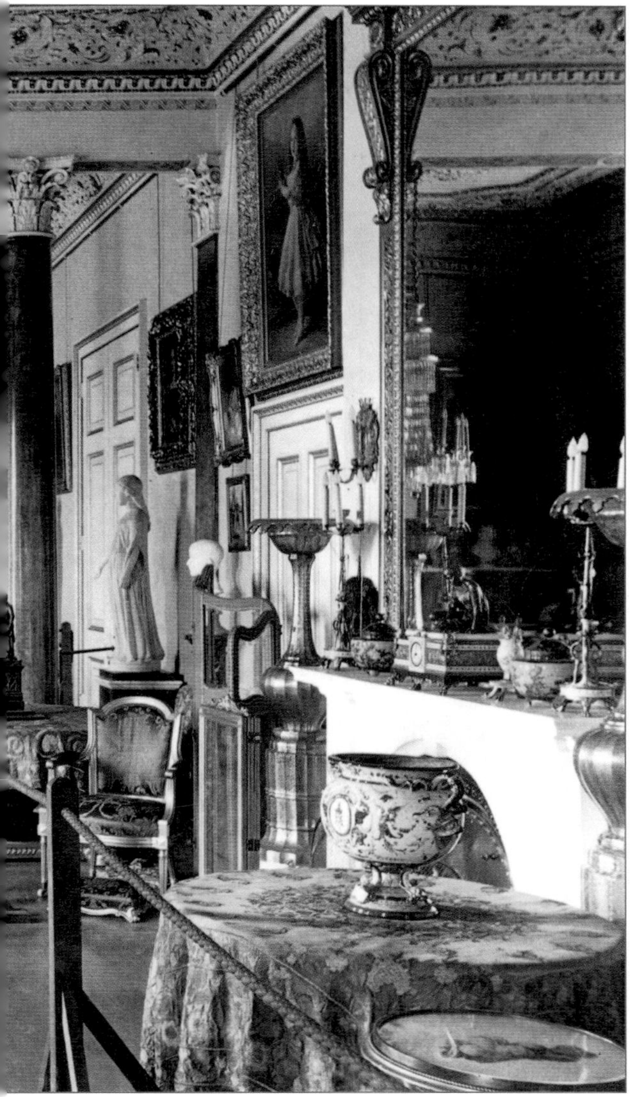

the expertise and practical help of Thomas Cubitt, the renowned London builder.

With the queen herself in residence - and destined to spend a considerable amount of her entire life at Osborne following the early death of her husband - the Isle of Wight had struck gold. Royalty and aristocracy on a global scale came now to the Island, as did Prime Ministers, Government officials and courtiers. They came mostly on business, summoned by, or seeking audience with, the head of state. But others came for fun - and very exclusive indeed was the fun to be had at the Royal Yacht Squadron, which was based across the River Medina from Osborne in the former Tudor stronghold of Cowes Castle (Henry VIII's 'West Cow') where guns were still being fired.

In 1813 a group of aristocrats and gentlemen had met in London to form what was known simply as The Yacht Club. They seem to have been largely motivated by a need to counter the take-over of London society and its clubs by Beau Brummel and the Dandies. The new club became even grander when it acquired the Royal prefix and in 1825 it began a long, and continuing, association with the Isle of Wight when it set up home at Cowes and restyled itself as the Royal Yacht Squadron. Some 23 years later, it moved from premises elsewhere in the town into the castle, which had been serving until then as the official residence of the Governor of the Island.

Modifications to the castle in the 17th and 18th centuries had left little more than the gun platform intact from the Tudor fort. From 1848 onwards, its cannon fire would signal nothing more hostile than intense competition for sailing glory. The Squadron would become the world's most exclusive club of any sort, and serve as the focal point for Cowes Week, international sailing's most prestigious regatta, and easily the most well-known event on the Isle of Wight's social and sporting calendar.

COWES, THE REGATTA 1903 50797b

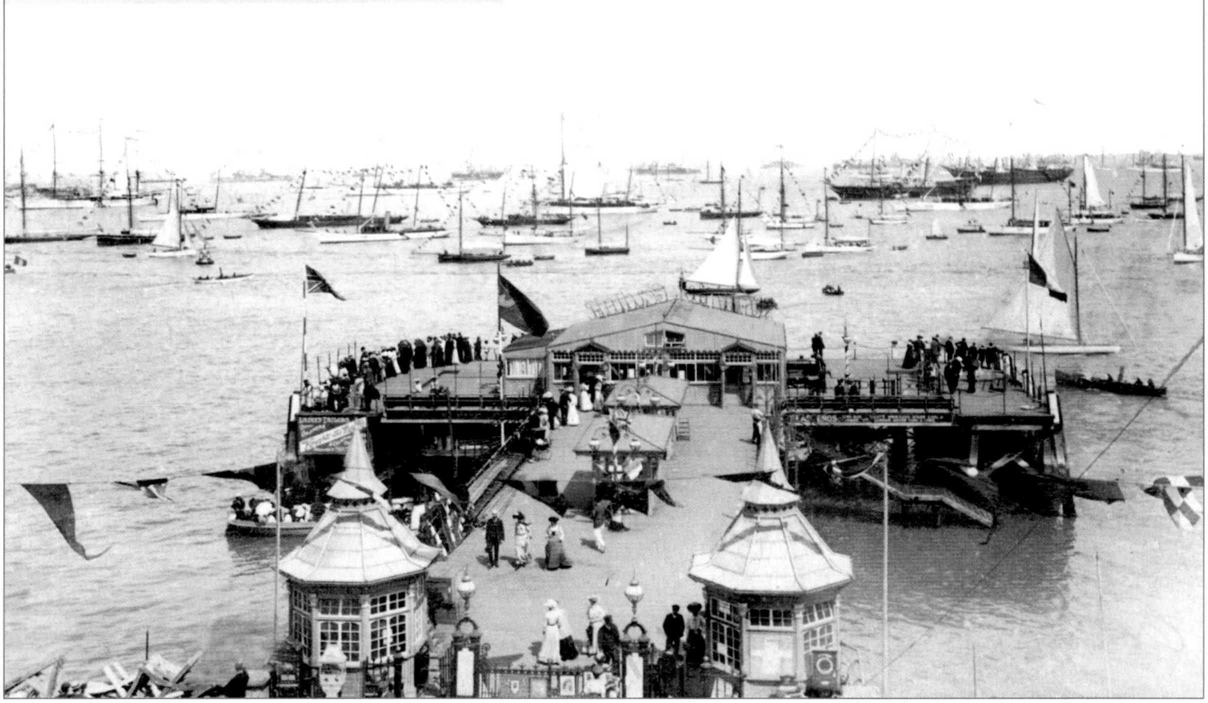

The sailing regatta is seen here in full swing. Victoria Pier (foreground) lasted exactly half a century following its opening in 1901.

The Squadron's arrival gave West Cowes a tremendous social boost, its subsequent development outstripping that of East Cowes across the river. Eventually, the 'West' prefix would officially be dropped altogether. It is Cowes pure and simple now, on the Isle of Wight and throughout the world. Yet it is far from the case that the history of Cowes, West or East, over the past 200 years has been tied to the rich and famous. The other side of the coin is pitted with industrial endeavour, and stamped throughout most of that time with the name of White.

Thomas White had acquired the old Nye shipyard in 1803, moving an already long established family business to Cowes from Broadstairs, Kent. It would expand into the most illustrious shipbuilding dynasty Cowes has ever known, contributing greatly to employment and economy throughout the Island. 'White's built - well-built' would be a simple, yet entirely accurate, marketing slogan for a company with an enviable international reputation under Thomas's grandson, John Samuel.

These were the 'headline' arrivals on the Island in the 19th century. Arriving in general had become progressively easier thanks to the development of cross-Solent ferry links. The Cowes-registered Isle of Wight Royal Mail

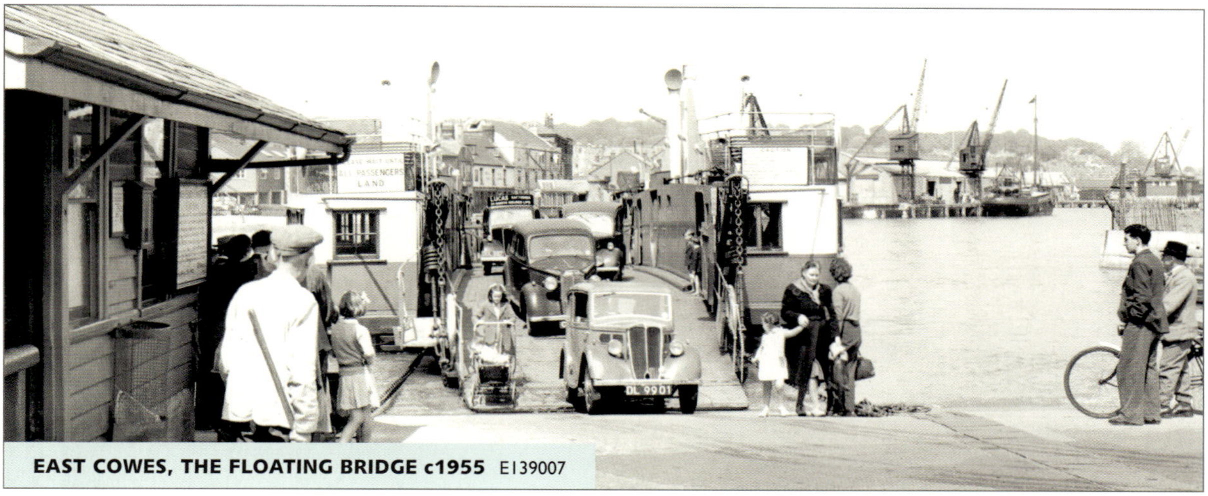

EAST COWES, THE FLOATING BRIDGE c1955 E139007

East and West Cowes were first connected by chain ferry - the floating bridge across the Medina river mouth - in 1859. The famous ferry link remains in service, still saving its users a lengthy inland detour via Newport.

Steam Packet Company had been running regular ferry services between the Island port and Southampton since 1820. Forty-one years later, the Company merged with a rival to form the Southampton, Isle of Wight and South of England Royal Mail Steam Packet Company Limited, famous for many years as the longest company title in England. A short-form was needed. Initially, it was 'The Isle of Wight Company.' Later it would become Red Funnel.

As noted in the previous chapter, the Ryde-Portsmouth ferry route had introduced regular paddle steamer services in 1825, while the Island's western ferry link, between Yarmouth and Lymington, saw its first steamship service in 1830. All this helped to bring people more easily to the Island, but onward travel within its confines was a serious problem until the advent of the railways in 1862.

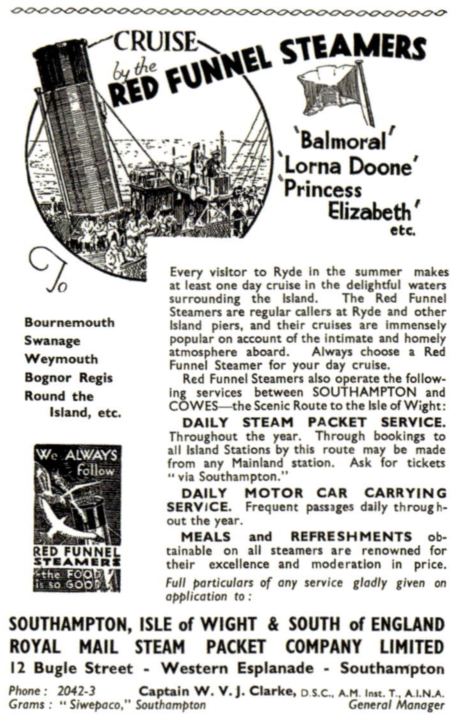

AN ADVERTISEMENT FOR RED FUNNEL CRUISES 1948
ZZZ04013 (Reproduced by kind permission of Red Funnel)

Paddle-steamers were still the norm when Red Funnel advertised cruises in 1948.

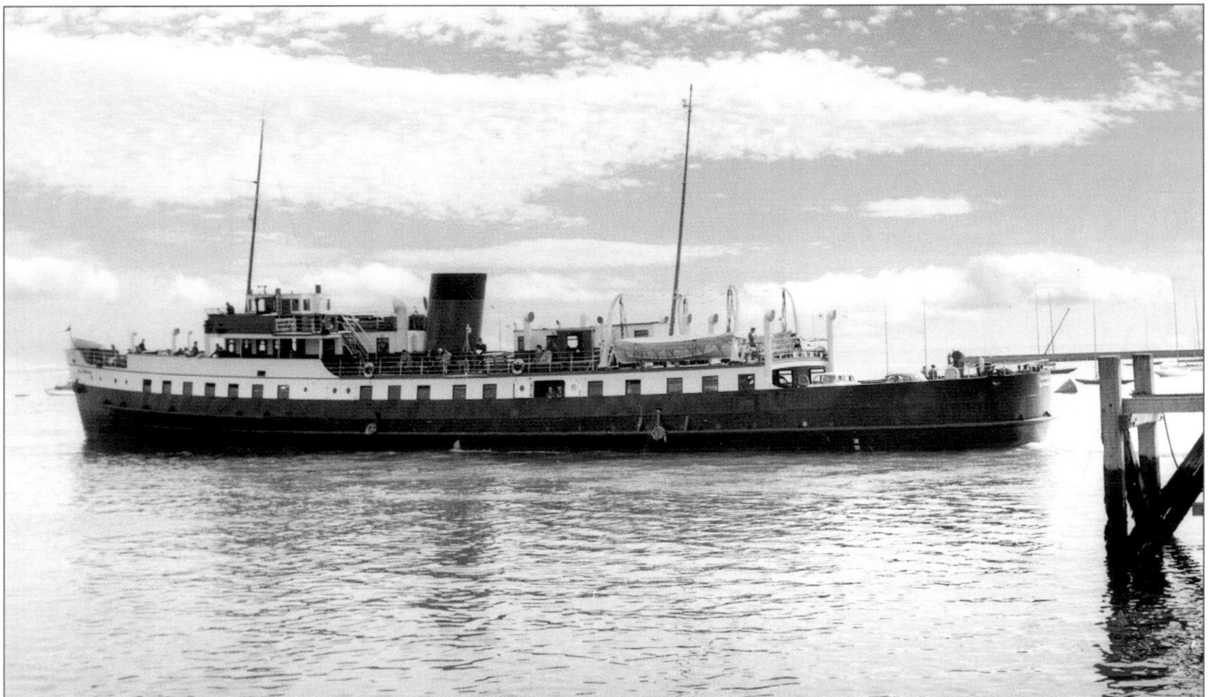

COWES, RED FUNNEL'S 'BALMORAL' LEAVING HARBOUR c1965 C173049

The now preserved MV 'Balmoral' is pictured near the end of her Red Funnel career.

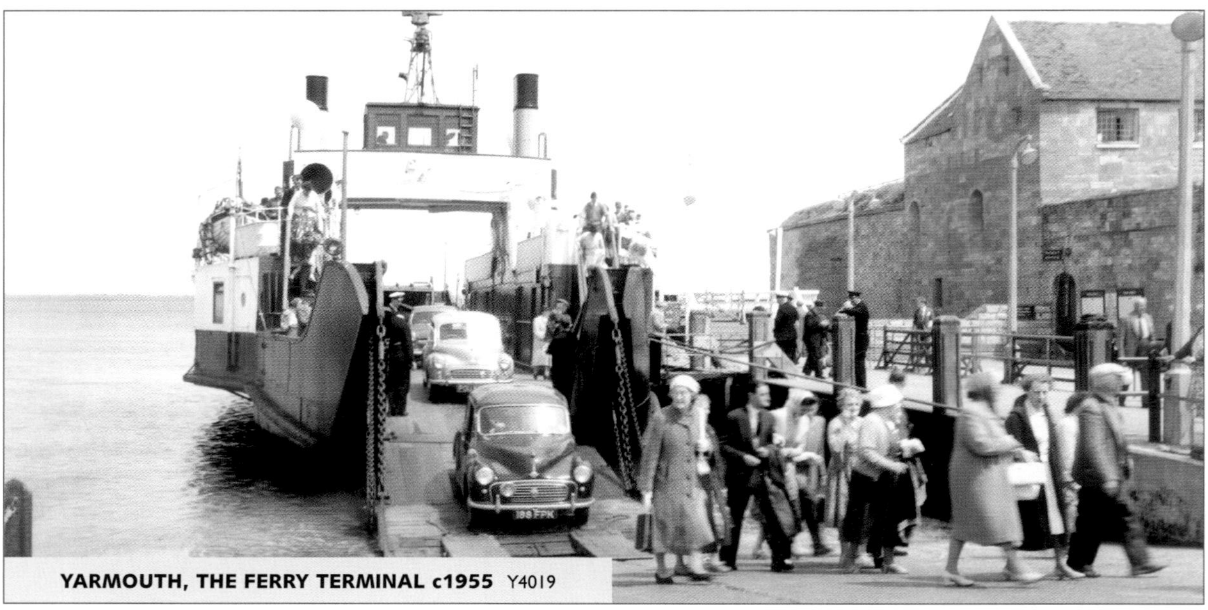

YARMOUTH, THE FERRY TERMINAL c1955 Y4019

Disembarkation facilities are rather better than this nowadays!

Did you know?

The First Railway

More than three decades before the opening of the Cowes & Newport Railway in 1862, the Island's first recorded rail system was developed by John Nash, the renowned Regency architect, at Hamstead, on the north-west coast. Nash bought land at Hamstead in 1806, significantly expanded the estate, transformed the dilapidated farmhouse into a fine residence, opened a brickworks and constructed a narrow gauge tramway - a roughly rectangular loop - to link the house, brickworks and quay. The extensive rail system seems to have had only a short life of a few years.

Cowes, yet to be eclipsed by Ryde as the principal ferry port, was linked to Newport in June of that year. Belatedly, the mid-Victorian 'railway mania' took off on the Island. The Isle of Wight Railway opened between Ryde and Brading, Sandown and Shanklin in 1864, extending to Ventnor two years later. The Ryde & Newport Railway followed in 1875, soon joining forces with the Cowes & Newport to form the Isle of Wight Central company. Still more companies promoted branch lines to link Sandown with Newport, via Merstone (opened 1880), Newport with Freshwater, via Yarmouth (1889), and, finally, the country junction of Merstone with St Lawrence, and eventually Ventnor (1900). The Isle of Wight Central took over most of these branches, the notable exception being the Freshwater, Yarmouth & Newport Railway which, although operated for a while by the Central, was still independent at the time of the Southern Railway take-over in 1923.

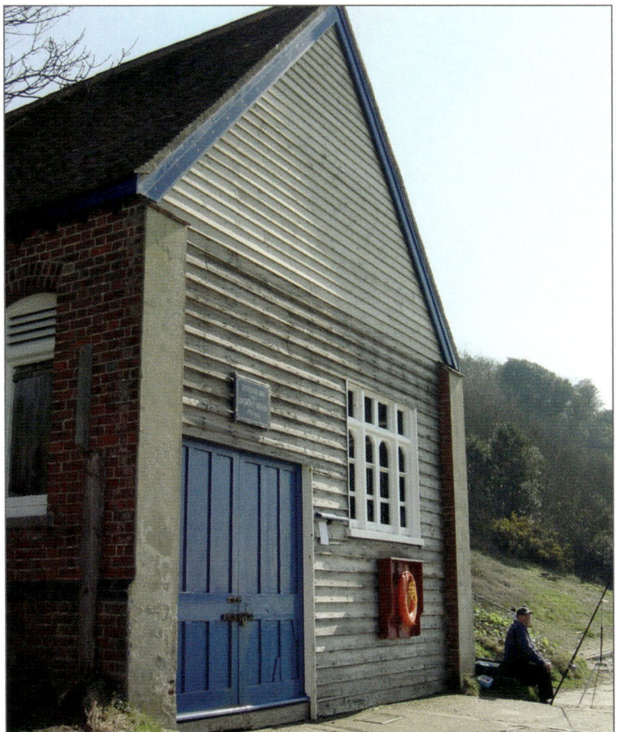

TOTLAND BAY, THE OLD LIFEBOAT HOUSE 2005
T65701k (Matt Searle)

Lifeboats were introduced to the Island in 1860. Only Bembridge and Yarmouth remain operational.

BRADING, THE TOWN c1883 16323

Brading is pictured a year after the reclamation of its Haven from the sea.

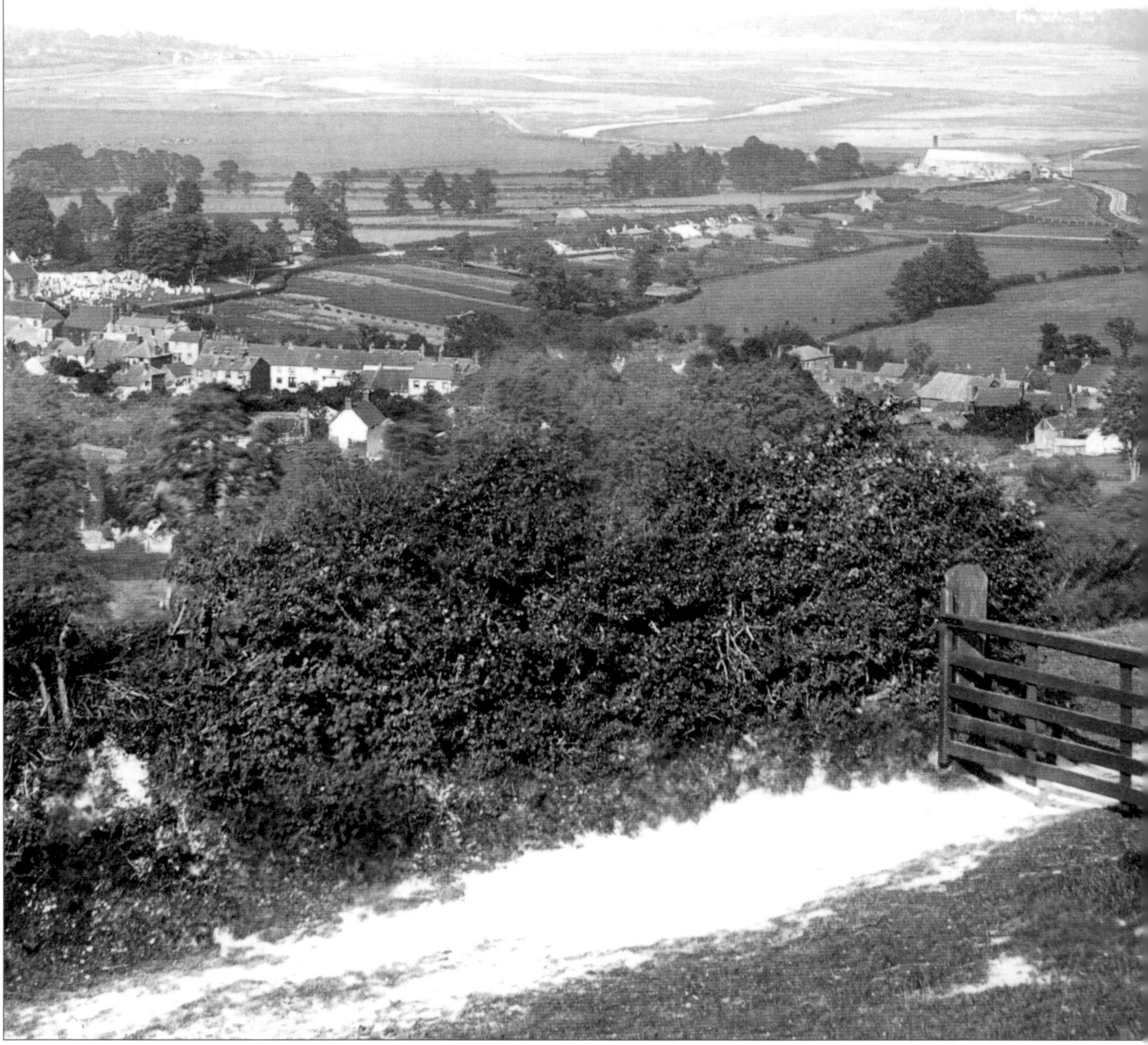

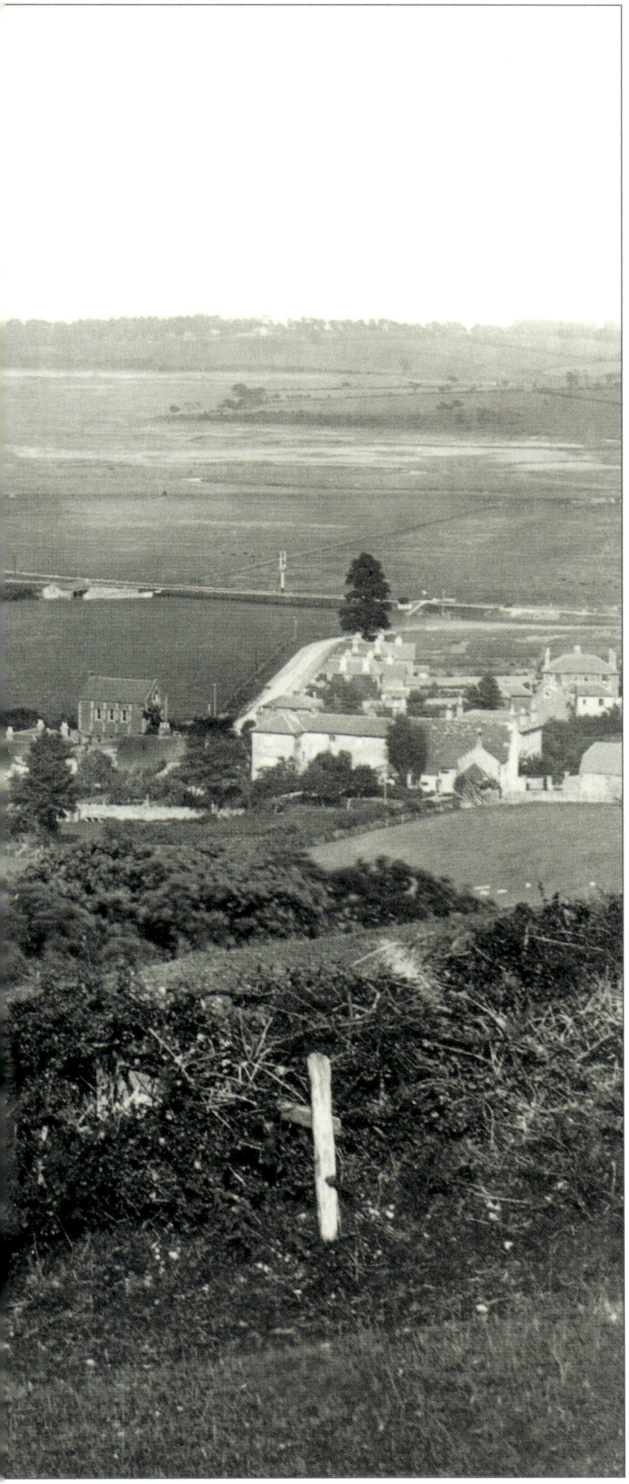

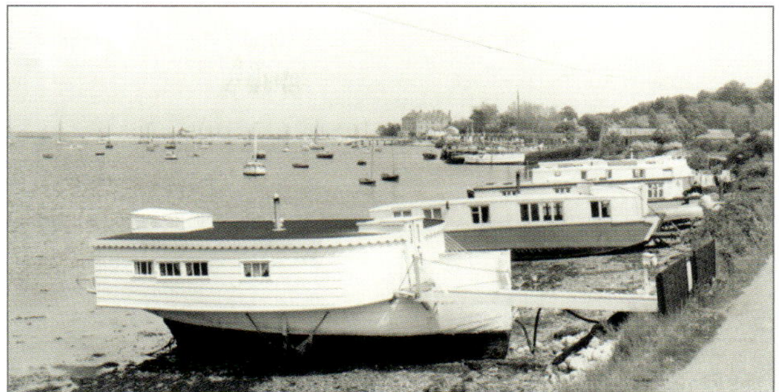

BEMBRIDGE, THE HARBOUR c1955 B64027

Bembridge is the harbour at the mouth of the Eastern Yar. To the right is the embankment which ended inland Brading's port status.

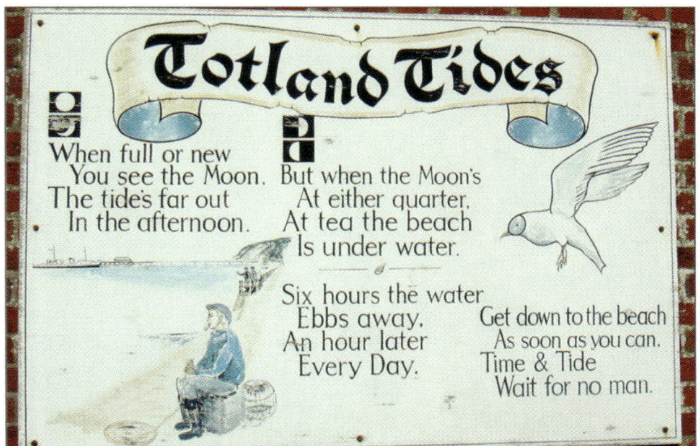

TOTLAND BAY, THE TIDES POEM 2005
ZZZ03990 (Matt Searle)

A poetic embellishment on the wall of the old Totland lifeboat house.

But that's not the complete picture. Ryde's station was linked by mainland companies with the town's pier-head in 1880 (see Topic Box, The Piers of Ryde) and, more significant than it sounds, the Isle of Wight Railway's sole branch line opened between the junction at Brading and Bembridge in 1882. This last scheme, delivered against a backdrop of financial scandal, finally achieved the permanent retreat of the sea from Brading

Haven thanks to the construction of the embankment that survives today - although long since rail-less - between St Helens and Bembridge. Before the scheme was completed, and the sea turned away, the branch line rails ran only as far as Brading Quay. Its grass-covered remains can still be traced on local footpath routes which, remarkably, also utilise sections of surviving sea wall embankments from the 16th-century reclamation schemes.

The coming of the railways was massively important to the Isle of Wight economy, making it infinitely easier to reach all the main centres of population, including the hitherto virtually inaccessible West Wight, and providing the means to bring the holidaying masses to rapidly expanding resorts. The latter were all subsequently equipped with seaside piers, that essential symbol of a thriving Victorian resort, though only Sandown of the east coast holiday towns possesses one now.

Ventnor thrived, and so did the patients of the Royal National Hospital for Diseases of the Chest. Given the accepted status of the town as a health resort, it was an obvious place to locate the hospital, which opened three years after the arrival of the railway. Patients travelled to Ventnor for a while on the 'Invalids' Express' and the hospital survived, until made redundant by modern medicine, for the best part of a century. Little remains of its once extensive buildings, now the site of Ventnor Botanic Garden and the Isle of Wight Smuggling Museum, but famous reminders abound of the Victorian legacy at nearby Bonchurch.

Ryde has the second-longest seaside pier in the country. Only Southend's is longer. The original wooden pier at Ryde opened in 1814, sufficiently long at 1,740 feet to allow ferries to berth even at low tide, when the sea retreats half-a-mile from the shore. By 1833, the pier had been lengthened to its present 2,250 feet

But Ryde Pier is really three piers in one. Built immediately east of the original structure, the second component pier opened in 1871 to support a horse-drawn tramway, which ran from the pier head as far as the pier gates and then through the town to provide a connection for steamer passengers with Ryde's original rail terminus at St John's Road, a mile to the south.

Intent on providing a smoother onward journey via Ryde to other Island destinations, the big mainland rail companies operating into Portsmouth - the London, Brighton & South Coast and the London & South Western - built a third pier to carry a double-track rail line from the pier head to Ryde Esplanade.

The 1880 'joint line' then ran inland, via a tunnel, to connect with the railway at St John's Road and open up direct train travel to the ferries from all rail-connected parts of the Island. The horse tramway was cut back to its pier section, sandwiched between the promenade and railway piers. It remained in use, operated by steam, electricity and, latterly, petrol railcars, until 1969.

Slightly further east was Victoria Pier, built in 1864 for a ferry service to Stokes Bay, Gosport. At 970 feet, it was unusable at low tide and became a public bathing station before its demolition shortly after the First World War.

The Piers of Ryde

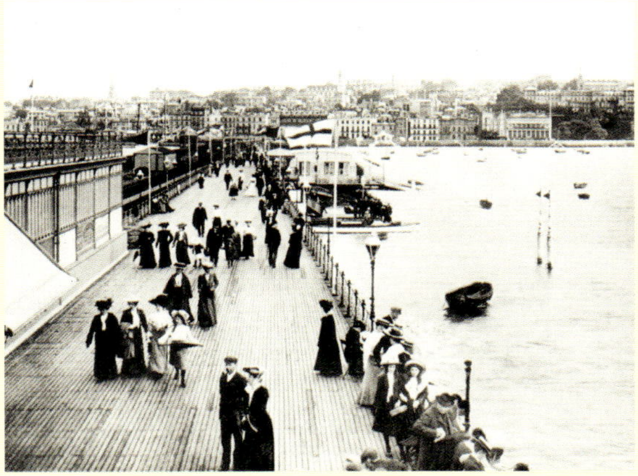

RYDE, THE PIER 1899 44304
Ryde Pier was a popular promenade for Victorians.

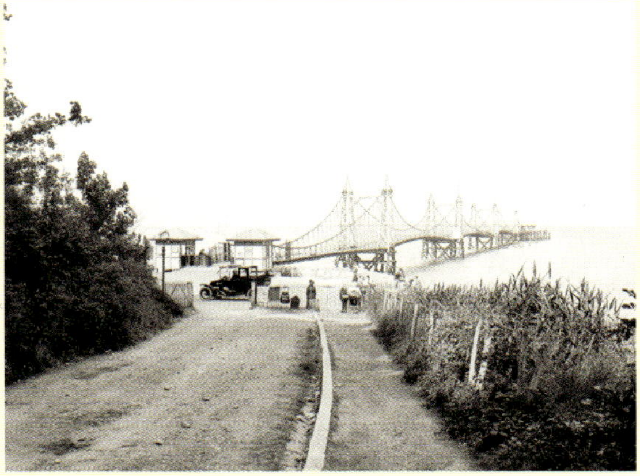

SEAVIEW, THE SUSPENSION PIER 1913 66340
The graceful suspension pier at Seaview was one of only two of its kind in England.

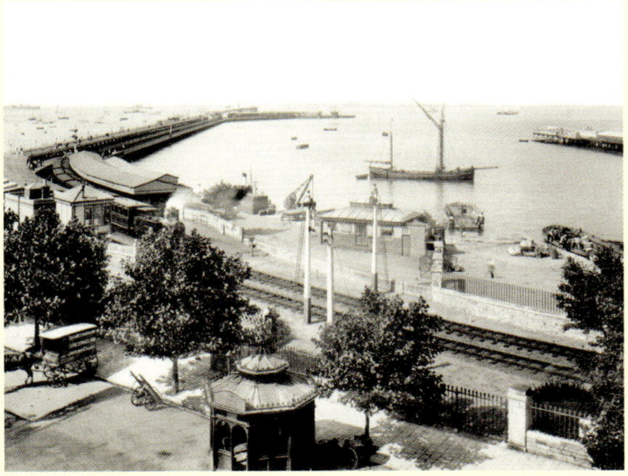

RYDE, THE PIER 1908 60567
This view shows Esplanade rail station (left) and the seaward ends of both Ryde Pier itself and Victoria Pier (right).

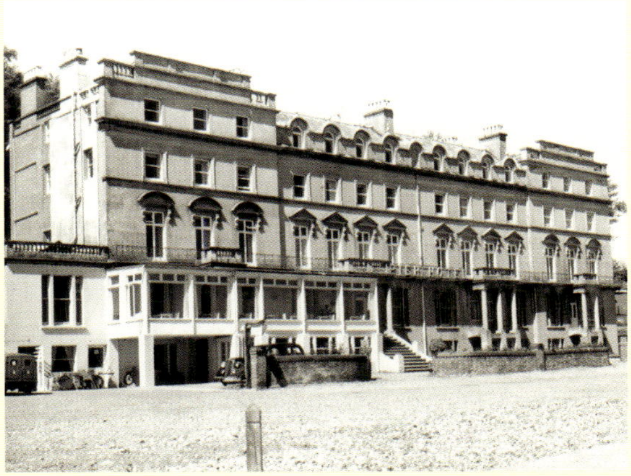

SEAVIEW, THE PIER HOTEL c1955 S87067
The hotel outlived the pier's demise in 1951 but its site is now occupied by housing.

VENTNOR, THE RAILWAY STATION 1908 60534

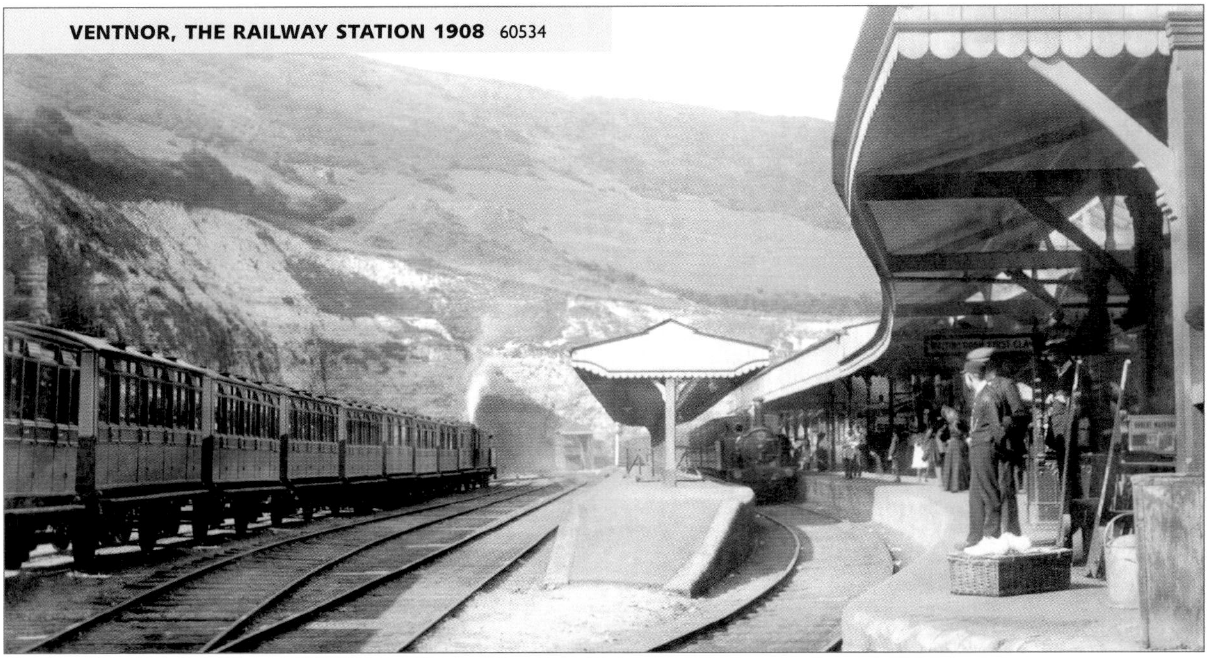

Ventnor's terminal station, opened in 1866, was built in a former quarry at the foot of St Boniface Down, the highest in the Island.

VENTNOR, THE ESPLANADE 1908 60527

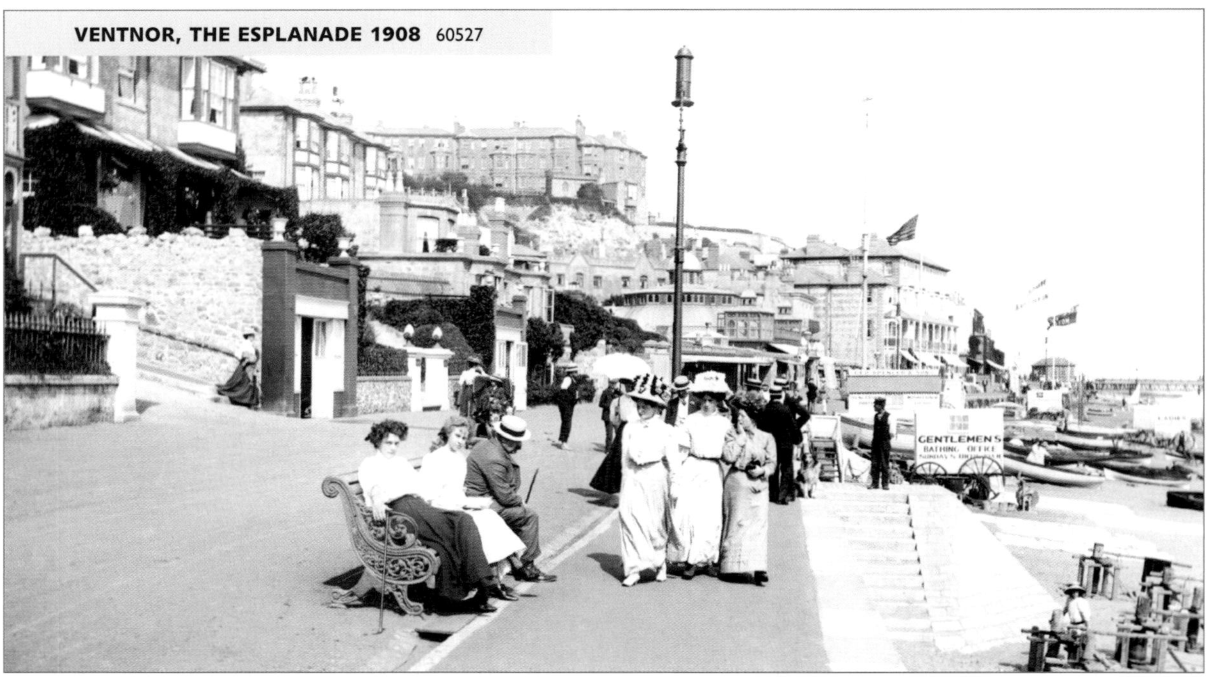

Ventnor began life as a resort in the Victorian era and was well established when this Edwardian view was taken.

VENTNOR, THE BOTANIC GARDEN LEAFLET 2005
ZZZ04019 (Reproduced by kind permission of Julian Winslow)

The equitable Ventnor climate now supports botanical treasures at the old hospital site.

Romantically situated between the sea and its idyllic village pond, Bonchurch inspired some of the greatest outpourings of Victorian

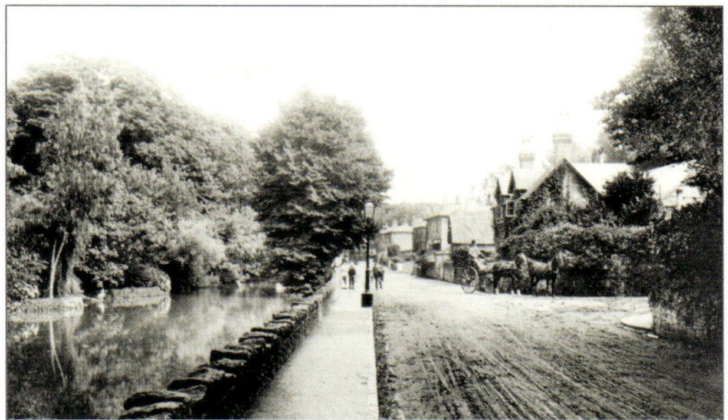

BONCHURCH, THE VILLAGE POND 1890 26151

The idyllic village pond was among the features of Bonchurch that were so inspiring to Victorian literary greats such as Algernon Swinburne and Charles Dickens.

(and later) literature. Charles Dickens wrote six chapters of 'David Copperfield' while renting Winterbourne, now a hotel. You can stay in the 'Copperfield Room' today. East Dene was the family home of the controversial poet Algernon Swinburne. Elizabeth Sewell, novelist and educationalist, lived for more than 30 years at Ashcliff, in The Pitts, while today's Bonchurch Manor Hotel was once the Hawthorndene school founded by the historian Canon Venables. Henry de Vere Stakpoole, Irish novelist of 'Blue Lagoon' fame, later lived at Cliff Dene. To the impressive list of writers with close Bonchurch links could be added William Adams, Alice Meynll, Edmund Peel, John Sterling, William Thackeray, Thomas Carlyle - and Tennyson.

Alfred Lord Tennyson provides the outstanding literary association with the Isle of Wight, though not principally at Bonchurch. The Victorian Poet Laureate lived

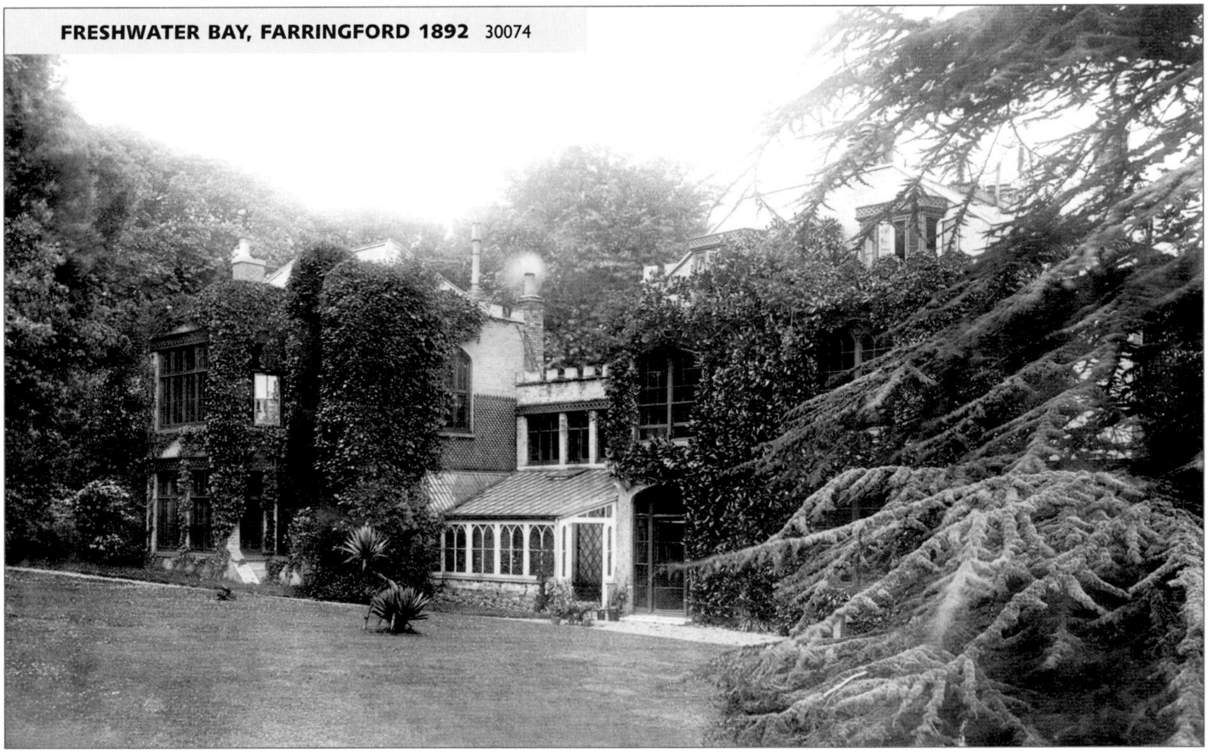

FRESHWATER BAY, FARRINGFORD 1892 30074

Farringford was the Island home of Alfred Lord Tennyson. This picture was taken in the year of the great poet's death.

in Farringford, a castellated late-Georgian house, set amid the ancient trees of its delightful park, south of the present shopping centre in Freshwater. He first took up residence there with his devoted wife Emily in 1853, acquiring the lease of the house three years later. It remained the couple's principal family home for the rest of their lives, although they were both at Aldeworth, their summer home in West Sussex, at the time of their deaths (Alfred died in 1892; Emily in 1895). They had been driven to seek greater seclusion away from the fans who repeatedly made for Farringford in search of a glimpse of their hero. Many of the great poet's finest works were composed on the Island.

Given his fondness for walking on the downs above Farringford, it was fitting that, after his death, High Down was officially renamed Tennyson Down in the poet's honour. His memorial stands there today. From it, the views across the Western Solent recall his most poignant poem, penned late in life as he contemplated death and what lay beyond. Tennyson's beautifully crafted 'Crossing the Bar' was reputedly written as he himself crossed to the Island on the ferry from Lymington.

Lewis Carroll at Sandown; George Eliot, Henry Longfellow and D H Lawrence at

Shanklin (and also Freshwater Bay, in the case of the latter); John Sterling at Ventnor; Thomas Macaulay at the nearby Undercliff; Alfred Noyes at St Lawrence; William Wordsworth, Karl Marx, Winston Churchill. It would take - and has taken - a whole book to list the entire catalogue of the names in the Isle of Wight's rich literary heritage before, during and after the years of Victoria. These writers, the presence of the queen herself and the railways each played their part in establishing, and then keeping, the Island at the forefront of the English tourism explosion, and as a very desirable place in which to live.

The population itself exploded, leaping by a staggering 10,000 between 1860 and 1870 alone. It was four times as high at the start of the 20th century as it had been 100 years earlier. Tourism brought thousands more across the Solent. It was just as well that the Island had by then a settled and uniform administrative system in place. Yarmouth, Newtown and Brading had all been disenfranchised by the turn of the century, no longer considered worthy of municipal status. Yarmouth and Brading still have town councils, but now at the grass roots 'parish' level of democracy. Newtown was the classic 'rotten borough,' for so long a town in name only (though still electing its own Members of Parliament!) It now snoozes peacefully in its natural state as a part of Calbourne parish.

The great reorganisation of local government at the close of the 19th century, which brought elected county councils into being, initially created waves of resentment throughout the Isle of Wight. The proposal was to place the Island within the administrative claws of Hampshire (initially under the title of the County of Southampton). This was something of an affront to a former self-governing Norman mini-state. A fierce, and ultimately successful, campaign was launched to preserve the Island's independence from the mainland giant, much against the Hampshire will. Wight has retained its county status ever since. Despite its close links, it is resolutely NOT part of Hampshire.

Second tier local government beneath strategic county level saw municipal boroughs continuing only in the old medieval town of Newport and the much younger Ryde, with the remaining towns and villages run by urban district councils, or the rural equivalent, as deemed appropriate. Several mergers followed

Did you know?

Isle of Wight Dialect

The Isle of Wight's distinctive local dialect, characterised by elongated vowels (hooam instead of home, for example) and including many words and phrases specific to the Island, has inevitably all but disappeared. Of the few dialect words that are still spoken, 'nammet' is probably the most common. It is the local equivalent of 'elevenses' and is derived from na-meeat (no meat), the Island's traditional mid-morning snack having been bread and cheese - brencheese in the local parlance.

in the 20th century, notably Ryde's takeover of St Helens and the amalgamation of the urban districts at Sandown and Shanklin. Much later, the whole system was swept away in favour of a two-borough second tier - Medina and South Wight - with the parishes beneath.

As is so often the case, there is a jarring French postscript to this otherwise progressive century on Wight. Concern, verging on panic, had spread through the country during a period of international uncertainty at the potential danger posed by France's development of new weaponry, especially from 'La Gloire', launched in 1859, the world's first ironclad warship. The British response saw the Island's coastal defences once again strengthened, mightily so this time. New gun batteries were put up east and west, protecting both approaches to the Solent and Spithead's anchorage. The remains of those at The Needles and Puckpool, east of Ryde, are open to the public today. Neither they nor the Island's other Victorian defences were ever called upon to fire on the French (though the rather more real German threat in the 1940s saw many of them reactivated) and it was the same for the ultimate examples of Lord Palmerston's infamous 'follies' - the sea forts strung out across the Eastern Solent to intimidate the potential enemy from an attack on Portsmouth.

Massively constructed were the forts of

SANDOWN, THE BEACH 1892 30048

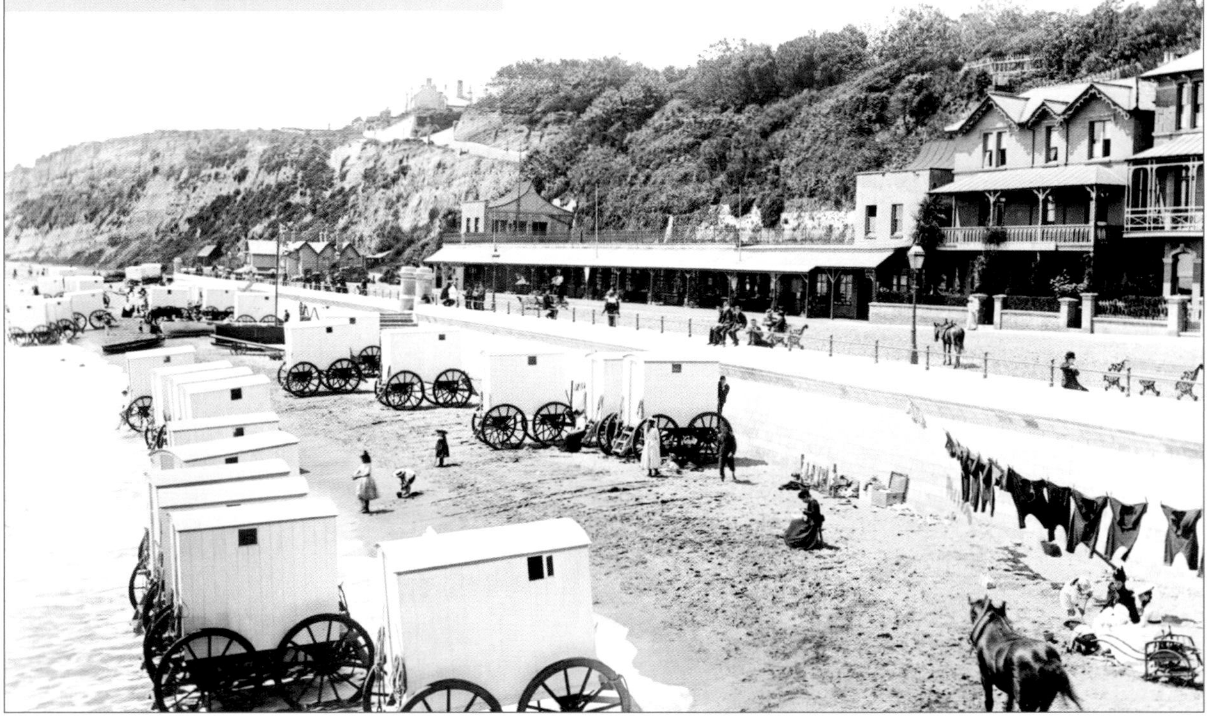

Easily reached by train, Sandown was thriving as a resort by the time this picture was taken.

SANDOWN, THE PIER 1895 36248

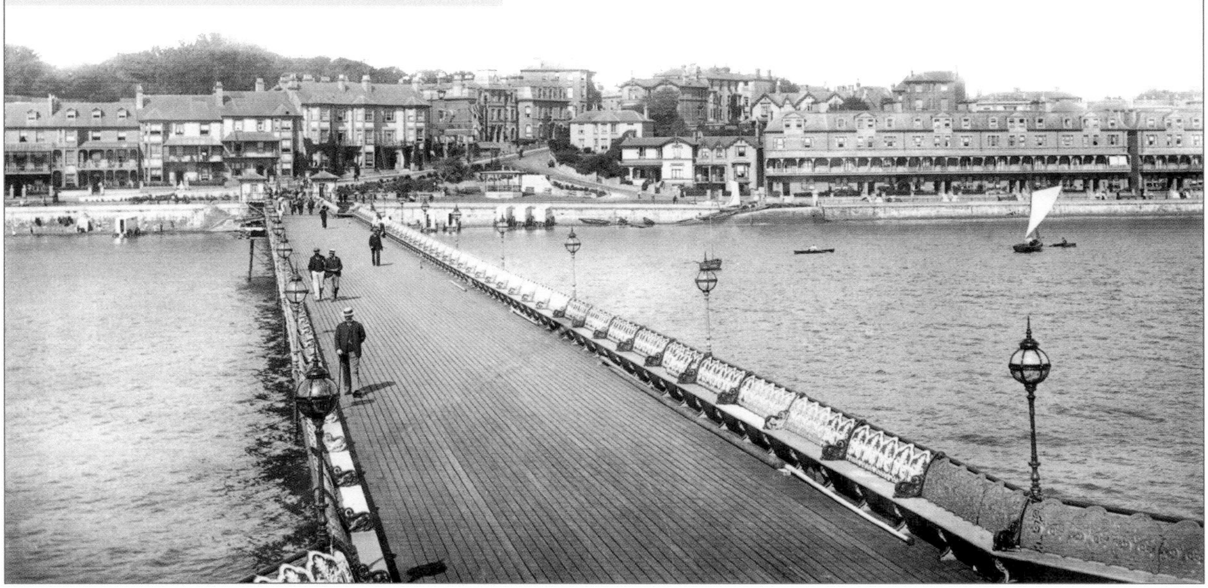

The pier was built in 1879, adding a major new attraction to the resort. Much altered, it thrives today.

TOTLAND BAY, THE PIER 1897 40385

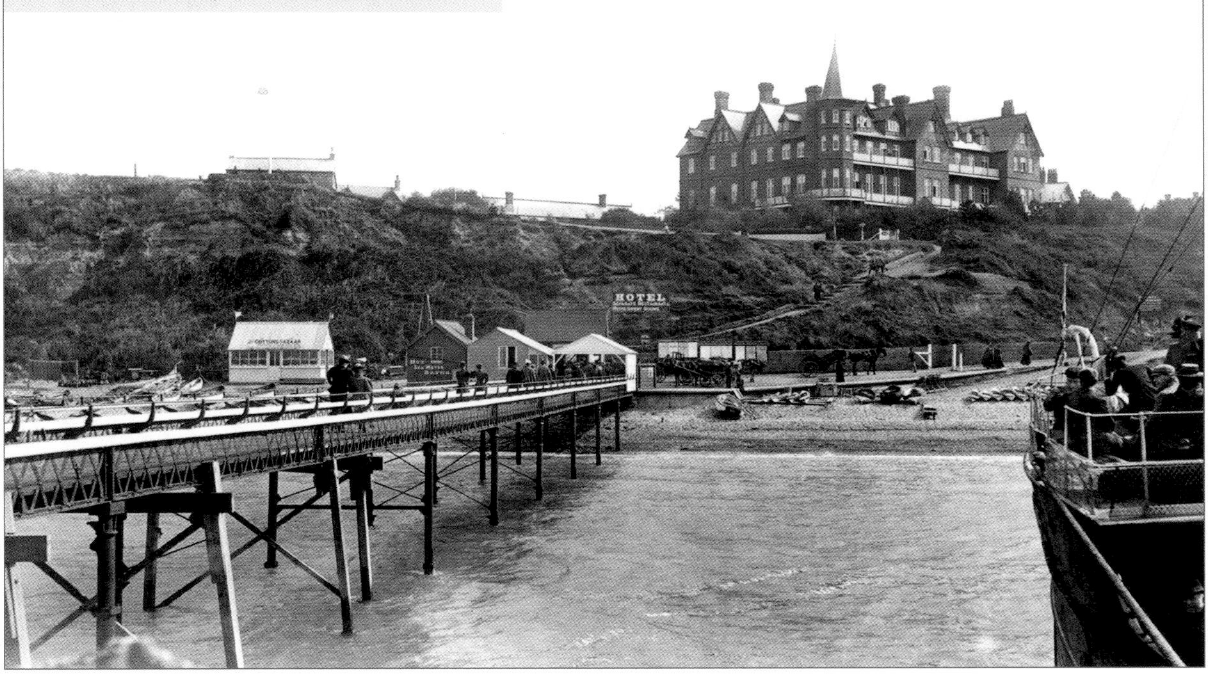

Even the smallest resorts had piers. Totland's, built in 1880, is one of the few survivors, although only partially open.

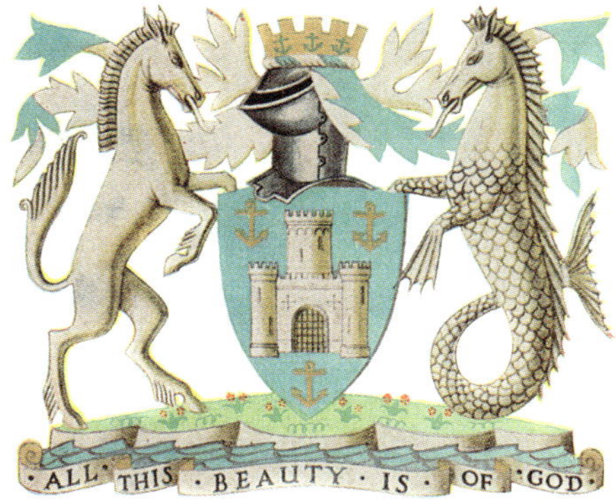

ISLE OF WIGHT COUNTY COUNCIL COAT OF ARMS
ZZZ04006 (Reproduced by kind permission of Isle of Wight Council)

'All this beauty is of God' - the proud message from the independent council.

Spit Bank (the one nearest Portsmouth), No Man's Land (nearest Ryde) and Horse Sand (roughly in the middle), as was the later addition of St Helens Fort, very close to the Island's north-east coast. They resemble stranded whales today and have been white elephants for most of their existence, right up to the 1980s, in fact. Then, Spit Bank was restored and opened to the public, a short launch service from the mainland providing access. No Man's Land and Horse Sand have since undergone startling interior up-market modernisation in private ownership. You'll need a lot of money to stay on them. Only St Helens Fort remains derelict, a last forlorn reminder of centuries of troubled relationships with the nearest Continental neighbour.

You can visit St Helens Fort, free of charge, but only once a year, when a very low tide allows a now traditional procession of people to reach it on foot, light bonfires and eat barbecued snacks. They are always careful to beat the tide back to the beach.

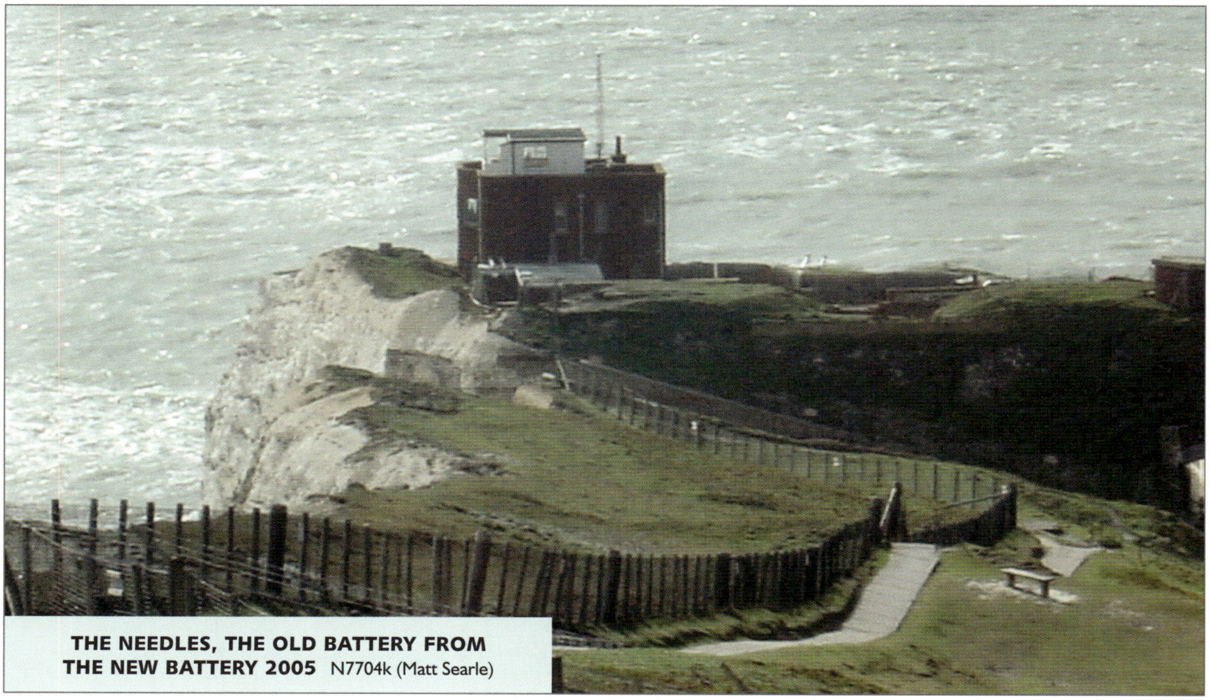

THE NEEDLES, THE OLD BATTERY FROM THE NEW BATTERY 2005 N7704k (Matt Searle)

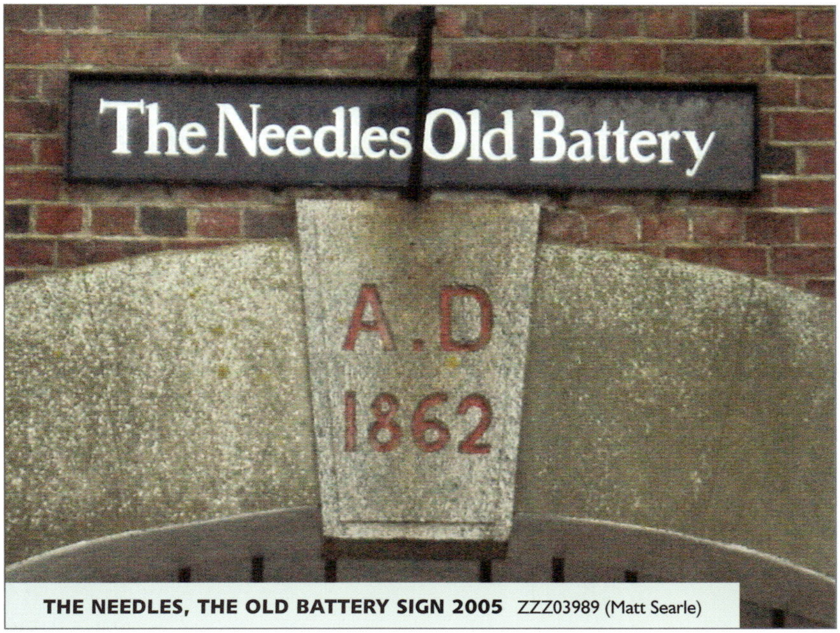

THE NEEDLES, THE OLD BATTERY SIGN 2005 ZZZ03989 (Matt Searle)

The Needles Old Battery was built between 1861 and 1863 as part of the defences against the French threat. It is now a tourist attraction.

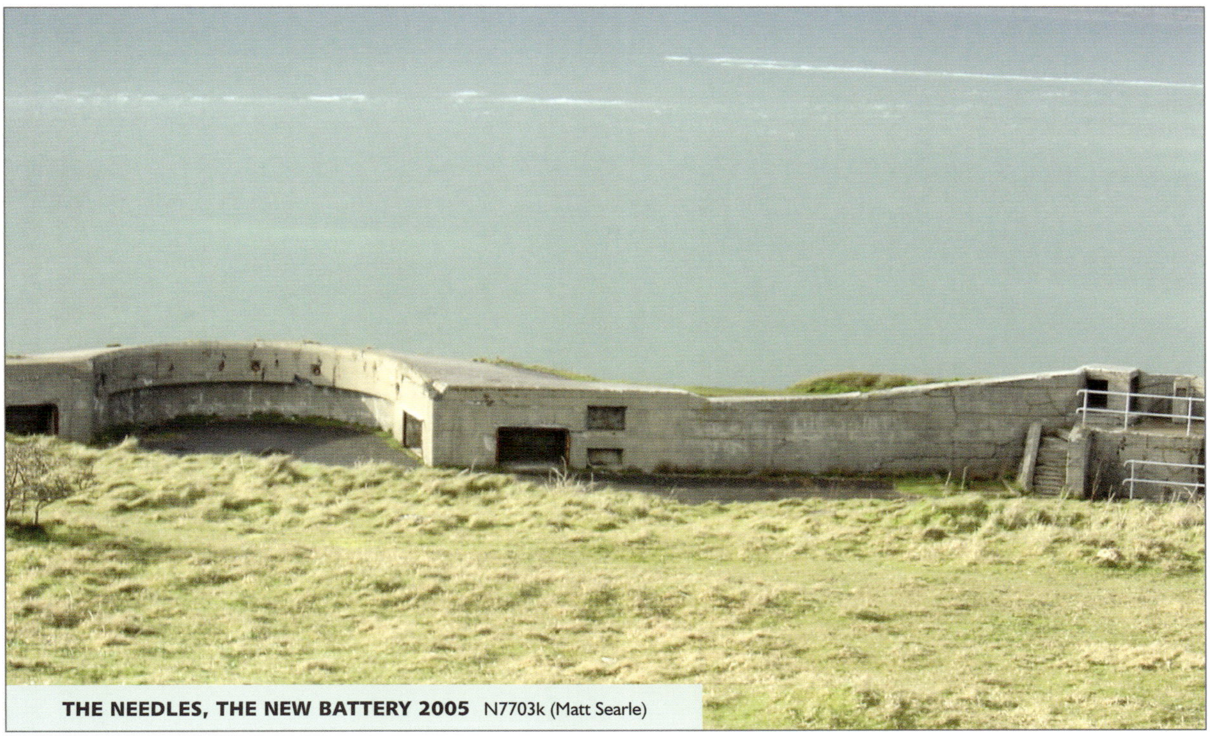

THE NEEDLES, THE NEW BATTERY 2005 N7703k (Matt Searle)

The New Battery, slightly further east, followed in 1893-95. This view of its remains was taken from the landward side, looking north.

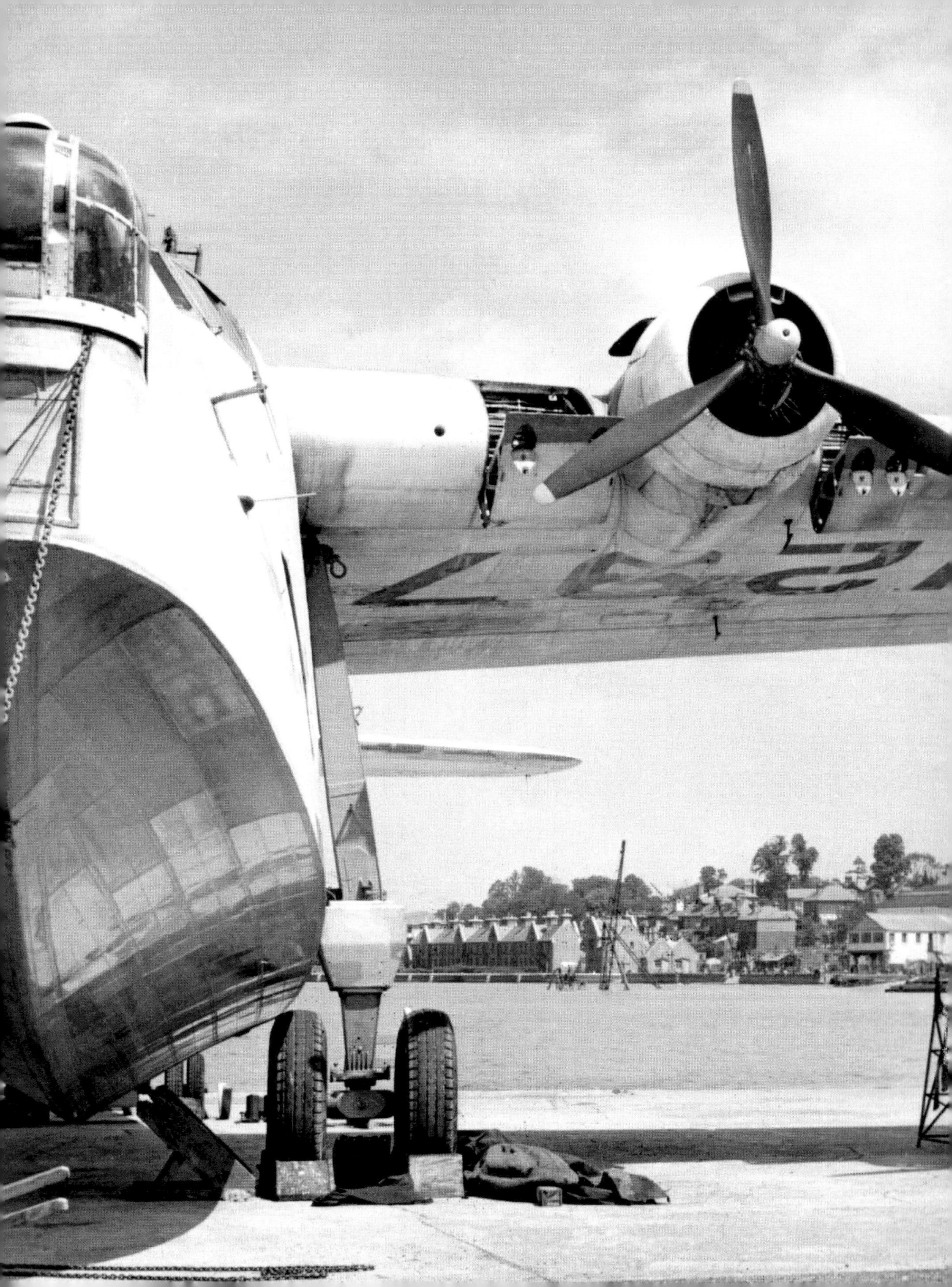

CHAPTER FIVE

Adjustments - The Modern Wight

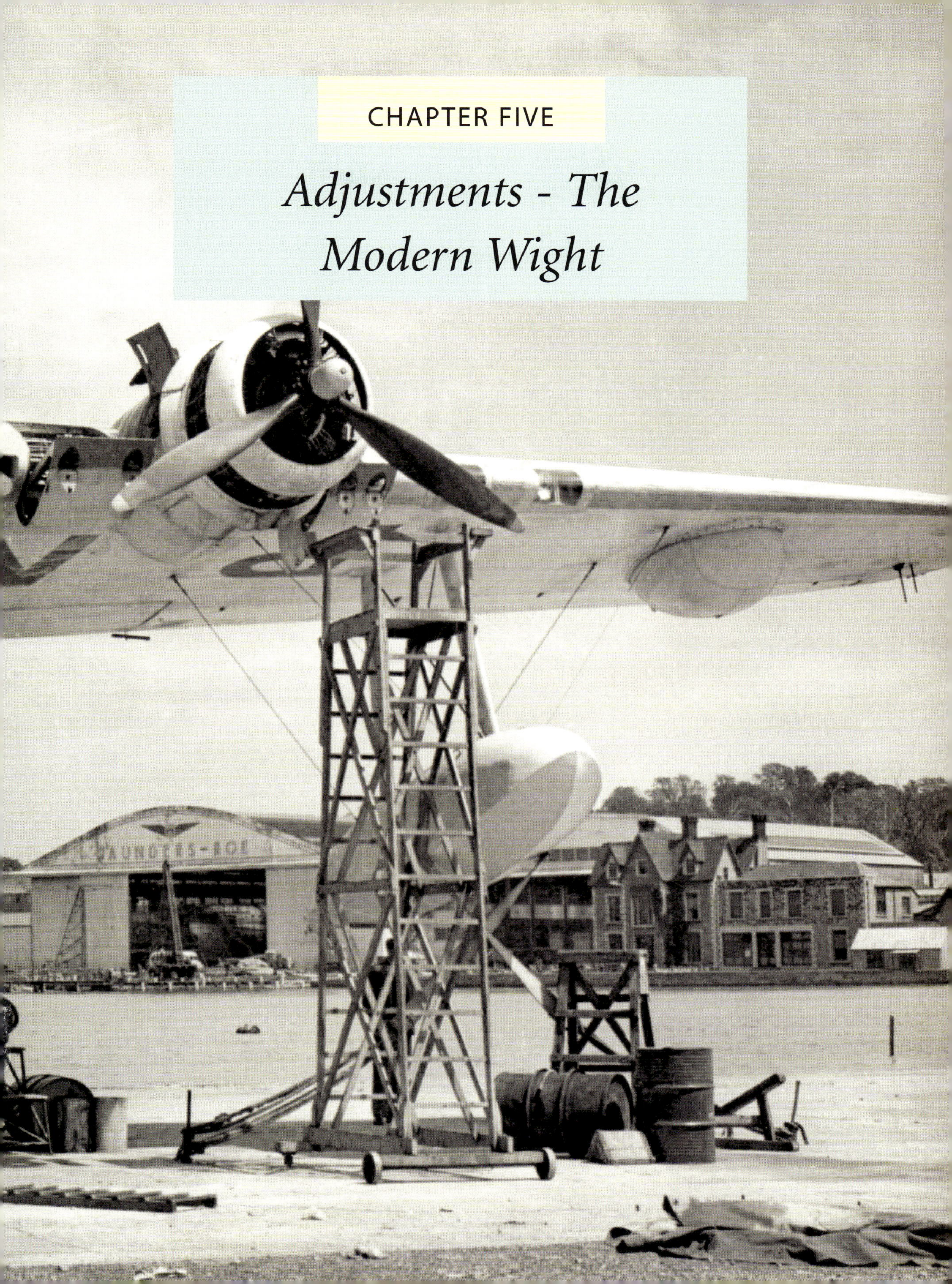

THE 20TH CENTURY WAS ALL about adjustments. Repeatedly, the Island had to respond to change, dramatically so at times, but there was also a lengthy list of notable achievements - if, at times, via reflected glory. Just before the turn of the century, in 1897, Guglielimo Marconi had crowned earlier land-to-ship experiments on the local coast by establishing the first wireless telegraph station in the world at Alum Bay. Four years later, the industrious, innovative and inventive Victorian era had finally run its course. Queen Victoria had, by then, been a long-time local resident, quite apart from her role as queen and empress, and had breathed her last at Osborne after years of grieving there for the long-departed Prince Albert. With her final journey in 1901 from Trinity Pier at East Cowes to her state funeral in London, the quintessential Victorian island she left behind was reflecting on the dramatic leap in its fortunes during the 57 years since she had first arrived among its people.

Amid the liberal helpings of shimmering glitter piled on the Wight by the Victorian stars, right up to the queen herself, it is perhaps easy to overlook the ordinary man and woman. Not everything in the garden isle (as it would be progressively called) was lovely at the turn of the century. There were slums in Newport (and for some years to come) and ten or eleven-hour days of hard toil for just 14s (70p) a week remained the norm for labourers, many of them still employed, just like generations of their ancestors, on the Island's farms. But, with flour and other foods now arriving in Cowes as cheap imports from North America and throughout the British Empire, they were eating much better. Meat, something of a luxury until then, was now regularly on the average family's menu.

Jack Jones, eminent Island historian and former curator at Carisbrooke Castle, has recalled the typical fare of a Newport family in the 1890s: 'Sunday dinner was always a beef roast, with baked potatoes and suet pudding. With beef at 2s-2/6d (10p - 12.5p) there was enough for cold meat on Monday and cottage pie on Tuesday while, later on in the week, stew made from beef cuttings at 4d (2p), rabbit pie or bacon and onion roll all varied the diet.' It was, he pointed out, 'all solid stodge, but hard work used up the calories.' Cake, though, was usually eaten only at Christmas!

The National Health Service was still half a century away but, led by Ryde's early example in 1842, several of the towns had their own hospitals, funded through local subscription, by the early years of the 20th century. The Island had earlier provided its poorest people with the first centralised workhouse in England - the House of Industry, north of Newport on the present hospital site. Now, it notched another notable 'first' with the 1904 setting-up of its library service, a model for others throughout Britain. The driving force behind that was Charles Seely, whose father, a Nottinghamshire coal-owner, had rescued Mottistone Manor from decline after purchasing it, together with the Mottistone Estate, in 1861. The Seely family played major roles in Island affairs throughout the 20th century, especially Charles's son, General Jack Seely, courageous soldier, Cabinet Minister,

Lord Lieutenant for more than 30 years and legendary coxswain of Brook lifeboat.

While life in the rural villages changed at a much slower pace, the availability of housing in the towns brought many people to within easy walking distance of the workplace. Manpower-intensive heavy industry had been confined to Cowes and East Cowes in the 19th century, and this would remain the case throughout the 20th. The long-established White's shipbuilding business adopted its most famous identity in 1898 when it became a public liability company registered as J Samuel White's, an internationally-respected brand for decades to come. By then, it had already diversified into heavy engineering and boiler-making. Its skilled, highly regarded workforce was fully utilised during the First World War, turning out destroyers, a job White's would be asked to repeat during the second global conflict in the 1940s. The company responded magnificently.

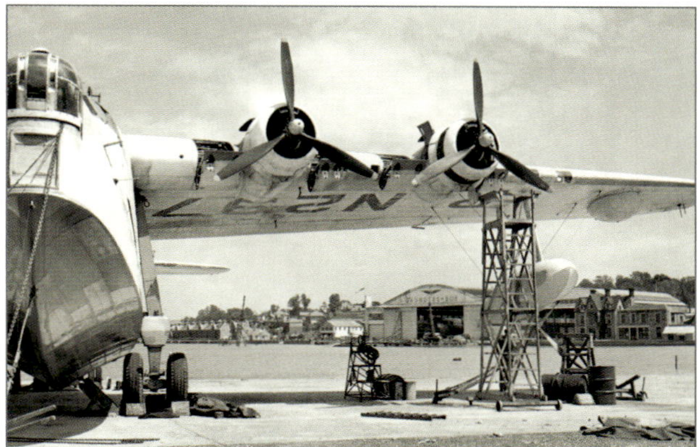

EAST COWES, THE SAUNDERS-ROE SEAPLANE BASE c1955 E139005

The wing of one of the company's flying boats frames the Cowes riverfront on the west bank.

The Island's other industrial giant was Saunders-Roe, initially a 1928 collaboration between boat builders S E Saunders and the aircraft manufacturers, A V Roe. Sea and air combined, and it would remain that way

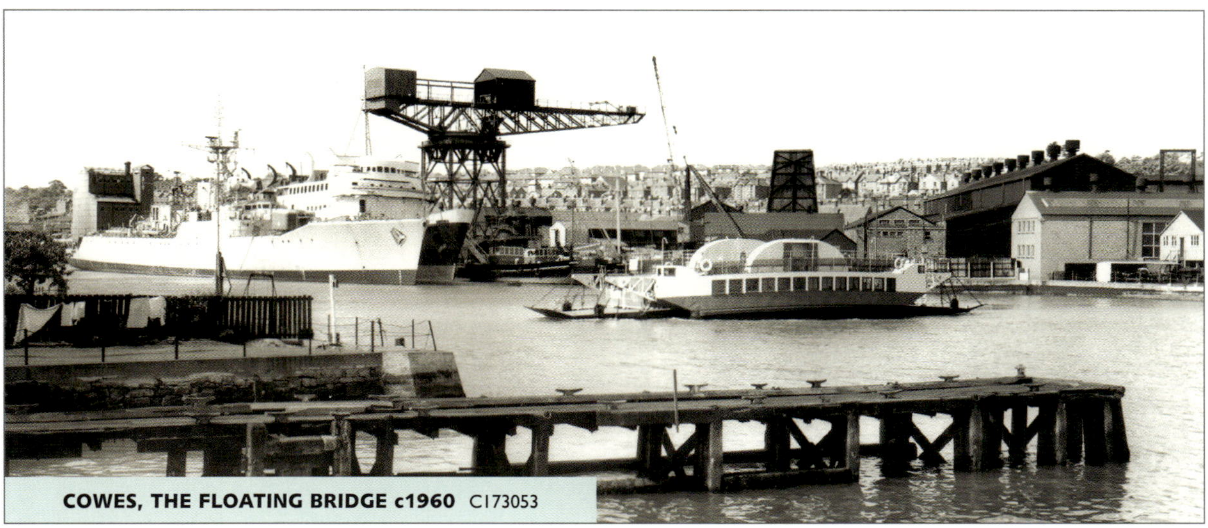

COWES, THE FLOATING BRIDGE c1960 C173053

This scene of industral Cowes shows floating contrasts: a ship for the Navy ... a bridge for the people. The 'hammer-head' crane survives today.

as the company expanded until, eventually, it became the Island's largest employer. As the century progressed, Saunders-Roe turned out an extraordinary number of seaplanes for Britain's war effort and developed giant flying boats for commercial passenger use throughout the world. There was a lot more to the company, too, as will be recalled later in the text.

The burgeoning tourist industry expanded still further through the era of Edwardian jollity and beyond, interrupted, of course, by the carnage of the First World War and hindered in the Twenties by global economic depression and industrial strife. Royalty continued to visit - and not just of the British kind. 'Kaiser Bill' sailed at Cowes, then drifted rapidly from popular esteem when war broke out and it was rumoured the Germans intended to annexe Wight as a sort of offshore Heligoland! In the main, though, the growing number of tourists brought money, employment and further prestige to the old queen's island. Travelling abroad was denied to all but the wealthiest, but the ferry crossing from Lymington, Southampton or Portsmouth gave the impression of a journey to a foreign land, quite distinct from mainland England. The sea journey was, and remains, an essential part of the Wight holiday experience. So the ferries got bigger and better.

Island rail companies, their steam trains hauled by small tank locomotives in their smart, distinctive liveries, worked hard to keep everyone on the move. The national grouping of the railways in 1923 saw all the Island companies swallowed up by the Southern Railway, which made immense improvements to the infrastructure, especially on the always-busy 'main line' between Ryde and Ventnor. Train travel was virtually unchallenged back then, but change was on the way. A portend of things to come arrived in the Twenties. Vehicles and livestock had been conveyed across the Solent from the early days of steam, but in towboats, hauled by the passenger steamers and, later,

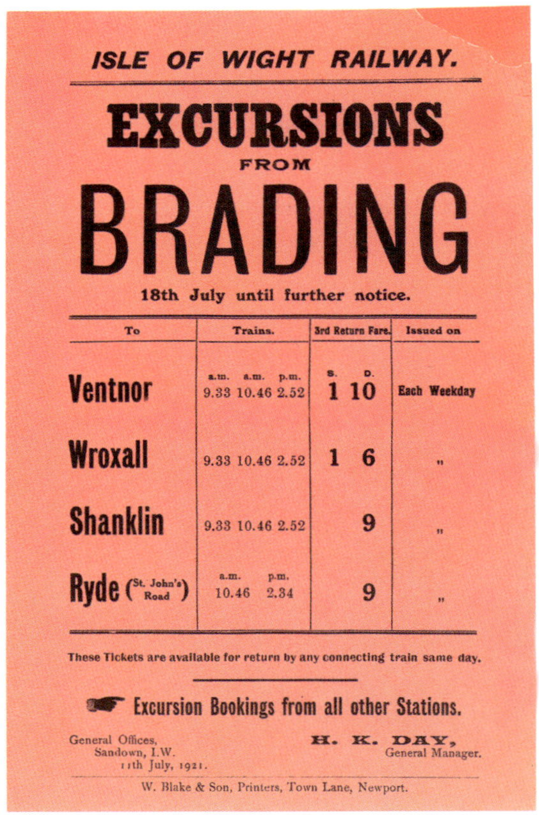
ISLE OF WIGHT RAILWAY.

EXCURSIONS

FROM

BRADING

18th July until further notice.

To	Trains.	3rd Return Fare.	Issued on
Ventnor	a.m. a.m. p.m. 9.33 10.46 2.52	s. d. 1 10	Each Weekday
Wroxall	9.33 10.46 2.52	1 6	"
Shanklin	9.33 10.46 2.52	9	"
Ryde (St. John's Road)	a.m. p.m. 10.46 2.34	9	"

These Tickets are available for return by any connecting train same day.

Excursion Bookings from all other Stations.

General Offices, Sandown, I.W. 11th July, 1921.

H. K. DAY, General Manager.

W. Blake & Son, Printers, Town Lane, Newport.

ISLE OF WIGHT RAILWAY HANDBILL 1921
ZZZ04004 (Author's Collection)

The Island's rail companies promoted cheap excursions throughout the network.

FISHBOURNE, THE CAR FERRY c1955 F140008

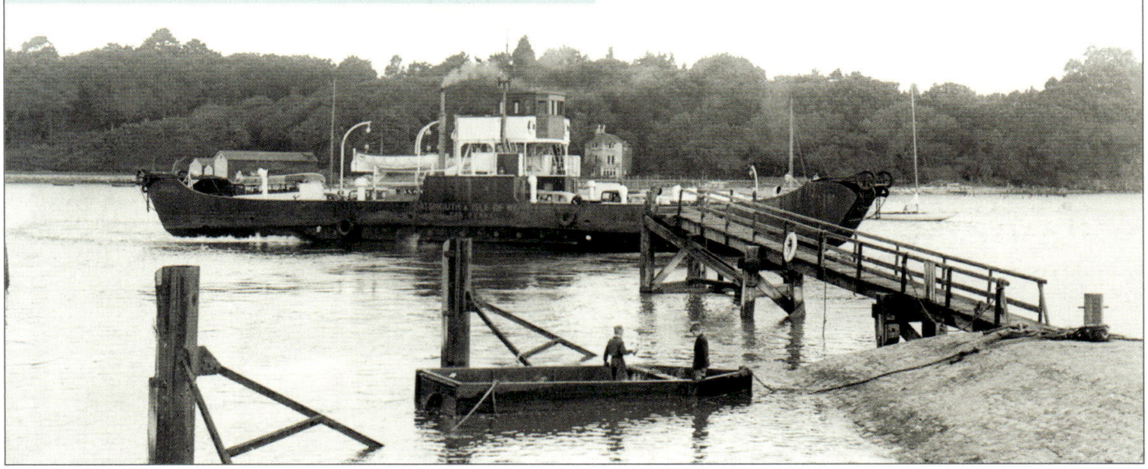

The British Railways-operated ferry is pictured arriving in Wootton Creek from Portsmouth.

by tugs. The Southern Railway, which had taken over the cross-Solent routes previously operated by the pre-grouping mainland rail companies (Ryde-Portsmouth and Yarmouth-Lymington) located a suitable site at Fishbourne, near the mouth of Wootton Creek, west of Ryde, for a new terminal and launched the first cross-Solent car ferry service to Portsmouth in 1927.

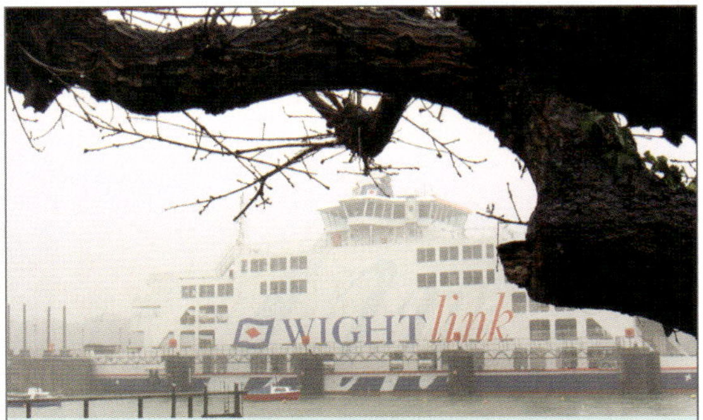

FISHBOURNE, THE CAR FERRY, WIGHTLINK'S 'ST CLARE' 2005 F140701k (Matt Searle)

Half a century later, the operator is Wightlink - and the ferry is considerably larger.

An alternative to the ferries for reaching the Isle of Wight has always, potentially at least, been the aeroplane. The 1930s saw the heyday of air travel to a number of Island airports, at Cowes (Somerton), Sandown (Lea) and Ryde (Westridge), and there were scheduled services after the Second World War, too. From Sandown, for example, it took 35 minutes to fly to Croydon in 1951. The airports at Ryde and Cowes have long disappeared and it's pleasure flights only from Sandown these days. In recent years there have been attempts to revive air passenger links, notably from Bembridge, the one other airport still operational, but regular services have proved difficult to organise. The need for Customs formalities is the main obstacle to flights making for destinations outside the UK, but Bembridge Airport's grass runways still host the Schneider Trophy race, reviving a hotly contested pre-war aerial spectacle, and scheduled air services may yet return.

Marketing the 'different-ness' of the Island became something of an art form. The most enduring example was the production of post cards featuring views of the 'Six Wonders of the Isle of Wight' - Ryde where you walk; Cowes you cannot milk; Newport you cannot bottle; Lake where there is no water; Freshwater you cannot drink; and Needles you cannot thread. And where else, would-be visitors were reminded, could you collect sand of just about all the colours of the rainbow other than at Alum Bay? Eventually, people would have to be forbidden - for their own good as well as that of the coastline itself - from clambering all over the towering cliffs in search of a particular hue. You can still buy the sand, of course, encased in a variety of decorated glass containers.

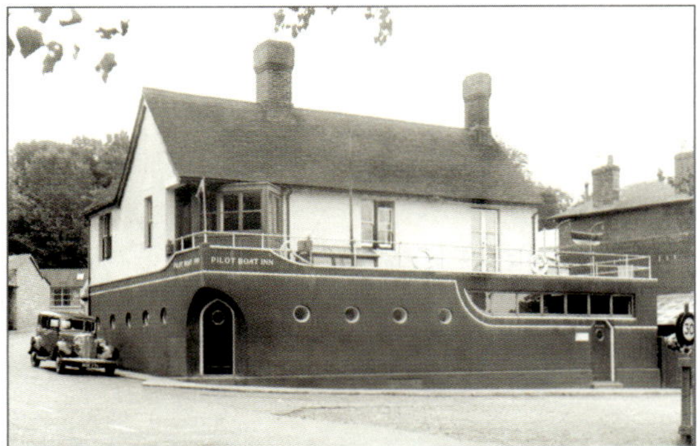

BEMBRIDGE, THE PILOT BOAT INN c1950 B64014

Another wonder of Wight - the boat you cannot sail in! It's still there today.

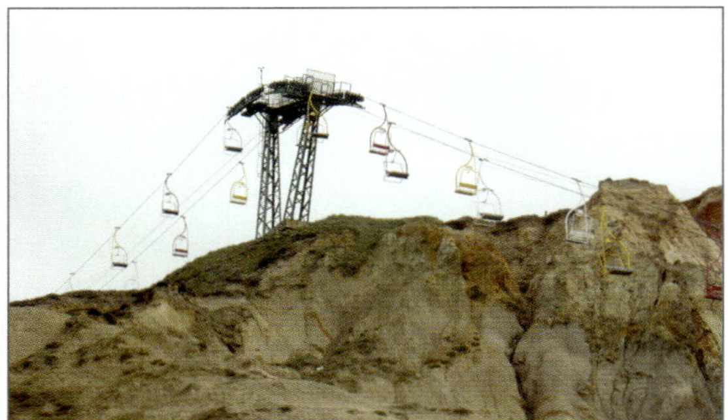

THE NEEDLES, THE CHAIRLIFT 2005
N7702k (Matt Searle)

The modern way of reaching the beach at Alum Bay from the Needles Pleasure Park.

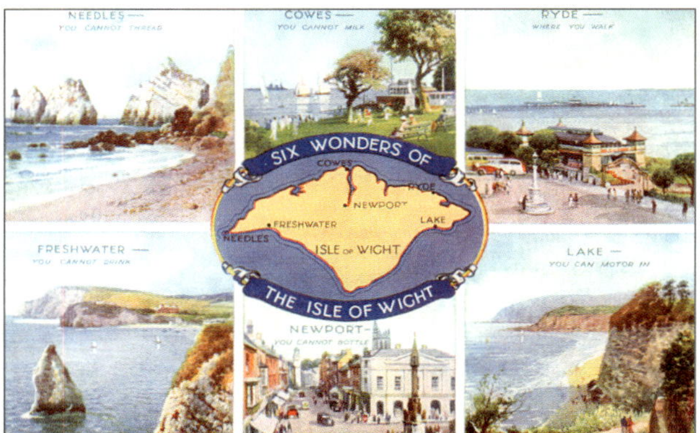

THE SIX WONDERS OF THE ISLE OF WIGHT
ZZZ04003 (Author's Collection)

A pre-war example of the Island's most popular post card.

Collecting shrapnel rather than coloured sand became a wartime hobby for local children when Adolf Hitler threw everyone else on the Island into a state of nervousness after crushing the French, taking the Channel Islands and training his binoculars across the English Channel at the wide expanse of beach in Sandown Bay. In a directive written during June 1940, he suggested the Isle of Wight should be taken by his forces as a possible bridgehead for a full-scale invasion of mainland England. He was a poor strategist, of course, and was later persuaded to concentrate his attentions to a much shorter crossing of the Channel further east before the Battle of Britain led to him calling off the whole thing. Although without knowledge of the Hitler directive, it was clear to the government in London, and obvious to everyone on Wight, that it had once again become England's 'front line' island, vulnerable to attack. This was ironic, for only months earlier the Island had been declared a 'safe haven' and a good place to send evacuated school children. The fall of France changed all that.

The Island coast was soon ringed by anti-invasion obstacles. Old coastal defences were reactivated, and new ones added. A garrison force eventually brought the number of military personnel on Wight up to more than 17,000. There were anti-aircraft gun sites, searchlight sites, submarine booms stretched across the Solent, a profusion of defensive 'pill boxes' and several radar stations. Permits were needed to enter or leave the Island. It was a restricted area - but try telling that to the Luftwaffe!

Much of the Battle of Britain was fought above the Island. Many aircraft from both sides came down, as did the bombs. Thwarted by intercepting Hurricanes and Spitfires, enemy pilots knew they'd get back to France a lot quicker without the bomb load. So out it went and, very often, it landed on the Isle of Wight. There were also raids on sensitive Island targets. RAF Ventnor, the radar station on St Boniface Down, was twice attacked by the Stuka dive-bombers in the summer of 1940, with significant loss of life, while the twin towns of Cowes and East Cowes were hit by the worst raid of all during a double-pronged strike in May 1942. There were many casualties and a fair amount of damage was inflicted on industrial sites and residential property alike. Cock-a-hoop, the enemy published an aerial photograph soon afterwards, outlining the targets they had hit in what they described, somewhat mischievously, as 'Cowes - the industrial heart of Great Britain.'

Mid-war, several terror attacks - the notorious tip and run raids - were unleashed against specific Island towns by a small number of enemy planes at a time. They were in and out in a flash, spouting cannon fire and dropping their bombs. Newport, Ryde, Ventnor and Shanklin, where a bomb was dropped on the Catholic Church while a service was in progress, all suffered serious damage. At Shanklin, the Luftwaffe virtually eliminated the hotels on the seafront. Revenge was gained later when the bombed-out buildings proved an effective hiding place for machinery and equipment associated with the extraordinary top-secret PLUTO (Pipe-Line Under the Ocean) project, devised to, quite literally, fuel the Allied advance from the Normandy beaches after the D-Day landings in June 1944. Its initial route across the Channel ran from Shanklin Pier to Cherbourg.

The Island was equipped with the first properly trained resistance force in Europe. Had the Germans landed, these men would have stayed behind in secret hideaways to hold up the enemy advance. Everyone else would have been evacuated. The enemy couldn't have used the seaside piers to come ashore, as most had their middle sections removed just in case the Germans were tempted.

The bald statistics of the Island's war? Bombs dropped (excluding countless incendiaries) - 1,748. Buildings destroyed or damaged beyond repair - 552. Buildings damaged but repairable - 10,873. Civilians killed - 214 (92 men, 90 women, 32 children). Seriously injured - 274. Number of air raid alerts - 1,594. Only Dover heard the sirens wail more times than the Island. Some safe haven!

When it was all over, the Island was quickly on invasion alert again, but this time from holidaymakers, desperate to escape for a few days from the austere post-war conditions at home. Many stories are told of the queues of luggage-laden returning tourists stretching down Ryde Pier as they awaited the ferry back to the mainland. The post-war holiday boom was matched by a boom in social housing on the Island, especially on the fringes of Ryde (at Binstead) and Newport (Pan).

But there was a battle ahead. In 1948 the nation's railways were nationalised, and

Bombed - by Beetles!

They gave a whole new meaning to the term 'live ammunition' and were without doubt the oddest of the many types of bomb dropped by the Luftwaffe on the Isle of Wight during the Second World War. When they came down in 1943 not far from Chale village, in the south of the Island, there was no explosion, no fire, just ... Colorado beetles!

This was the first recorded drop in Germany's 'beetle bomb' offensive against the vital British potato crop. Presumably, German intelligence was aware of the Island's wartime status among the nation's top potato-growing counties - but they were over-precise in the delivery. The crude cardboard boxes used were each filled with exactly 100 or 50 beetles, so the young evacuees employed to round them up knew precisely how many they had to catch!

The children were sworn to secrecy to avoid the risk of panic in Britain and the extraordinary 'beetle bomb' episode remained 'hush hush' right up until 1970.

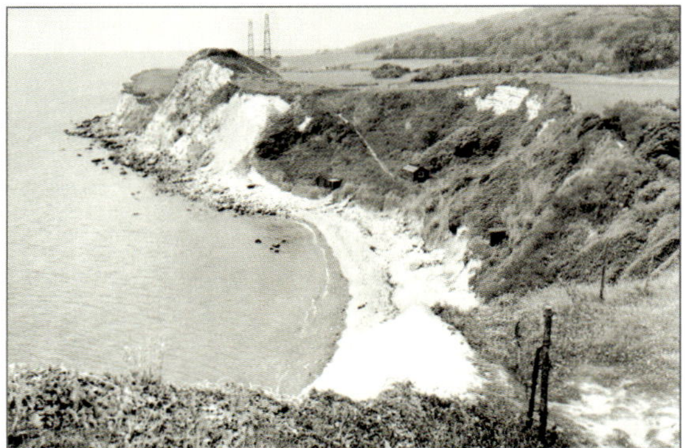

ST LAWRENCE, WOODY BAY c1955 S573029

The pylons of Woody Bay's wartime radar station are visible in the background.

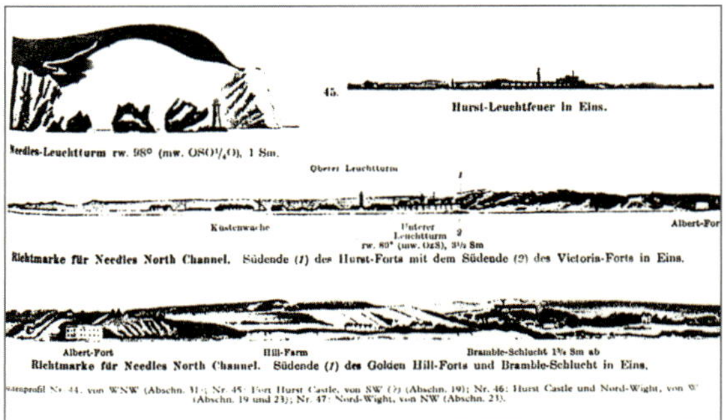

WEST WIGHT - A GUIDE FOR THE LUFTWAFFE
ZZZ04007 (Author's Collection)

A profile prepared for Luftwaffe pilots of the Island's far western coastline.

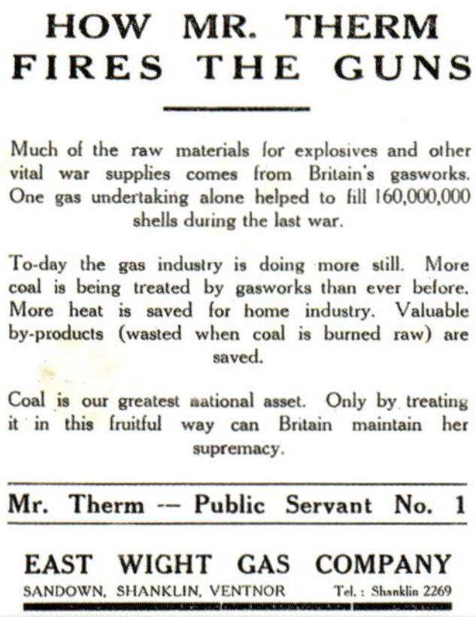

WARTIME ADVICE FOR ISLANDERS
ZZZ04008 (Author's Collection)

A newspaper advertisement explains how the gas company was helping the war effort.

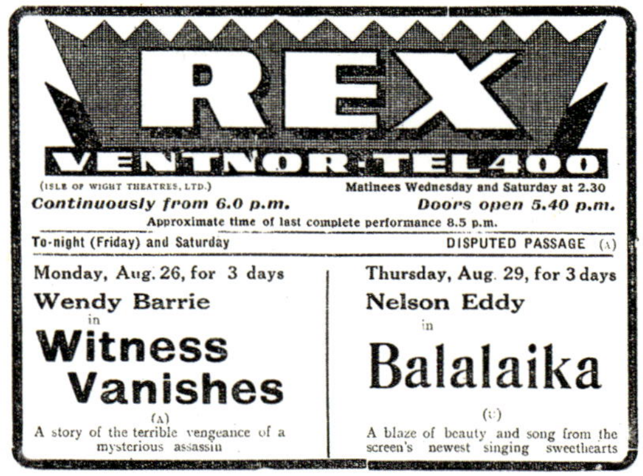

WARTIME ADVERTISMENT FOR THE REX CINEMA
ZZZ04009 (Author's Collection)

And in Ventnor - wartime attractions at the town's now-closed cinema.

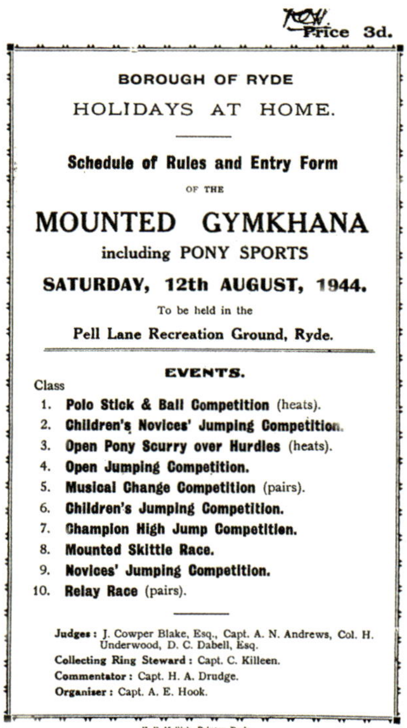

Price 3d.

BOROUGH OF RYDE

HOLIDAYS AT HOME.

Schedule of Rules and Entry Form

OF THE

MOUNTED GYMKHANA

including PONY SPORTS

SATURDAY, 12th AUGUST, 1944.

To be held in the

Pell Lane Recreation Ground, Ryde.

EVENTS.

Class
1. **Polo Stick & Ball Competition** (heats).
2. **Children's Novices' Jumping Competition.**
3. **Open Pony Scurry over Hurdles** (heats).
4. **Open Jumping Competition.**
5. **Musical Change Competition** (pairs).
6. **Children's Jumping Competition.**
7. **Champion High Jump Competition.**
8. **Mounted Skittle Race.**
9. **Novices' Jumping Competition.**
10. **Relay Race** (pairs).

Judges: J. Cowper Blake, Esq., Capt. A. N. Andrews, Col. H. Underwood, D. C. Dabell, Esq.
Collecting Ring Steward: Capt. C. Killeen.
Commentator: Capt. H. A. Drudge.
Organiser: Capt. A. E. Hook.

[illegible], Printer, Ryde

RYDE'S WARTIME GYMKHANA
ZZZ04010 (Author's Collection)

It might have been wartime, but there was still room for fun in Ryde.

British Railways was not impressed with the prospect of maintaining a complex, wholly self-contained, but antiquated network, with all its attendant maintenance facilities, on the Isle of Wight. They began lopping the branches. First to go, in 1952, was the delightful, but always hopelessly uneconomic, line from Merstone to Ventnor West. There was much more of a rumpus when BR proposed closure of the Freshwater and Bembridge branches, together with some of the intermediate stations on the Ryde-Newport line. Allegations of deliberate false accounting by the rail authorities were raised, and with a bagful of evidence to support them. The lines and stations closed anyway in 1953, followed by the cross-country link between Newport and Sandown in 1956.

That left just the principal routes (Ryde-Shanklin-Ventnor and Ryde-Newport-Cowes). Dr Richard Beeching said they should go too.

Did you know?

England's First Carnival

Ryde is widely accepted as the location for the first-ever street carnival in England. Following an initial torchlight procession in 1887, celebrating Queen Victoria's Diamond Jubilee, the town organised a 'Grand Carnival' in August of the following year, the first adoption in England of the term 'carnival' for a street procession. Ryde Carnival remains a major event on the Island's annual social calendar, increasingly characterised in recent years by striking Latin-American influences.

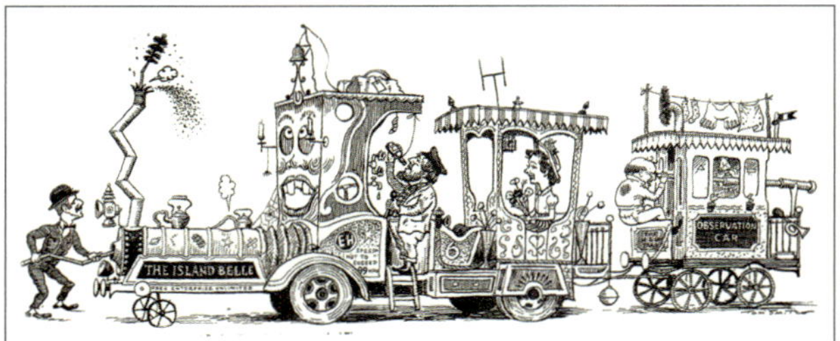

RYDE CARNIVAL 1951 ZZZ04012
(Reproduced by kind pemission of Isle of Wight County Press)

The 1951 Ryde Carnival - cartoon-style.

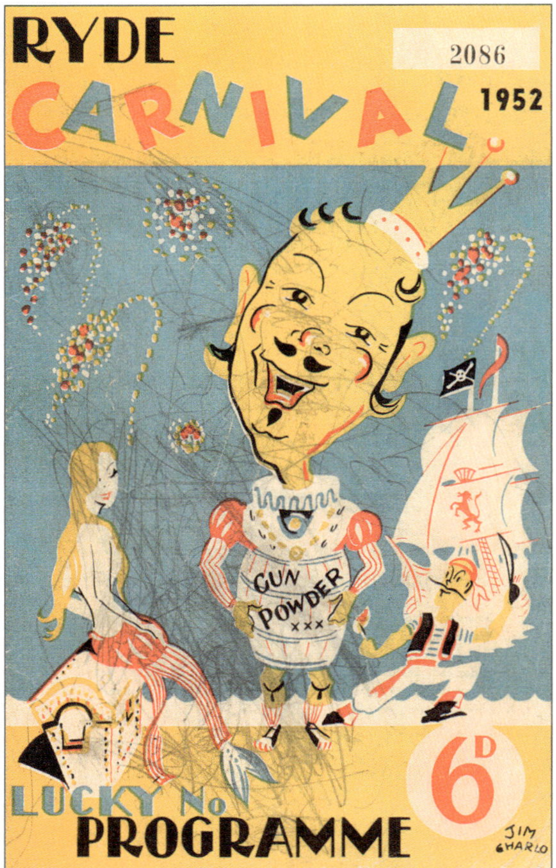

RYDE CARNIVAL ZZZ04011 (Author's Collection)

The cover of Ryde's 1952 carnival programme.

There was outcry. The Island mobilised and the arguments raged, amid more allegations of dodgy figures and broken promises to the Island. After an almighty fight, the Ryde-Cowes route eventually succumbed in February 1966 and, to intense local rage, Shanklin-Ventnor followed in the April. But the fight to save the most heavily used section, between Ryde and Shanklin, was won. It has been operated since then by hand-me-down London Underground units, the oldest trains by far on the national system. There have been all sorts of closure rumours, but also a determination on the Isle of Wight that this is one bit of railway it is going to hang on to.

Today, as Island Line, it is run efficiently, is both quick and very cheap to use, and is the top-performing railway in the country. Virtually everyone is agreed that the congested Island roads simply couldn't cope with the knock-on effect of rail closure. The future is uncertain, but the resolve to keep the line is absolute.

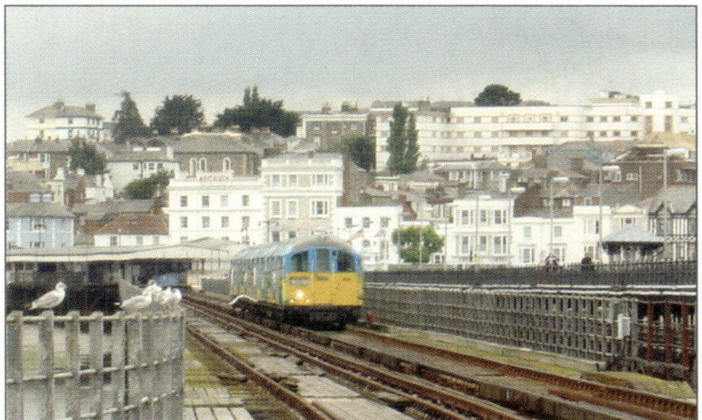

RYDE, A VIEW OF A TRAIN FROM PIER HEAD 2005
R76704k (Matt Searle)

One of Island Line's ex-Underground trains on a Shanklin service - a view from Pier Head station.

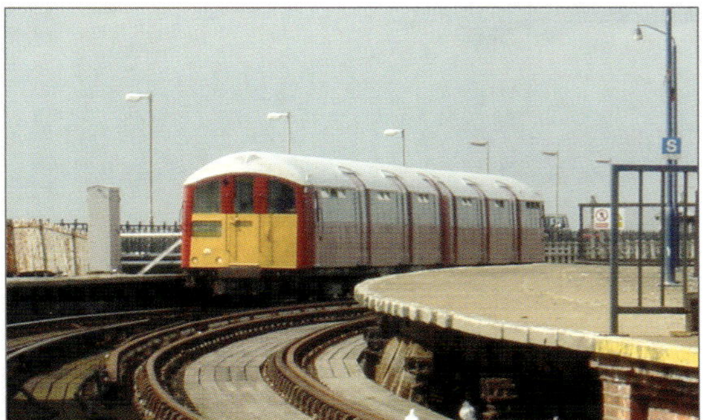

RYDE, THE ESPLANADE STATION 2005
R76705k (Matt Searle)

Ryde Esplanade station is at the pier entrance - soon to be re-developed as part of a 'gateway' interchange.

NEWPORT - A LOST STATION ZZZ04005
(Author's Collection)

Newport was once the hub of a complex rail system. It closed in 1966 but a feasibility study has backed re-opening of the station.

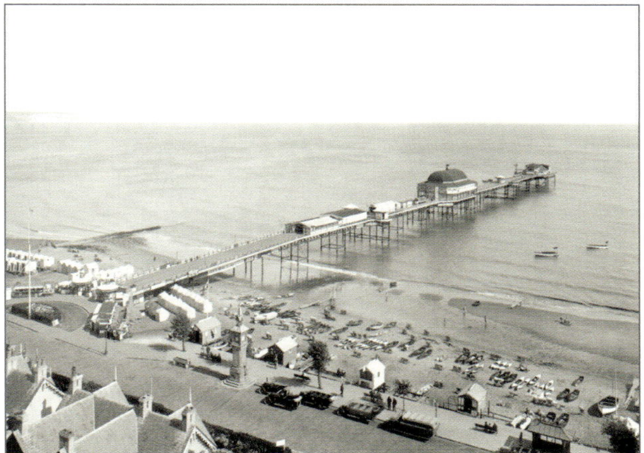

SHANKLIN, THE PIER 1927 80456

The Victorian pier was a casualty of hurricane-force winds in 1987.

Another tremendous battle was successfully waged by something of an unholy Isle of Wight alliance when there were plans in the 1960s to site a nuclear power station at Hamstead, between Cowes and Yarmouth, one of the quietest and most beautiful spots on the Island's coast. Islanders have proved fearsome fighters when mainland-run interests threaten their homeland.

There was tremendous local pride in 1959 when Saunders-Roe unveiled the world's first hovercraft, the SR.N1, at East Cowes. Sir Christopher Cockerell famously used a baked bean tin in his early experiments with the air riding principle. The SR.N1 resembled nothing on earth, but did have more than a passing resemblance to a flying saucer. Bigger, better models were turned out by Saunders-Roe both before and after its takeover by Westland's and later absorption in the British Hovercraft Corporation. In 1965 the world's first hover ferry service opened between Ryde

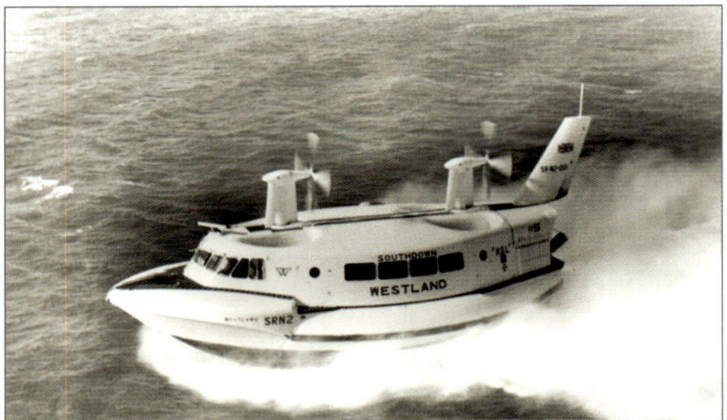

RYDE, AN EARLY HOVERCRAFT - THE SR.N2 c1965 R76049

The SR.N2, seen in Westland's branding, undergoes trials off Ryde.

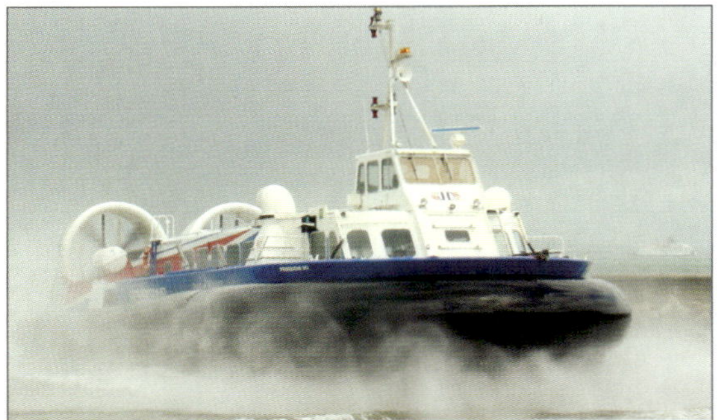

RYDE, HOVERTRAVEL'S FREEDOM 90 - THE MODERN SUCCESSOR 2005 R76701k (Matt Searle)

Hovertravel's Freedom 90 arrives at Ryde.

and the mainland. It still runs to Southsea today, operated by Hovertravel, a tremendous success story.

Saunders-Roe was also closely involved when the UK dipped its toes into the Space Age. A site was laid out high above the sea on the south side of West High Down, close to The Needles, so that the Island company could test-fire the engines it had manufactured at East Cowes for the Black Knight and Black Arrow rockets. The rockets themselves were later put through their paces in Woomera, Australia. Test firing on The Needles headland was carried out between 1956 and 1971 before the site - like the British space programme soon afterwards - was abandoned. It's now a ghostly, incongruous promenade to nowhere on the edge of the cliffs. Information boards tell the story.

Today, what used to be Saunders-Roe is now part of GKN Aerospace Services. Sadly

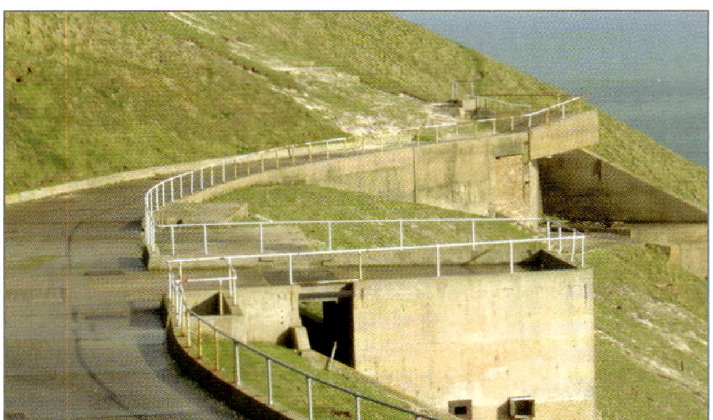

THE NEEDLES, THE ROCKET-TEST SITE 2005
N7701k (Matt Searle)

Possibly the most bizarre tourist attraction on the Island, the abandoned rocket-test site retains its fascination.

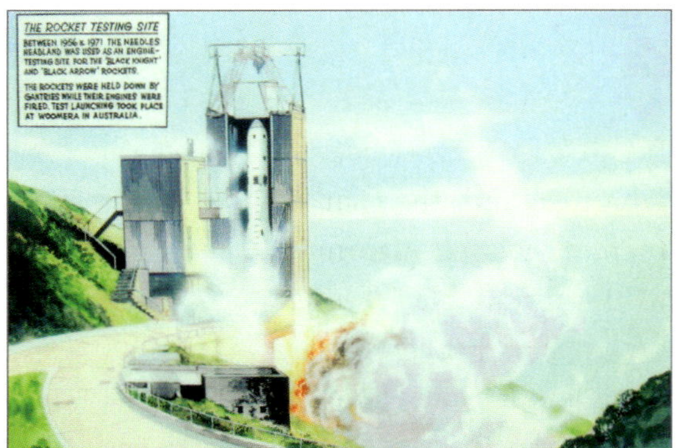

THE NEEDLES, THE ROCKET-TESTING INFORMATION PANEL 2005 ZZZ03987 (Matt Searle)

An information panel gives visitors an idea of what it used to be like.

for the Island, the company has retreated significantly from East Cowes, greatly reducing the employment opportunities there. Many of its redundant buildings were demolished in 2005. J Samuel White's departed completely from Cowes back in 1965 after 160 years in business. During that time, it had turned out a huge number of ships - from cross-Channel steamers to the many warships it built for naval fleets worldwide. Destroyer production for the Royal Navy in the Second World War was carried out at break-neck speed, but never at the expense of quality workmanship.

White's helped sustain the town for a very long time and one of its ships, the Polish destroyer 'Blyskavica', possibly saved it from total destruction when she was in port for a mid-war refit. On the night of the Cowes Blitz in 1942, she fired repeatedly at the Luftwaffe until her guns were white hot. Unlike her makers, she remains afloat, preserved in Poland. Happily, Cowes hangs on to other famous names linked to its maritime heritage, which is now mainly concerned with serving the many yachtsmen/women who still frequent the port. Walk along Medina Road for the evidence: sailmakers Ratsey & Lapthorn and the Clare Lallow yard are still there, and still functioning. They were known to the inimitable Uffa Fox, yachtsman, boat designer and so much else besides. They are known today to another noteworthy resident, the round-the-world yachtswoman, Dame Ellen MacArthur.

Hovercraft excepted, the Island's most famous post-war industrial product was the Islander light aircraft, a dream realised for its developers, John Britten and Desmond Norman. Many of them - and many derivatives - were turned out at the Bembridge Airport base of Britten-Norman. It was the subject of successive takeovers after running into financial problems, but that does not mask the undoubted triumph of this innovative machine, its name recalling not only its development on Wight but also its unrivalled island-hopping capabilities worldwide. Another trail-blazer was Jim McMahon, Australian partner of Britten and Norman, whose revolutionary Micronair approach to aerial crop-spraying, run from Bembridge Fort, won global success. As, more recently, did Richard Noble, who smashed the world's land-speed record in the Isle of Wight-developed Thrust 2.

Did you know?

The Last Island Governor

The assassination by the IRA in 1979 of Earl Mountbatten of Burma deprived the Isle of Wight of its last Governor. Lord Louis had been formally installed to the post by Queen Elizabeth II amid great pageantry at Carisbrooke Castle in July 1965. No successor has been appointed in the years since his death. The last Island Governor actually to live at the castle was Princess Beatrice, installed in 1896, who revived the ages-old tradition by using the castle as a summer residence. She died in 1944.

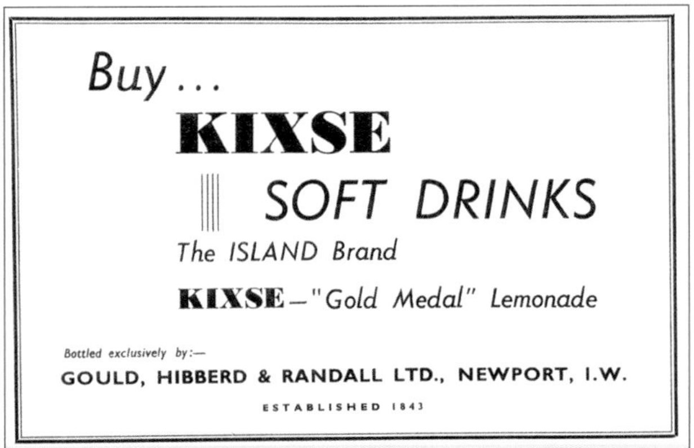

AN ADVERTISMENT FOR KIXSE - THE ISLAND BRAND c1964 ZZZ04014 (Author's Collection)

Great stress has always been placed on the origin of Island-produced products.

More recently still, the Island itself trail-blazed by pioneering unitary local authority in England. The Isle of Wight Council now runs all front-line services, with a network of town and parish councils beneath it. Wight had its own police force until 1947 but it's now part of the Hampshire and Isle of Wight Constabulary (the 'and Isle of Wight' bit was shamefully not officially added until many years into the merged force's existence). Despite the residency down the years of some of Britain's most notorious criminals at the three neighbouring prisons (Parkhurst, Albany and Camp Hill), serious crime is rare. Prisoners were once kept in hulks, moored in the Medina river mouth. A hospital in the redundant Albany Barracks at Parkhurst opened as a prison, initially for young offenders, in 1838, beginning the Island's long and famous association with locking up the nation's villains. Today's inmates cause the Island few problems. The odd one or two escape from time to time, but getting out of jail is one thing. Getting off the Island, as Charles I found to his cost, is quite another!

People still work for an independent fire and rescue service on the Island, though the lighthouses at The Needles and St Catherine's Point are fully automated and the coastguard operation is run largely from the other side of the Solent. Primary healthcare services are concentrated on the much enlarged and modernised St Mary's Hospital, opposite the prisons, north of Newport. There was controversy over the centralisation policy, not least because it brought to an end Ryde's long-established Royal Isle of Wight County Hospital. Now, the concern is more to do with retaining key medical care facilities on the Island rather than a ferry or helicopter ride away on the mainland.

Such issues, say some people, would be resolved if the Island declared itself independent, Jersey-style. The Vectis National Party had a real go at pushing that particular cause a few decades ago, though their choice of name was a trifle ironic. Vectis was hardly independent under the Romans! The Island did manage to issue its own stamps during a national postal strike and has cheekily produced its own version of Euro coinage - but only for fun, you understand!

More serious has been the adjustment to modern tourism patterns. The Island can no longer rely on the traditional 'bucket and spade' holidaymaker crossing the Solent for a two-week stay. The availability of cheap package holidays abroad effectively put an end

When the Island Rocked

Probably no other events in the recent history of the Isle of Wight have succeeded in propelling it to the glare of international attention as did the three great pop festivals held at the end of the 1960s.

The first, near Godshill on August Bank Holiday 1968, featured headline acts The Crazy World of Arthur Brown and Jefferson Airplane on its bill, but was somewhat eclipsed by the three-day 1969 follow-up at Wootton, rounded-off, as The Beatles looked on, by the legendary Bob Dylan.

Then, amid the surreal surroundings of the rural West Wight at Afton Farm, came the five-day festival to top them all. Absolutely massive in scale, rivalled only by the USA's 1969 Woodstock festival in New York State, and hotly controversial, this is widely recalled - especially by the countless thousands who attended and the Islanders whose attitudes towards it ranged from awe and youthful, rebellious delight through to open hostility - as the last great event of the Sixties, even though it was not actually held until August 1970. Afton Farm's line-up included Joan Baez, Leonard Cohen, The Doors, The Who and, sadly, an obviously exhausted Jimi Hendrix, who was dead three weeks later. The Sixties were finally put to rest. It was the end, too, for the mighty, chaotic Isle of Wight pop festivals. Like Jimi Hendrix, they were every bit a product of their time.

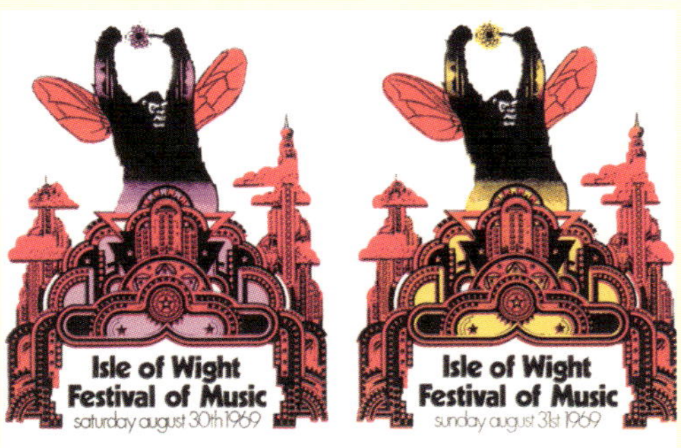

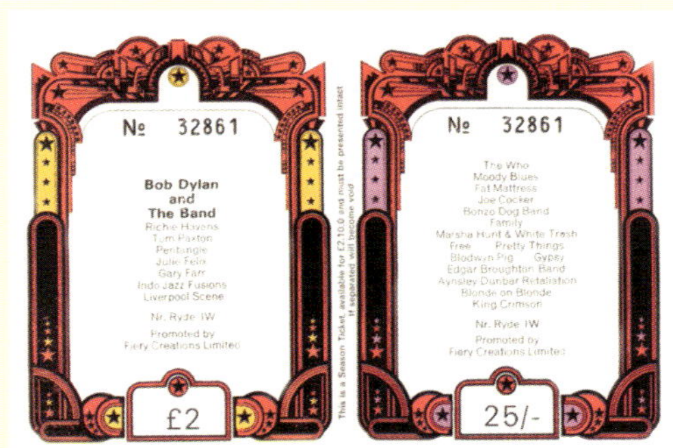

ISLE OF WIGHT FESTIVAL OF MUSIC TICKETS 1969
ZZZ04015 (Author's Collection) and ZZZ04016 (Author's Collection)
Tickets for the festival starring Bob Dylan - the artwork speaks of the era.

to that. So Wight has had to find new ways to tempt the choice-happy tourist. Sensibly, it is promoting the natural attractions afforded by its stunningly beautiful landscape with major walking and cycling events and other 'green tourism.' Its springtime walking festival, making the most of an extensive, well-signed footpath network, has quickly become the UK's largest. The rich heritage is also high on the marketing agenda. It's an extraordinary microcosm of the nation's overall history, all the way back to the dinosaurs.

A great deal of investment has gone into equipping Newport's shopping centre with big-name stores. At Ryde, ongoing regeneration is rightly making the most of the Victorian legacy and will be capped when the long-awaited 'gateway' interchange (train, bus, taxi) is built on the Esplanade. Yarmouth has in recent years been given a new road bridge across the Western Yar. They're still talking about a bridge over the River Medina. Meanwhile, the chain ferry keeps clanking across.

Wight still inspires the arts. It's pop chart-toppers have ranged from Craig Douglas, a Newport milkman in the Fifties, to Level 42's Mark King, still one of rock music's most respected artistes. The Island still organises major music festivals - echoes of the mighty pop fests in 1968, 1969 and 1970 (see Topic Box, page 113). Ryde's Raymond Allen penned one of television's most enduring sit-coms in 'Some Mothers Do 'Ave 'Em' (watch out for the local street names when next you watch an episode) and Anthony Minghella, also from Ryde, established himself among the world's leading film directors with the Oscar-winning 'The English Patient', after his parents had made the family name one of the best-known on the Island with their ice cream factory. Island talent is not wafer-thin!

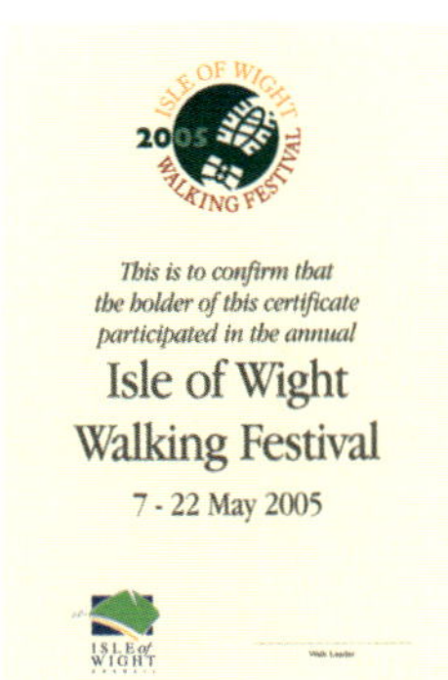
This is to confirm that the holder of this certificate participated in the annual
Isle of Wight Walking Festival
7 - 22 May 2005

ISLE OF WIGHT WALKING FESTIVAL 2005
ZZZ04018 (Reproduced by kind permission of Isle of Wight Council)

A certificate for those taking part in the country's largest walking festival.

The Island now has a resident population in excess of 120,000 and must deal with the fact that a large, and growing, proportion is retired. The congested roads are a major concern. Railway revival offers the best solution, but it costs. The car ferries get bigger and bigger, but still more vehicles would flock to the Island if there were a fixed link, and you'll always find somebody making the case for one. To most Islanders (especially the Caulkheads - those actually born on Wight) it's the daftest idea. The Isle of Wight needs to stay detached. It deserves to after all those centuries of invasion.

Did you know?

The Solent Tunnel

Proposals for a fixed link between the Isle of Wight and the mainland are nothing new. The Victorian era spawned several schemes, the most notable of which was the Solent Tunnel project of the South Western & Isle of Wight Junction Railway in 1901. This envisaged a rail link from the Lymington branch line in Hampshire to a point between Causeway Crossing and Yarmouth Station at the western end of the Island's Freshwater, Yarmouth & Newport Railway, via a 2 mile 500 yard tunnel beneath the Solent. Trial borings were carried out before the project was abandoned.

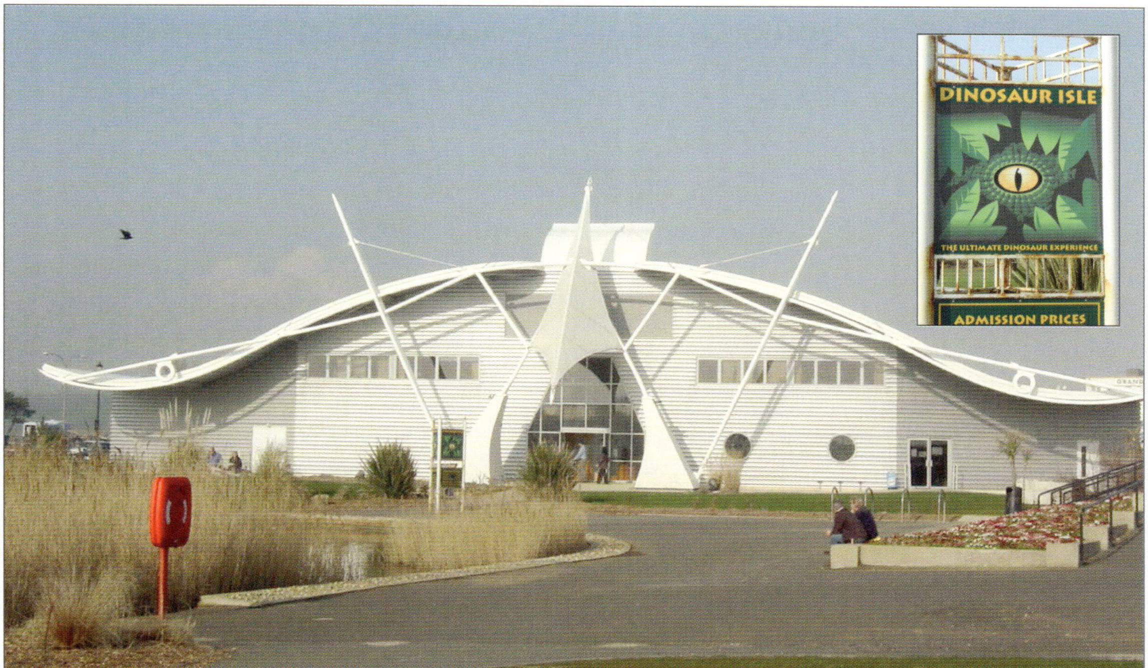

SANDOWN, THE DINOSAUR ISLE MUSEUM AT YAVERLAND 2005 ZZZ03993 (Sarah Miller)
INSET: SANDOWN, THE DINOSAUR ISLE MUSEUM SIGN 2005 S57703k (Matt Searle)

Striking architecture evokes the subject matter at one of the Island's newest attractions.

The Island's most modern ferry, it operates between Cowes and Southampton.

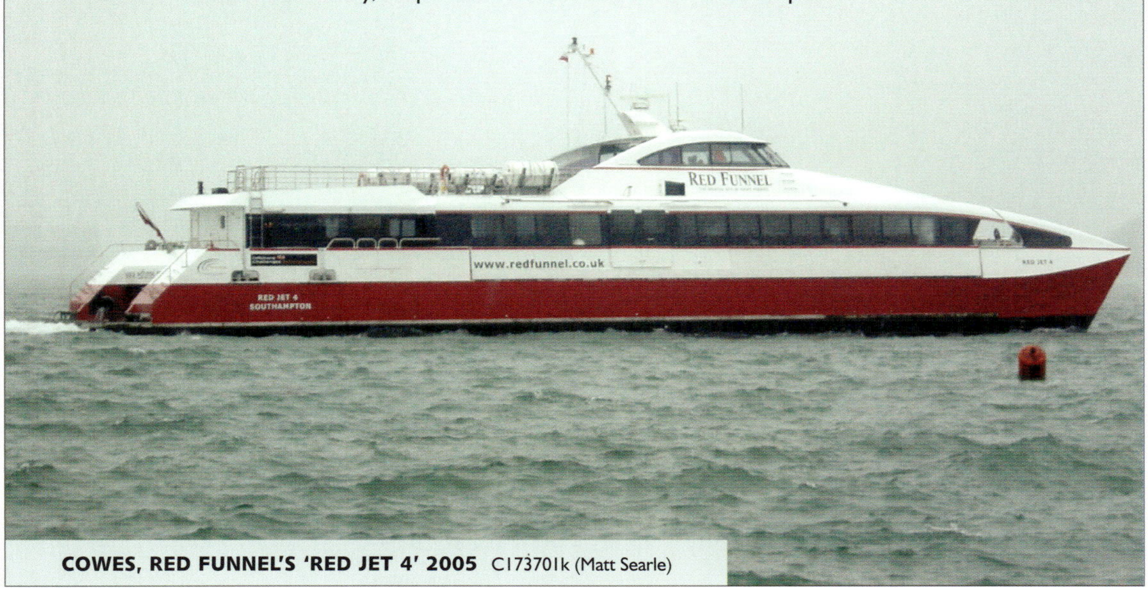

COWES, RED FUNNEL'S 'RED JET 4' 2005 C173701k (Matt Searle)

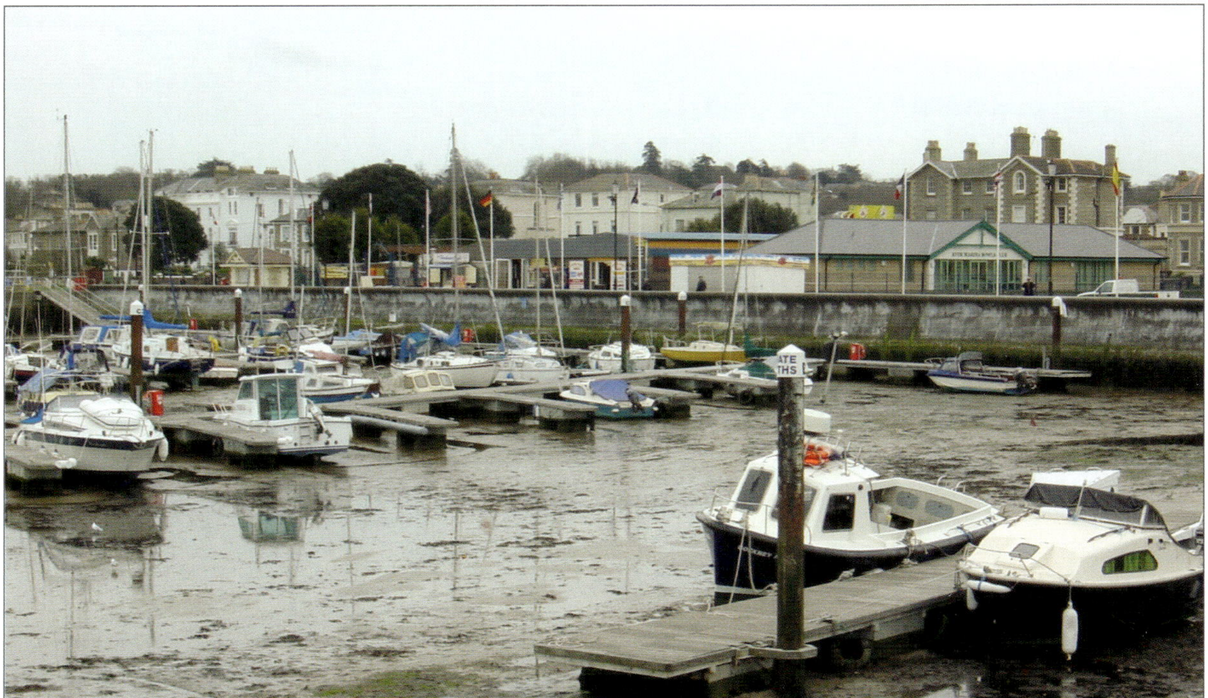

RYDE, THE HARBOUR MARINA 2005 R76702k (Matt Searle)

Pictured at low tide, this is the Island's newest harbour, a project of the former Medina Borough Council.

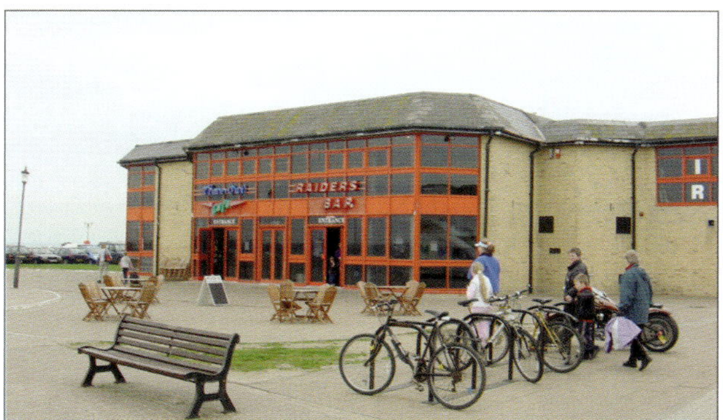

RYDE, PLANET ICE 2005 R76703k (Matt Searle)

The ice rink - home of Wight Raiders ice hockey team - is a recent seafront development at Ryde.

ISLE of WIGHT
COUNCIL

THE MODERN IMAGE 2005
ZZZ04017 (Reproduced by kind permission of Isle of Wight Council)

The logo of the Island's unitary authority.

ACKNOWLEDGEMENTS

Preparation of this work would not have been possible without the considerable help I have received from Matt, my son, and Sarah Miller, his girlfriend. Their photography and copy checking (and, in the case of Matt, computer wizardry!) has been invaluable. My sincere thanks go to them both.

SELECTED BIBLIOGRAPHY

Adams, R B	*Red Funnel and Before, 1986*
Allen, P C	*The Railways of the Isle of Wight, 1928*
Barber, Thomas	*Picturesque Illustrations of the Isle of Wight, 1811*
Bede (trans. Shirley Price)	*A History of the English Church and People, 1955*
Davenport Adams, W H	*The History, Topography and Antiquities of the Isle of Wight, 1856*
Eldridge, R J	*Newport Isle of Wight in Bygone Days, 1952*
Graham, Norman	*IWCC: A Centenary Souvenir, 1990*
Green, Margaret	*Churches of the Isle of Wight, 1969*
Hinton, Brian	*Message to Love: The Isle of Wight Festivals, 1995*
Hockey, Dom S F	*The Charters of Quarr Abbey, 1991*
Hyland, Paul	*Wight: Biography of an Island, 1984*
Jones, Jack and Johanna	*The Isle of Wight: An Illustrated History, 1987*
Lane, Marian	*Piers of the Isle of Wight, 1996*
Robbins, Michael	*The Isle of Wight Railways, 1963*
Searle, Adrian	*Isle of Wight at War, 1989*
Searle, Adrian	*Isle of Wight Folklore, 1998*
Wheeler, Jack	*St Thomas' Church, Ryde, 1972*
Wilson, Lawrence	*Portrait of the Isle of Wight, 1965*
Winter, C W R.	*The Ancient Town of Yarmouth, 1981*
Winter, C W R.	*The Manor Houses of the Isle of Wight, 1984*
Winter, C W R.	*The Enchanted Isle, 1990*
Worsley, Sir Richard	*The History of the Isle of Wight, 1781*

In addition to the above list, innumerable other works - books, booklets, magazines, newspapers, pamphlets etc - have been consulted, many of them housed with the excellent collection of local publications in Newport's Lord Louis Library. My thanks to the staff there for their time and guidance.

Ottakar's Bookshops

Ottakar's bookshops, the first of which opened in Brighton in 1988, can now be found in over 130 towns and cities across the United Kingdom. Expansion was gradual throughout the 1990s, but the chain has expanded rapidly in recent years, with many new shop openings and the acquisition of shops from James Thin and Hammicks.

Ottakar's has always known that a shop's local profile is as important, if not more important, than the chain's national profile, and has encouraged its staff to make their shops a part of the local community, tailoring stock to suit the area and forging links with local schools and businesses.

Local history has always been a strong area for Ottakar's, and the company has published its own award winning local history titles, based on text written by its customers, in recent years.

With a reputation for friendly, intelligent and enthusiastic booksellers, warm, inviting shops with an excellent range of books and related products, Ottakar's is now one of the UK's most popular booksellers. In 2003 and then again in 2004 it won the prestigious Best Bookselling Company of the Year Award at the British Book Awards.

Ottakar's has commissioned The Francis Frith Collection to create a series of town history books similar to this volume, as well as a range of stylish gift products, all illustrated with historical photographs.

Participating Ottakar's bookshops can be found in the following towns and cities:

Aberdeen
Abergavenny
Aberystwyth
Andover
Ashford
Ayr
Banbury
Barnstaple
Basildon
Berkhamsted
Bishop's Stortford
Boston
Brentwood
Bromley
Bury St Edmunds
Camberley
Canterbury
Carmarthen
Chatham
Chelmsford
Cheltenham
Cirencester
Coventry
Crawley
Darlington
Dorchester
Douglas, Isle of Man
Dumfries
Dundee
East Grinstead
Eastbourne
Elgin
Enfield
Epsom
Falkirk
Fareham
Farnham
Folkestone
Glasgow
Gloucester
Greenwich
Grimsby
Guildford
Harrogate
Hastings
Haywards Heath
Hemel Hempstead
High Wycombe
Horsham
Huddersfield
Inverness
Isle of Wight
Kendal
King's Lynn
Kirkcaldy
Lancaster
Lincoln
Llandudno
Loughborough
Lowestoft
Luton
Lymington
Maidenhead
Maidstone
Market Harborough
Milton Keynes
Newport
Newton Abbot
Norwich
Oban
Ormskirk
Petersfield
Portsmouth
Poole
Redhill
St Albans
St Andrews
St Neots
St Helier
Salisbury
Sheffield
Stafford
Staines
Stevenage
Sutton Coldfield
Teddington
Tenterden
Tiverton
Torquay
Trowbridge
Truro
Tunbridge Wells
Twickenham
Walsall
Wilmslow and
Alderley Edge
Wells
Weston-super-Mare
Windsor
Witney
Woking
Worcester
Yeovil

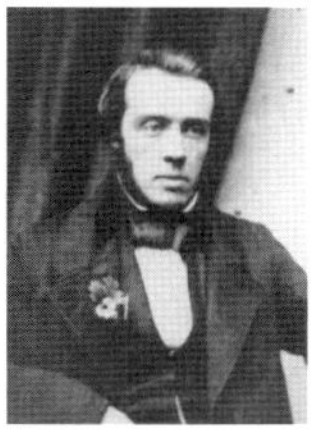

Francis Frith

Pioneer Victorian Photographer

Francis Frith, founder of the world-famous photographic archive, was a complex and multi-talented man. A devout Quaker and a highly successful Victorian businessman, he was philosophical by nature and pioneering in outlook. By 1855 he had already established a wholesale grocery business in Liverpool, and sold it for the astonishing sum of £200,000, which is the equivalent today of over £15,000,000. Now in his thirties, and captivated by the new science of photography, Frith set out on a series of pioneering journeys up the Nile and to the Near East.

He was the first photographer to venture beyond the sixth cataract of the Nile. Africa was still the mysterious 'Dark Continent', and Stanley and Livingstone's historic meeting was a decade into the future. The conditions for picture taking confound belief. He laboured for hours in his wicker dark-room in the sweltering heat of the desert, while the volatile chemicals fizzed dangerously in their trays. Back in London he exhibited his photographs and was 'rapturously cheered' by members of the Royal Society. His reputation as a photographer was made overnight.

By the 1870s the railways had threaded their way across the country, and Bank Holidays and half-day Saturdays had been made obligatory by Act of Parliament. All of a sudden the working man and his family were able to enjoy days out, take holidays, and see a little more of the world.

With typical business acumen, Francis Frith foresaw that these new tourists would enjoy having souvenirs to commemorate their days out. For the next thirty years he travelled the country by train and by pony and trap, producing fine photographs of seaside resorts and beauty spots that were keenly bought by millions of Victorians. These prints were painstakingly pasted into family albums and pored over during the dark nights of winter, rekindling precious memories of summer excursions. Frith's studio was soon supplying retail shops all over the country, and by 1890 F Frith & Co had become the greatest specialist photographic publishing company in the world, with over 2,000 sales outlets, and pioneered the picture postcard.

Francis Frith had died in 1898 at his villa in Cannes, his great project still growing. By 1970 the archive he created contained over a third of a million pictures showing 7,000 British towns and villages.

Frith's legacy to us today is of immense significance and value, for the magnificent archive of evocative photographs he created provides a unique record of change in the cities, towns and villages throughout Britain over a century and more. Frith and his fellow studio photographers revisited locations many times down the years to update their views, compiling for us an enthralling and colourful pageant of British life and character.

We are fortunate that Frith was dedicated to recording the minutiae of everyday life. For it is this sheer wealth of visual data, the painstaking chronicle of changes in dress, transport, street layouts, buildings, housing and landscape that captivates us so much today, offering us a powerful link with the past and with the lives of our ancestors.

Computers have now made it possible for Frith's many thousands of images to be accessed almost instantly. The archive offers every one of us an opportunity to examine the places where we and our families have lived and worked down the years. Its images, depicting our shared past, are now bringing pleasure and enlightenment to millions around the world a century and more after his death. For further information visit: www.francisfrith.co.uk

FREE PRINT OF YOUR CHOICE

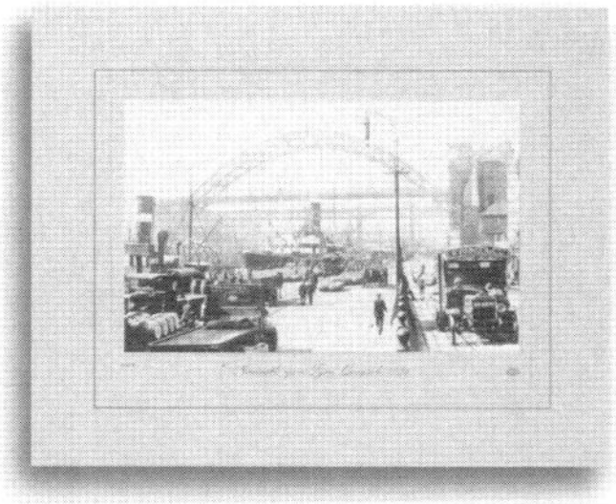

Mounted Print
Overall size 14 x 11 inches (355 x 280mm)

Choose any Frith photograph in this book.
Simply complete the Voucher opposite and return it with your remittance for £2.25 (to cover postage and handling) and we will print the photograph of your choice in SEPIA (size 11 x 8 inches) and supply it in a cream mount with a burgundy rule line (overall size 14 x 11 inches).
Please note: photographs with a reference number starting with a "Z" are not Frith photographs and cannot be supplied under this offer.
Offer valid for delivery to one UK address only.

***PLUS:* Order additional Mounted Prints at HALF PRICE - £7.49 each** (normally £14.99)
If you would like to order more Frith prints from this book, possibly as gifts for friends and family, you can buy them at half price (with no additional postage and handling costs).

***PLUS:* Have your Mounted Prints framed**
For an extra £14.95 per print you can have your mounted print(s) framed in an elegant polished wood and gilt moulding, overall size 16 x 13 inches (no additional postage and handling required).

IMPORTANT!

These special prices are only available if you use this form to order . You must use the ORIGINAL VOUCHER on this page (no copies permitted). We can only despatch to one UK address. This offer cannot be combined with any other offer.

Send completed Voucher form to:
The Francis Frith Collection, Frith's Barn, Teffont, Salisbury, Wiltshire SP3 5QP

CHOOSE A PHOTOGRAPH FROM THIS BOOK

Voucher *for FREE and Reduced Price Frith Prints*

Please do not photocopy this voucher. Only the original is valid, so please fill it in, cut it out and return it to us with your order.

Picture ref no	Page no	Qty	Mounted @ £7.49	Framed + £14.95	Total Cost £
		1	Free of charge*	£	£
			£7.49	£	£
			£7.49	£	£
			£7.49	£	£
			£7.49	£	£
			£7.49	£	£
			* Post & handling		£2.25
			Total Order Cost		£

Please allow 28 days for delivery.
Offer available to one UK address only

Title of this book ....
I enclose a cheque/postal order for £ ....
made payable to 'The Francis Frith Collection'

OR please debit my Mastercard / Visa / Maestro / Amex card, details below

Card Number

Issue No (Maestro only) Valid from (Maestro)

Expires Signature

Name Mr/Mrs/Ms ....
Address ....
....
....
.... Postcode ....
Daytime Tel No ....
Email ....

ISBN: 1-84567-747-1 Valid to 31/12/08